Immigration and Nationalism

Latin American Monographs, No. 18
Institute of Latin American Studies
The University of Texas at Austin

Immigration and Nationalism

ARGENTINA AND CHILE, 1890–1914

➤➤➤

BY CARL SOLBERG

PUBLISHED FOR THE *Institute of Latin American Studies*
BY THE UNIVERSITY OF TEXAS PRESS, AUSTIN

Requests for permission to reproduce material from this work
should be sent to:
  Permissions
  University of Texas Press
  P.O. Box 7819
  Austin, TX 78713-7819
  http://utpress.utexas.edu/index.php/rp-form

Library of Congress Catalog Number 76-99916

ISBN 978-1-4773-0501-0, paperback
ISBN 978-1-4773-0502-7, library e-book
ISBN 978-1-4773-0503-4, individual e-book

To My Parents

PREFACE

The question of immigration aroused bitter controversy in Argentina and Chile during the quarter century preceding World War I. In the press, in parliamentary chambers, in essays, novels, and plays, citizens of both republics intensely pondered, discussed, and debated the changes that the European influx was bringing about. Their concern reflected a growing awareness that immigration, along with foreign capital and European technology, was sweeping away traditional social and economic patterns and leaving an uncertain future.

This acrimonious debate over immigration stimulated the rise of nationalism, which began to replace the cosmopolitan social and economic theories Argentines and Chileans had accepted since the mid-nineteenth century. But Argentine and Chilean nationalism before World War I differed sharply in form and in emphasis. While Argentine intellectuals were propagating cultural and nostalgic nationalism, the Chilean version concentrated primarily on economic problems. In order to help explain the rise of two distinct currents of nationalist thought, this study aims to examine and compare the responses to immigration that took place in the two republics.

In Argentina and Chile the masses decisively influenced neither the official immigration policy nor the formulation of nationalistic ideologies designed to counteract immigration. Although rural workers and urban laborers sometimes expressed hostility against the foreigners, political decision making was not based on mass opinion. With this in mind, the present study focuses its attention on the Argentine and Chilean upper classes, which in both republics still held an effective monopoly of political, economic, and social power. It was the upper classes, along with the middle social groups in the case of Chile, that consciously attempted to discredit immigration and to propagate nationalism. These upper and middle classes acted not out of ethnic or religious prejudice but because immigration was threatening their power and status.

The comparative approach dictated a topical organization for this study. Among the major themes to emerge from the research were the cosmopolitan social theories used to justify immigration, the reaction that appeared against immigrant businessmen and professionals, the identification of foreigners as the cause of urban social problems, the hostility aroused by immigrant political participation, and the eventual intellectual rejection of cosmopolitanism in favor of nationalism.

The research drew upon a wide variety of source material. Parliamentary debates, for example, revealed the viewpoints of the elites when immigration policy was discussed in the political arena. The principal newspapers, which frequently analyzed or debated the impact of immigration, were another prime source, particularly for Chile. Journalism flourished in that country, where each political party maintained its own daily paper to express its social and economic views. The variety and depth of coverage of the Chilean newspapers partially compensated for a paucity of scholarly journals and reviews during the 1890–1914 period. A third important source included the publications of economic interest groups. Among them were the journals of agricultural and industrial associations in both countries and of mining groups in Chile. Scholarly journals and literary reviews were valuable, particularly in the case of Argentina. During the 1890–1914 period, only a few such reviews appeared regularly in Chile, but one may find discussion of the immigration question in at least a dozen reputable Argentine journals. Popular magazines, including *Zig Zag* in Chile and *Caras y Caretas* in Argentina, sometimes cast the response to immigration in a humorous or satirical vein.

The works of Argentine and Chilean intellectuals comprised perhaps the single most important source. Many of these writers, particularly in Argentina, revealed upper-class thinking and viewpoints on the question of immigration. In an attempt to garner a consensus of intellectual opinion I have examined the works of the social and economic essayists who wrote specialized studies about immigration, as well as books, pamphlets, and articles by a wide variety of scholars, ranging

from educators to psychologists and criminologists. Literature in the
form of novels, poetry, and short plays (sometimes called *sainetes*)
provided valuable insights, particularly for Argentina. Chilean literature, which still dealt mainly with universal themes rather than with
national social questions, was not as rich a source.

Travel and research in Latin America for purposes of this study
were made possible by a National Defense Foreign Language Fellowship (Title VI) and by a Stanford University Graduate Fellowship.
Collections of material that proved to be of great value were at the
Library of the Facultad de Filosofía y Letras of the University of Buenos Aires, at the Library of the Banco Tornquist in Buenos Aires, and
at the Biblioteca Nacional in Santiago. To the many employees and
officials of these and other libraries I consulted, I express my deep
appreciation. I would like to thank Dauril Alden, Stanley G. Payne,
David Potter, John D. Wirth, and John J. Johnson for their criticisms
of the manuscript. Finally, all English translations of Spanish sources,
unless specifically noted, are my own.

CONTENTS

MAPS

TABLES

ILLUSTRATIONS

Immigration and Nationalism

Argentina and Chile

Political Divisions

1914

INTERNATIONAL BOUNDARY
PROVINCIAL BOUNDARY

0   50   100   200   300   400 miles

SCALE

CHAPTER ONE

"To Govern Is to Populate": The Justifications of Immigration

›››

THE SIXTY MILLION EUROPEANS who emigrated during the nineteenth century stimulated economic development, hastened social change, and invigorated cultural life in numerous countries scattered around the globe, but the emigrants also helped bind these countries to Europe's economy. By the mid-nineteenth century, an international economic system centered in Europe had integrated world production and distribution more completely than ever before. Europe's voracious industries and growing population demanded raw materials and foodstuffs, which improved transportation and banking facilities enabled her to obtain in the underdeveloped regions of Asia, Africa, and the Americas. To pay for these imports, she sent manufactured goods and the capital that resulted from the profits of manufacturing to the farthest corners of the earth. At the same time, the increasing European imports of farm, forest, and mine products created labor shortages in many regions, thereby inducing workers from all parts of Europe to migrate abroad. Goods, money, and men all flowed out of Europe in astonishing quantities to tie the world more closely together, to stimulate worldwide economic growth, and to give the European industrial nations ownership and control over much of the economic activity in the rest of the world.

New theories were needed to justify this international economic system, for the mercantilist and protectionist ideas popular in previous centuries conflicted with the free-trade ideal. Liberal economics, which European thinkers formulated to meet nineteenth-century needs, taught that maximum general prosperity would result when manpower, goods, and capital were free to respond to world-market demand and supply. Economic wisdom, according to the liberal theorists, dictated that each nation should do everything possible to integrate its economy into the international system. By the mid-nineteenth century European books were spreading the new theories everywhere, while foreign students who attended European universities were embracing liberal economic principles and disseminating them among the educated populace of their homelands.

Argentina and Chile were two countries in which liberal economic theory became influential by the mid-nineteenth century. During the decades following independence from Spain, the two republics had devoted much energy to problems of political organization but had neglected material development. As the upper classes became aware of the vast potential profits possible in the export trade, national attention began to shift away from political questions toward economics. Chile in 1833 and Argentina in 1853 wrote constitutions that not only opened the way to eventual resolution of the fundamental organizational problems previously keeping both countries in an uproar, but that also encouraged foreign participation in economic development. A new era of relative civil peace and order dawned, and the upper classes hastened to welcome European capital, technology, and manufactures.

Although numerically small, the ruling elites possessed immense power in Argentina and Chile. The existing constitutions proclaimed popular sovereignty, but, in both countries, the upper classes almost completely controlled politics, largely through the abundant opportunities for electoral corruption existing at all levels of government.[1]

[1] Good descriptions of the electoral corruption that the Argentine and Chilean upper classes employed to retain political power include Peter Snow, *Ar-*

The elite families also strongly influenced intellectual life in both Argentina and Chile. They owned most of the leading newspapers and journals, provided the administration and teaching staff of the universities, and patronized literature and the arts.

The same groups that controlled politics and intellectual life were also at the apex of the social pyramid. Aloof, proud, and remote, the elite classes were difficult to enter, particularly in Argentina. To achieve upper-class status, one generally required the prestige that only an old, respected Spanish family name could confer. Most of the leading families of both republics had gained their power during the colonial period when the Spanish crown had granted them huge expanses of land. Many of these families joined forces to lead the movements for independence; after it was achieved, they furnished the political leaders of the new nations. Prior to about 1900 no other social group could challenge upper-class pre-eminence. The middle social strata contained small, fragmented groups that generally identified with the elites. The urban working classes were only beginning to become aware of their potential power, while rural laborers remained almost totally outside the political arena.

In Argentina the economic base of the upper class was ownership of the nation's richest land, the incredibly fertile soil of the riverside or littoral region comprising the provinces of Buenos Aires, Santa Fe, and Entre Ríos. Fifty families owned a total of 4,600,000 hectares of land in Buenos Aires, the richest province. Along with the powerful landed families from Santa Fe and Entre Ríos and those from the province of Córdoba, this group formed the core of the Argentine elite.[2] These landed families had not enjoyed great wealth during most of the nineteenth century, when lack of demand for agricultural and

---

gentine Radicalism, pp. 5–6; Miguel Ángel Cárcano, Sáenz Peña: La revolución por los comicios, pp. 131–134; Ricardo Donoso, Alessandri, agitador y demoledor, I, 72–74; Julio César Jobet, Ensayo crítico del desarrollo económico-social de Chile, p. 115.

[2] These statistics on landownership appear in Gaston Gori, El pan nuestro, p. 120. This social history is an excellent source of information on the origins and extent of the Argentine landed elite's power. For insight into the economic bases of Argentine upper-class power, see Sergio Bagú, Evolución histórica de

pastoral products discouraged large landholders from exploiting their properties. By around 1880 European demands for Argentine beef and wheat began to climb just at the time when improvements in ocean transport were enabling Argentina to become a full-fledged competitor in the European market. Between 1890 and 1912 Argentine exports quintupled from 100,000,000 to 500,000,000 gold pesos.[3]

This prosperity gave the large landed families tremendous economic power. They became wealthy enough to indulge their every whim, which frequently included fine horses for their favorite sport of polo, the latest European fashions, and palatial houses on the country *estancia*, in Buenos Aires, and often in Paris. "Rich as an Argentine" became a common phrase on the French Riviera to denote extreme wealth. Allied with the landed interests to form the rest of the Argentine upper class were the owners of the nation's largest commercial houses, banks, and export-import firms, all centered in the city of Buenos Aires.[4]

Unlike those in Argentina, large landowners no longer dominated the Chilean upper class by 1890. To the contrary, the power of Chile's landed oligarchy had declined steadily since the War of the Pacific (1879–1884), during which Chile seized from Peru and Bolivia the nitrate-rich regions of Tarapacá and Antofagasta. This area, at the time, was the world's only important source of sodium nitrate, an ingredient for explosives much in demand by the Great Powers. Nitrate became Chile's principal export, and nitrate mining enriched many Chilean families. Along with commercial and banking magnates, they were gradually able to marry into the landed elite. Financial power

---

la estratificación social en la Argentina, p. 37. This comprehensive analysis of Argentine social and economic history, heavily documented and containing valuable statistics, unfortunately has not been published. Also valuable is Thomas F. McGann, *Argentina, Estados Unidos y el sistema interamericano, 1880–1914*, trans. Germán O. Tjarks, especially pp. 31–32.

[3] Ernesto Tornquist & Cía. Ltda., *El desarrollo económico de la República Argentina en los últimos cincuenta años*, pp. 133–134.

[4] Oscar E. Cornblit, Ezequiel Gallo (hijo), and Alfredo A. O'Connell, "La generación del 80 y su proyecto: Antecedentes y consequencias," in Torcuato S. Di Tella, et al., *Argentina, sociedad de masas*, p. 31.

rather than the prestige of family name began to be the touchstone for membership in the Chilean upper class.[5]

The native-born populations of both countries were too small to provide the necessary manpower for the flourishing export economy that the Argentine and Chilean elites envisioned. Chile, a country of about 300,000 square miles, had about 1,600,000 inhabitants in 1860, while in the same year a scant 1,200,000 inhabited Argentina's huge territory of over 1,000,000 square miles. Large sections of both nations, including Chile's extensive territories south of the central valley, the enormous area of Argentine Patagonia, and much of the rich Argentine pampas, remained almost completely empty.

Immigration appeared essential if Argentina and Chile were to partake of the benefits offered by the international economic system. In 1852 the Argentine political thinker Juan Bautista Alberdi had summarized the prevailing mood among his country's ruling elite when he proclaimed: "To govern is to populate." Some of Chile's most respected nineteenth-century writers, including Vicente Pérez Rosales and Benjamín Vicuña Mackenna, expressed similar views.[6] During the 1850's governments in both countries began to follow these ideas by instituting liberal immigration policies, and well before 1890 Argentina and Chile officially threw open their gates to virtually unrestricted entry. Argentine immigration legislation, dating from 1876, opened the nation to all but obvious undesirables like the insane and those

---

[5] Two works on the changing composition of the Chilean elites are Alberto Edwards Vivas, *La fronda aristocrática*, fifth edition, p. 16, and Raúl Alarcón Pino, *"La clase media en Chile," orígenes, características e influencias*, p. 81.

[6] Alberdi's slogan of 1852 was frequently quoted by writers on immigration for the next half century. For the original statement, see Juan B. Alberdi, *Bases y puntos de partida para la organización política de la República Argentina*, p. 219. In Chile, Pérez Rosales wrote a justification of immigration as part of *Recuerdos del pasado*, his autobiography, which is now regarded as one of the gems of national literature. Vicuña Mackenna, an influential statesman, presented a detailed argument for promoting immigration in his *Bases del informe presentado al supremo gobierno sobre la inmigración estranjera por la comisión especial nombrada con ese objeto y redactada por el secretario de ella.*

with communicable diseases. Chile enacted no immigration restrictions at all during the period before 1914 and simply allowed any foreigner to enter.

Several powerful economic interests in each country strongly supported liberal immigration policies during the 1880–1914 period. These groups were convinced that prosperity and growth required a steady flow of cheap labor. They expected, moreover, the European laborers to form a large, servile working class that would augment upper-class wealth but would not challenge the prevailing social hierarchy or distribution of economic power.

Industrialists composed probably the weakest economic group to support immigration in either country. Since industrialization still was in a rudimentary stage characterized by small plants and artisan shops, its promoters as yet wielded little influence. Nonetheless, industrial interests clamored vigorously and sometimes successfully for the governments to promote immigration.

Many European artisans and skilled workers had come to Argentina during an economic boom that pushed up salaries between 1880 and 1888,[7] but this immigration slowed after an economic recession hit Buenos Aires in 1890. Business revived during the mid-1890's, but industrial immigration did not, which caused the Unión Industrial Argentina, an association representing most Argentine industrialists, to complain that employers were suffering from a lack of adequate labor and especially from a shortage of skilled workers. The Unión Industrial time and again unsuccessfully petitioned the government to subsidize the passage of skilled workers.[8] Urban entrepreneurs favored immigration of unskilled laborers for an additional reason—to form a large pool of potential strikebreakers. Some railway companies, for example, utilized the government's virtually unrestricted immigration policies to import workers from Spain and Italy during the numerous

---

[7] Luis V. Sommi, *La revolución del 90*, second edition, p. 41.

[8] "La inmigración y la industria," *Boletín de la Unión Industrial Argentina*, III (March 27, 1890), 1; "Inmigración y emigración," ibid., VII (June 1, 1895), 19–20; "Inmigración," ibid., XXVI (April 15, 1912), 5.

railroad strikes of the 1890's.[9] Buenos Aires' prestigious *La Nación* commented during a rash of walkouts in 1905 that the immigrants "will be an extremely useful element at the present time, for if well utilized, they can contribute effectively to the solution of strikes that have been declared or will be declared."[10]

Few industrial workers emigrated spontaneously to Chile, an isolated country about which little information existed in Europe. But demand for skilled labor in Chile was strong, and the owners of the nation's nascent industries continually complained about the lack of workers such as plumbers, electricians, machinists, and, above all, foremen of all kinds. Employers were not interested in trying to solve this shortage through promoting vocational education to train the native born. The publications of the Sociedad de Fomento Fabril, the organization representing Chilean industry, made it clear that most employers considered native-born Chilean labor hopelessly slow and inept.[11]

To obtain foreign workers the Sociedad de Fomento subsidized passages for selected European workers and their families. But the national government for years remained deaf to pleas of industrialists to share the expenses of immigrant subsidies. President José M. Balmaceda, a friend of national industry, induced Congress to include a subsidy in the budgets of 1889 and 1890, but he lost office in 1891 and his successors did not promote state support for industrial immigrants until the late 1890's.[12] To attract specialized workers in key industries that the state wished to develop, the government in 1898 began to offer free third-class passage to Chile, free freight for up to two tons of machines and tools, and free transport within Chile from

[9] Adrián Patroni, *Los trabajadores en la República Argentina*, p. 41.

[10] *La Nación*, October 3, 1905, p. 5.

[11] Carlos Vattier, "Apuntes sobre la industria nacional en Chile," *Boletín de la Sociedad Nacional de Minería*, third series (January 31, 1901), p. 26; see also Pedro Luis González, "La inmigración," *Boletín de la Sociedad de Fomento Fabril*, XX (September 1, 1903), 315; and "Operarios estranjeros para los ferrocarriles del estado," ibid., XIX (May 1, 1902), 182.

[12] For the Sociedad's position on this issue see Sociedad de Fomento Fabril, *Inmigración libre*, p. 3. The budget appropriations for immigration subsidies are found in Chile, Presidente, *Lei de presupuestos de los gastos jenerales de la administración pública de Chile.*

the port of arrival to the immigrant's destination. Although Congress expanded these provisions in 1905 to include passage for families of subsidized immigrants, in practice the actual number of free passages depended on the size of the annual congressional appropriations for the scheme, which varied greatly from year to year.[13]

Entrepreneurs and contractors of large construction projects, particularly railroads, formed another influential economic interest group that backed immigration. The contractors of the Argentine railroads relied on immigrant labor and recruited 20,000 Italian workers in 1905 alone.[14] Chile traditionally had supplied construction laborers to other South American countries, but, during an acute labor shortage between 1905 and 1908, the contractors of the railroad from the Chilean port of Arica to La Paz, Bolivia, hired at least 500 Orientals.[15] Railroad construction created auxiliary demands for foreign-born labor, for example, to cut and finish ties in the forests of the Argentine Chaco.[16] Public works in large cities created additional demands for immigration. Construction of the Buenos Aires water system created jobs for 7,500 foreign workers in 1905.[17]

Chile's powerful mining industry added its weight to the construction and industrial interests that had been urging the government to promote immigration. The mine operators, who formed the Sociedad Nacional de Minería, became particularly alarmed during the 1905–1908 labor shortage. High wages in public works and railroad construction were luring some nitrate miners away from the searing deserts of northern Chile, and those who remained were demanding higher wages. With increased labor costs imminent, the Sociedad de Minería in 1906 petitioned the government quickly to recruit and fi-

[13] Ramón Briones Luco, *Glosario de colonización*, pp. 311–313. This work provides detailed information on immigration laws and decrees through 1901. One may consult the 1905 decree in Chile, *Boletín de las leyes i decretos del gobierno*, 2 vols., (Santiago, 1905), I, 802–809.

[14] *La Nación*, November 4, 1905, p. 6.

[15] Chile, Cámara de Diputados, *Boletín de sesiones*, sesiones extraordinarias, December 7, 1907, p. 297 (hereafter abbreviated *B.S.C.D.*).

[16] *La Nación*, June 26, 1897, p. 3; August 2, 1905, p. 7.

[17] Ibid., November 4, 1905, p. 6.

nance a large and steady current of European immigration. To encourage the government to act, the mine owners raised the specter that lack of manpower might force a drop in nitrate exports, taxes on which annually provided about 50 per cent of the national government's income.[18] Congress responded by appropriating 2,500,000 pesos to subsidize immigration for 1908, and the legislators further agreed to let the mine owners' European agents select prospective immigrants.[19]

In their quest to obtain cheap labor, the mine owners did not overlook Oriental immigration. One powerful group of nitrate operators, known as the Combinación Salitrera, began in 1907 to apply pressure on the government to back the importation of Japanese and Chinese. Braving a storm of racist-tinged opposition that appeared in the newspapers, the operators emphasized that Oriental workers were orderly, diligent, and willing to work at low wages. The government hastened to assure the Combinación that while it could not finance the proposed immigration, neither would the state oppose it. But with the demise of Chile's short-lived economic boom in 1908, the mine operators rapidly lost interest in importing Oriental workers, only a few thousand of whom arrived before 1914.[20]

In contrast with Chile, where mining formed one of the most important productive sectors, Argentina's key economic activities were agriculture and stock raising. Both required a large and growing labor supply throughout the 1890–1914 period. In Buenos Aires province, center of cattle production, the need for immigrant labor paralleled the rapid expansion of Argentine meat exports. Buenos Aires stockmen had viewed agriculture, and those who practiced it, with haughty disdain until the late 1880's, when Europe's sudden hunger for Argentine

[18] The petition is reprinted in "El problema de la inmigración," *Boletín de la Sociedad Nacional de Minería,* third series (October–November, 1906), pp. 364–368, and in *La Unión,* November 30, 1906, p. 3. Information on the contribution that nitrate export taxes made to the government's revenue is in Clark Winston Reynolds, "Development Problems of an Export Economy: The Case of Chile and Copper," *Essays on the Chilean Economy,* p. 334.

[19] "Servicio de inmigración," *Boletín de la Sociedad Nacional de Minería,* third series (January 31, 1907), p. 48.

[20] *El Mercurio,* May 20, 1907, p. 3; *La Unión,* June 19, 1913, p. 7.

meat created a demand for vast quantities of cattle feed, particularly alfalfa. The value of alfalfa lands increased tremendously; a French observer reported in 1910 that a hectare purchased at 30 or 40 pesos some years previously now brought 450 pesos.[21]

Suddenly aware that agriculture could be a lucrative business, the Buenos Aires landed interests began to call loudly for the immigration of rural workers. The landowners began to co-operate in the search for European workers with the ruling groups in Santa Fe and Córdoba, provinces that had been encouraging immigration since the late 1860's.[22] Through the Sociedad Rural, the nation's most influential lobbying organization, the landowners of the littoral provinces strongly supported unrestricted immigration of agricultural laborers during the entire 1890–1914 period.[23] Landowning interests also exerted pressure on the government to construct reception facilities for the newly arrived Europeans and to organize their distribution to agricultural areas. In response Congress appropriated over three million pesos to build a large and well-equipped immigrant hotel, which opened in Buenos Aires in 1910.[24]

To justify this sudden interest in immigration, spokesmen for the landed groups developed arguments claiming that the foreigner was a better agriculturist than the native-born Argentine. Perhaps the meth-

[21] Jules Huret, *La Argentina de Buenos Aires al Gran Chaco*, trans. E. Gómez Carrillo, I, 171; on rising land values, see Cárcano, *Sáenz Peña*, p. 23, and Gaston Gori, *El pan nuestro*, p. 30. Data on the price of land in Santa Fe province is found in Ezequiel Gallo (hijo), "Santa Fe en la segunda mitad del siglo XIX. Transformaciones en su estructura regional," *Anuario del Instituto de Investigaciones Históricas*. VII (1964), pp. 145, 150–151.

[22] Manuel Bejarano, *La política colonizadora en la provincia de Buenos Aires (1854–1930)*, mimeographed, pp. 9, 23, 48–49, 56.

[23] Emilio Lahitte, "Correspondencia sobre nuestra inmigración, *Anales de la Sociedad Rural Argentina*, XXVIII (January 31, 1894), 46–47. For opinion of the *Sociedad Rural* after 1894, see "Exportación e inmigración," ibid., XXX (January 31, 1896), 148–150; "Colonización e inmigración," ibid., XLV (November–December, 1910), 142–143.

[24] Argentine Republic, Congreso Nacional, *Diario de Sesiones de la Cámara de Diputados*, June 19, 1905, pp. 647–649 (hereafter abbreviated *D.S.C.D.*); Argentine Republic, Congreso Nacional, *Diario de Sesiones de la Cámara de Senadores*, December 1, 1910, p. 85 (hereafter abbreviated *D.S.C.S.*).

ods of the southern Italian farmers left something to be desired, but this was more than compensated for by their patience, energy, and frugality.[25] At the same time, the creole agricultural worker was portrayed as lazy, frivolous, and totally lacking in ambition.[26] One rich landowner who himself had emigrated to Argentina as a young man wrote a short novel, *Las cien hectáreas de Pedro Villegas*, which contrasted a French immigrant's loving care of the land with the wasteful and primitive techniques of his creole employee. The Argentine, who believed it impossible to support a family on one hundred hectares of rich agricultural land, had to be trained and guided by his French employer before becoming a successful farmer.[27]

During periods of labor shortage in rural areas, cries for increased immigration became particularly intense. In 1903 and again in 1905 agricultural interests complained that the corn crop might rot for lack of harvest labor.[28] As a solution to situations like this, some landowners proposed government subsidies to pay immigrant passages. The government had experimented with prepaid passages during the late 1880's, but after 1890 most national leaders agreed with liberal economists that subsidies were wasteful in a country that continued to attract many foreigners spontaneously. In 1899, however, Deputy Manuel Gálvez (not to be confused with the writer of the same name) asked Congress to appropriate eleven million pesos to finance passages. Pointing out that an average of only 14,217 Europeans annually had arrived to stay during the 1891–1896 period, Gálvez argued at length that spontaneous immigration did not supply the needs of agriculture. This proposal received the support of the *Revista Económica*, a publi-

[25] Alois E. Fliess, *La producción agrícola y ganadera de la República Argentina en el año 1891*, pp. 102–103.

[26] Examples are Agustín Álvarez Suárez, *Breve historia de la provincia de Mendoza*, p. 7; Alejandro Calzada, "Enseñanza de la crisis," *Revista argentina de ciencias políticas*, VIII (August 12, 1914), 499; and Ezio Colombo and Carlos M. Urien, *La República Argentina en 1910*, I, 147.

[27] Godofredo Daireaux, *Las cien hectáreas de Pedro Villegas*, pp. 9, 13, 19, 29.

[28] Estanislao S. Zeballos, "Problemas conexos con la inmigración," *Revista de Derecho, Historia y Letras*, XV (June, 1903), 545; *La Nación*, July 9, 1905, p. 5.

cation representing landed interests,[29] but Congress did not act and the question was at any rate resolved when spontaneous immigration began to increase substantially in 1904.

The reliance of Argentine agriculture on foreign labor was poignantly illustrated in 1911 and 1912 when the Italian government banned all emigration to Argentina. This prohibition, provoked by a diplomatic spat over sanitary conditions on immigrant ships, deeply alarmed agricultural interests. "It seems that we are living in a nightmare," complained La Prensa,[30] but disaster was averted by an increase in Spanish immigration, by government pressure on the steamship lines forcing them to double the return trip fare to Europe, and by greater utilization of the existing labor force.[31]

Additional support for massive immigration came from the owners of plantations in Argentina's remote northern territories. Through the Unión Industrial Argentina, these men proclaimed the first public support of Asiatic immigration in Argentina. The Orientals, it was claimed, "were excellent, active, and intelligent laborers" who would provide the intensive care that semitropical plantation crops require. In agreement, La Nación's editorials appealed to the government to support non-European immigration. The Japanese were by no means an inferior race, claimed this newspaper, for they were clean, active, hardworking, and very intelligent.[32] But Argentine opinion continued to view Asiatic immigration dimly and the government refused to recruit Orientals, only a few hundred of whom actually arrived before 1914.[33]

Unlike Argentina, agricultural production in Chile was not expanding rapidly nor was it primarily oriented toward the export market.

---

[29] D.S.C.D., July 31, 1899, p. 555; "Inmigración: Importante proyecto con este fin," Revista Económica, third epoch, I (August 10, 1899), 213.

[30] Robert F. Foerster, The Italian Emigration of Our Times, p. 276; La Prensa, August 1, 1911, p. 7.

[31] La Vanguardia, August 30, 1911, p. 1.

[32] "Inmigración," Boletín de la Unión Industrial Argentina, XXVI (April 15, 1912), 5; La Nación, February 5, 1910, p. 6, February 18, 1910, p. 10, June 24, 1912, p. 9.

[33] For the beginnings of Japanese immigration to Argentina, see James Lawrence Tigner, "The Ryukyuans in Argentina," Hispanic American Historical Review, XLVII (May, 1967), pp. 203–205.

As they had in centuries past, the great landowners of the rich central valley, the principal agricultural region, relied for their labor supply on the servile and obedient native-born *inquilinos,* workers tied to the land by the strong bonds of custom and paternalism. Assured of a steady labor supply, the landed interests seldom supported government-sponsored immigration. They also opposed plans to colonize the southern frontier provinces of Cautín and Malleco, which the government had seized from the Araucanian Indians during the 1880's. Immigration, the great landowners feared, might create a new agricultural region in the south to challenge their traditional monopoly of the national market. When President Balmaceda began an ambitious plan to colonize the frontier in the late 1880's, he encountered powerful landowner-based opposition.[34] The agrarian interests and their principal political spokesman, the Conservative party, remained hostile to government subsidized immigration until 1905. During the Chilean economic boom beginning in that year, agricultural laborers began to leave the great estates of the central valley, attracted by high wages elsewhere.[35] Threatened with a labor shortage or an increased wage bill, agricultural interests began to urge the government to recruit European workers to supply the needs of the mines and the public works projects.

The Sociedad Nacional de Agricultura, which represented the large landowners and had never favored immigration in the period since 1890, suddenly reversed its position. "Cost what it may," emphasized the group's publication, "immigration, immediate and abundant immigration . . . ought to be the fundamental objective of the government's program."[36] In Congress representatives of agricultural interests echoed Senator Fernando Lazcano, who worried, "I don't know how the wheat crop will be harvested this year, when the high wages paid on the great public works have lured away the country folk and left only women and children behind." He went on to plead that the gov-

[34] Hernán Ramírez Necochea, *Balmaceda y la contrarrevolución de 1891,* p. 145.
[35] *B.S.C.D.,* sesiones extraordinarias, December 7, 1907, p. 297.
[36] "La inmigración," *Boletín de la Sociedad Nacional de Agricultura,* XXXVII (November 15, 1906), 768–769.

ernment send two ships at once to Spain and Italy to bring workers to Chile.[37] Ironically, Congress heard agricultural interests ask for the first time for better treatment of immigrants to Chile and in particular for the establishment of adequate immigrant reception facilities in the major seaports.[38]

But by the latter part of 1908 the economic boom had suddenly died and manpower again became relatively plentiful.[39] When workers began to drift back to the estates, agricultural interests abruptly abandoned their short-lived support of immigration. The need of the hour was now held to be strict government economy, and agriculture called for an end to all state immigration subsidies.[40] Immigration was now, according to *El Mercurio*, "a positive economic damage for the country," which at any rate could be encouraged anew during any future economic revival.[41] The only other occasion when Chilean agriculture supported immigration before World War I occurred during an economic boomlet in 1912 and 1913.[42]

Chilean agriculture was the only major economic interest in either republic that did not consistently support liberal immigration policies during the period beginning in 1890 and closing with the outbreak of the First World War. Industrialists in both countries and mining groups in Chile frequently urged their governments to promote immigration, both to supply skilled workers and to make available a constant supply of cheap unskilled labor. But the Argentine agricultural and livestock industries comprised the group that most directly required continued massive immigration. Argentina had become one of the

[37] Chile, Senado, *Boletín de sesiones*, sesiones extraordinarias, November 7, 1906, p. 172 (hereafter abbreviated *B.S.S.*).

[38] *B.S.S.*, sesiones extraordinarias, January 2, 1907, p. 1043. The decree of March 1, 1905, establishing the immigrant hostelry is reprinted in *Boletín de la Sociedad de Fomento Fabril*, XXII (July 1, 1905), 419–420.

[39] Luis Navarrette, "El alcoholismo, la inmigración i la falta de brazos," *Revista de Educación Nacional*, III (November, 1907), 264–265.

[40] "Servicio de inmigración," *Boletín de la Sociedad Nacional de Agricultura*, XXXVIII (December 15, 1907), 724–725.

[41] *El Mercurio*, December 1, 1907, p. 5.

[42] "La escasez de brazos," *Boletín de la Sociedad Nacional de Agricultura*, XLIII (June 15, 1912), 333–334.

world's great agricultural exporters by the end of World War I, but it was still a sparsely populated nation that in the absence of modern mechanized techniques could expand farm production and exports only as long as immigrant labor continued to arrive. Argentine national prosperity, in other words, was directly linked to massive European immigration. Chile's economy was also tied closely to the international market, but the production of that nation's chief export, nitrates, did not require massive European immigration. The mining interests pleaded for skilled European miners, but, except for brief periods of labor shortage, Chilean miners, together with Bolivian and Peruvian migrants, were able to supply all the unskilled manpower that nitrate extraction required.

The economic groups desiring European or Asian labor were able to draw upon and utilize elaborate theories to justify immigration, theories that intellectuals in Argentina and Chile were preparing. Building upon the cosmopolitan ideas of nineteenth-century liberals like Alberdi in Argentina and Vicuña Mackenna in Chile, intellectuals in both countries during the quarter century preceding World War I developed a comprehensive justification of immigration that made it virtually synonymous with modernization. The European, they predicted, would shake both nations out of the traditional colonial mold and make them powerful, dynamic, and civilized. According to the intellectuals, the foreign-born population would promote not only economic development but also political stability and cultural progress.

Positivist social philosophy, popular in both Argentina and Chile since the 1880's, formed the ideological substructure for this justification of immigration. As it was understood in Latin America, positivism taught that society could be objectively or scientifically observed and that universally applicable social laws would emerge from this observation. Theoretically, any country whose government shaped social and economic policy in accordance with these laws would enjoy material and cultural progress. Argentine and Chilean positivism also absorbed many doctrines of economic liberalism. In particular, liberal economists and positivist social scientists agreed that a nation would prosper and progress when maximum international mobility of labor existed.[43]

Questions of race preoccupied Argentine and Chilean thinkers no less than economic problems. As late as 1914, many intellectuals based their evaluation of racial problems on the biological determinist theories that Count Gobineau, Gustave Le Bon, and Herbert Spencer had popularized in Europe. Under the influence of positivism, Argentine and Chilean writers raised these ideas to the status of social laws. These pseudoscientific racial theories, which considered non-whites inherently inferior and condemned racial mixture, found a sympathetic audience in Latin America, partly because they reinforced a long-standing creole disdain for the Indian.[44] In both countries the upper classes were predominantly creole, that is white and of Spanish descent, but the lower social levels commonly were mestizo, of mixed Spanish and Indian descent. The elite groups and most intellectuals scorned the dark-skinned masses as biologically and culturally inferior.[45]

The mestizo population, it was assumed in Argentina and Chile, would never foster progress and development. Typical of the intellectual climate of the time were the racial theories of the Argentine sociologist Lucas Ayarragaray that claimed the mestizo population was inherently degenerate physically and morally.[46] The mixed blood,

[43] For discussion of positivism as understood in Argentina and Chile, see William Rex Crawford, *A Century of Latin American Thought*, pp. 95–142, and Leopoldo Zea, *Dos etapas del pensamiento en Hispanoamérica*, pp. 175–371. Of the voluminous Argentine and Chilean literature analyzing positivism, the following works proved valuable for this study: José Ingenieros, *Socialismo y legislación del trabajo*, p. 5; Edwards Vivas, *La fronda aristocrática*, pp. 40–45; and Guillermo Subercaseaux, *Historia de las doctrinas económicas en América y en especial en Chile*, pp. 40–45.

[44] Magnus Mörner, *Race Mixture in the History of Latin America*, p. 108. This work contains a valuable analysis of Latin American racial attitudes since the Iberian conquest.

[45] Kalman H. Silvert, "Los mitos sociales chilenos," *Revista de la Universidad (La Plata)*, III (January–March, 1958), 109; Sergio Bagú. *La sociedad de masas en su historia*, p. 23. These two works comment on race attitudes in Chile and Argentina, respectively.

[46] Lucas Ayarragaray, *La constitución étnica argentina y sus problemas*, pp. 7–11.

Ayarragaray wrote in 1904, is a dull creature, "incapable of grasping synthetic concepts and advanced methods of reasoning."[47] Chilean writers similarly heaped scorn on their own countrymen of mixed Indian and European blood. One essayist contended that Chilean mestizos were phlegmatic, sickly, morally weak, unambitious, inconstant, dirty, and dishonorable.[48] An influential newspaper agreed that Chilean blood was "exhausted," and "carries within itself the seeds of stagnation."[49]

The solution to this racial problem, alleged some intellectuals, was gradually to whiten the population by means of large-scale mixture of the swarthy mestizos with European immigrants. Ayarragaray thought that a mestizo would have to be bred with whites for at least three generations before an individual would emerge capable of "assimilating European civilization."[50] But, according to Argentine and Chilean writers, not all immigrant races were equally desirable. Northern Europeans allegedly were superior and would contribute much more to the evolution of the mestizos than southern or eastern Europeans. The worship of the Anglo-Saxon and the German was particularly strong in Chile, whose leading newspaper, *El Mercurio*, assured its readers in 1898 that the Italian and Spaniard were "too much like us in habits, customs, education, ideas, and industries," and that the northern European was a preferable immigrant.[51]

Across the Andes, however, Italians enjoyed greater racial prestige and also were praised by many Argentine writers as bearers of a distinguished cultural tradition. Furthermore, the reputation of the Spanish immigrant began to improve in Argentina by 1910, largely because of the growing influence of the intellectual movement known as Hispanicism. Emphasizing that unique and valuable cultural traditions united Spain and her former American colonies, Hispanicism attracted prominent Argentine support including the social essayist Manuel

---

[47] Lucas Ayarragaray, *La anarquía argentina y el caudillismo*, p. 244.
[48] Felix del Campo N., "Pro inmigración," *Boletín de la Sociedad de Fomento Fabril*, XXI (May 1, 1904), 187.
[49] *La Lei*, September 27, 1898, p. 1.
[50] Ayarragaray, *La constitución étnica*, p. 15.
[51] *El Mercurio*, March 2, 1896, p. 2.

Ugarte and University of La Plata President Joaquín V. González, who was also an author of some renown. Both men claimed that the Spanish were far more desirable immigrants than other Europeans.[52]

While intellectuals admired the northern European, the Italian, or the Spaniard, they generally viewed Syrian, Jewish, or Oriental immigrants with a dislike approaching disgust. These groups, it was claimed, had deteriorated biologically to such low levels that they could contribute nothing to the improvement of the mestizo. Journalists in both countries led this defamation. Bitter newspaper articles frequently appeared condemning Syrians, Jews, and Orientals as inherently disease ridden, immoral, and lazy.[53]

But, allegedly, if these "inferior" races were kept out, gradual intermarriage between foreigners and the native born would produce one of the world's most beautiful and noble peoples. A variety of Argentine authors expressed this conviction. The novelist Francisco A. Sicardi foresaw the Argentine of the future as physically and morally "almost at a state of human perfection."[54] Florencio Sánchez, Argentina's most famed twentieth-century dramatist, reached a similar conclusion. His play *La gringa* resolved a conflict between native-born Argentines and Italian immigrants by joining the two races in marriage. From this union, he exclaimed, "the virile race of the future" would emerge.[55] Manuel Gálvez, a young nationalist writer critical of some of the effects of immigration, at times became infected with enthusiasm about the contribution foreigners were making to Argentina's future.

[52] Manuel Ugarte, *El porvenir de América Latina*, p. 36; see also Joaquín V. González, *La Argentina y sus amigos: Discursos sobre política internacional, 1906–1910*, in *Obras completas*, IX, 189.

[53] Numerous journalists of the period argued that these immigrant groups were racially inferior. See *La Nación*, November 20, 1890, p. 1, December 14, 1908, p. 6, and June 19, 1914, p. 11, for criticism of the Jews; *La Prensa*, September 10, 1910, p. 12, *La Nación*, February 27, 1910, p. 8, and *El Mercurio*, April 13, 1908, p. 1, for criticism of the Syrians and Lebanese; and *La Prensa*, July 21, 1912, p. 10, November 10, 1913, p. 6, *La Nación*, July 24, 1912, p. 9, and *El Mercurio*, August 4, 1906, p. 5, for criticism of the Chinese and Japanese.

[54] Quoted in Emma Napolitano, "Francisco A. Sicardi," *Instituto de Literatura Argentina: Sección de Crítica*, II (1942), 401.

[55] Florencio Sánchez, *La gringa*, in Dardo Cúneo, ed., *Teatro completo de Florencio Sánchez*, third edition, p. 144.

The mixture of Basque, Armenian, Spanish, Italian, and Argentine, Gálvez predicted, would produce a new race "predestined in the near future to a magnificent destiny."[56]

Improving the mestizo population through intermarriage with Europeans was only one justification that intellectuals developed for large-scale immigration. Another common assertion was that immigration was the ideal source for the dense populations both nations allegedly needed to advance culturally and economically. In addition, writers in both countries feared that without greater populations, Argentina and Chile might lose sovereignty over part or even all of their national territories.

From the viewpoints of economics and geography, the concern many Chilean intellectuals voiced about their country's lack of population was hardly justified. Natural increase had added over one million inhabitants to the Chilean population between 1860 and 1895, and relatively little empty land suitable for agriculture remained, even in the frontier provinces. Population density per square mile of arable land was much higher than in the Western Hemisphere nations receiving large numbers of immigrants. In 1907, for example, Chile counted 149 people per arable square mile, while the United States contained 62 and Argentina only 8.[57]

Chilean writers disregarded these hard facts and formulated a myth that their nation was relatively unpopulated. They usually pointed to the virgin forests of the south, stretching across thirteen degrees of latitude between Puerto Montt and the settlements Chile had established on the Strait of Magellan. With these lands, one writer exclaimed, "we are far below a normal population density."[58] Echoing this argument, Santiago Aldunate B., long-time Chilean minister to Italy, pointed out that, since Chile's population density in 1909 was only one-sixteenth that of Switzerland, Chile should aim to multiply its population sixteen times to reach a total of fifty million![59] These

56 Manuel Gálvez, *El solar de la raza*, pp. 61–62.
57 Mark Jefferson, *Recent Colonization in Chile*, p. 51.
58 Felix del Campo N., *La inmigración europea en Chile como servicio del estado*, p. 15.
59 Santiago Aldunate B., "Inmigración i propaganda," *Boletín de la Sociedad de Fomento Fabril*, XXVI (May 1, 1909), 238–239.

authors overlooked the rough terrain and harsh climate of the far south, which make the area unsuitable for agriculture without enormous capital investment.

Fear of Argentine economic and political aggression was a principal motivation for this Chilean concern with population growth and immigration. As recently as 1860 the estimated population of Chile had outnumbered that of Argentina, but massive immigration gave the latter nation clear numerical superiority by 1900.[60] When war threatened between the two countries during the late 1890's, Chilean journalists urged the government to follow the Argentine example by encouraging a large and steady current of immigration on which Chile's industrial and military power could be based.[61] Otherwise, warned one editorialist, Chile would become only "a poor backwater compared to Argentina.[62]

Voices such as these called for more government financial support to subsidize immigrant passages and to advertise Chile among prospective immigrants in Europe. El Mercurio, furthermore, urged the government to stimulate Italian immigration by establishing and subsidizing a direct shipping line from southern Europe to Chilean ports.[63] Also necessary, many writers thought, was a thorough reform of the government's disorganized and corrupt colonization and immigration departments. Criticism of these agencies became particularly loud after the collapse of an attempt in 1896 and 1897 to colonize the rainy and cold island province of Chiloé with Europeans.

The Chilean government's immigration agents had recruited hundreds of colonists in large northern European cities for the Chiloé

[60] Walter F. Willcox, "Increase in Population of the Earth and of the Continents since 1650," in Walter F. Willcox, ed., International Migrations, II, 77.

[61] See, for example, editorials in El Mercurio of October 5, 1898, p. 2, and of December 4, 1900, p. 2. Also reflecting this theme was "Inmigración libre," Boletín de la Sociedad de Fomento Fabril, XVII (December 1, 1900), 362.

[62] La Lei, June 11, 1903, p. 1. Similar fears were expressed during congressional debates on immigration policy. See, for example, speech of Enrique MacIver, B.S.C.D., sesiones ordinarias, January 11, 1892, pp. 521–523.

[63] El Mercurio, April 24, 1896, p. 2, January 16, 1897, p. 2, June 23, 1907, p. 3; Belisario García, "Chile, como país colonizador," La Revista de Chile, III (December 1, 1899), 342.

venture. Lacking agricultural experience, the colonists arrived on the densely forested island, whose rainfall sometimes totaled 180 inches annually, to find that the government's colonization service had done almost nothing to help them become established. Ill-planned and underfinanced, the venture floundered by the end of 1897 when most of the three hundred families of colonists left in disgust for the mainland or for Europe, where their tales of the Chiloé fiasco embarrassed Chilean attempts to recruit colonists for other schemes.[64] In 1902 the minister of foreign affairs and colonization declared that reform could wait no longer and presented a comprehensive plan to reorganize the colonization and immigration services.[65] But Chile's lethargic Congress took no action and the government continued to create immigration bureaus and agencies without any rational scheme.

Like their colleagues in Chile, Argentine intellectuals were proclaiming loudly that rapid population growth was essential to national progress. This concern grew intense after the second Argentine census, taken in 1895, revealed that the population barely had reached four million and that virtually the entire interior of the republic remained a desert, as Domingo F. Sarmiento, the nation's most famous writer, had described it in 1845.[66] The need for population was so great, editorialized La Nación in 1899, that at least 200,000 immigrants should arrive yearly for the indefinite future. Fourteen years later the national population had surpassed seven million, but the economist Pedro Ezcurra wrote that Argentina would be able to fulfill its potentialities only if the population doubled every twenty years.[67]

Argentine writers grew particularly alarmed when they directed their

[64] The whole unfortunate affair is described in W. Anderson Smith, *Temperate Chile*, p. 67; *La Lei*, September 10, 1897, p. 1; García, "Chile, como país colonizador," p. 344; Alfredo Weber S., *Chiloé: Su estado actual, su colonización, su porvenir*, pp. 158–159; Chile, Ministerio de Relaciones Exteriores, Culto i Colonización, *Memoria* (1897), pp. 18–19. See also D. C. M. Platt, "British Agricultural Colonization in Latin America," *Inter-American Economic Affairs*, XIX (Summer, 1965), 28.

[65] Chile, Ministerio de Relaciones Exteriores, Culto i Colonización, *Memoria . . . presentada al Congreso Nacional de 1902*, I, 224–234.

[66] Domingo F. Sarmiento, *Facundo: Civilización i barbarie*, p. 27.

[67] *La Nación*, February 28, 1899, p. 4; Pedro Ezcurra, "Inmigración," *Revista de Derecho, Historia y Letras*, XLIV (April, 1913), 503.

attention to the immense empty territories of Patagonia. After an 1895 estimate revealed that only 300 of Neuquén Territory's 24,000 inhabitants were Argentine and the rest Chilean, a few Buenos Aires journalists began to sound the alarm that their country's sovereignty over the distant southern regions was in peril.[68] To convince national opinion that the south must be populated rapidly, two respected intellectuals attempted to publicize Argentina's weakness in Patagonia.

Roberto J. Payró, a reporter for *La Nación* as well as a novelist and social essayist, traveled extensively in Patagonia in 1898 in preparation for his book *La Australia argentina*. Dismayed by the desolation of Argentine Patagonia, Payró compared its tiny, backward towns with the flourishing Chilean settlements on the Strait of Magellan. Patagonia would continue to stagnate, Payró predicted, unless the government actively directed immigration to the area.[69]

Four years after Payró's book appeared, Gabriel Carrasco, a respected economist, reiterated the Chilean threat to the south in his book *De Buenos Aires al Neuquén*. Carrasco, who also traveled widely in Patagonia, was alarmed to report that at least three-quarters of Neuquén Territory's population was still Chilean and that the neighboring republic controlled nearly all Neuquén commerce and mining. To counteract the presumed Chilean threat against continued Argentine political control, Carrasco called for rapid settlement of the area with European immigrants, who he assumed would become loyal to Argentina.[70]

These books perhaps helped to direct national opinion toward the need to settle the south with European immigrants, which by the first years of the new century had become a major public issue. In 1901 *La Prensa* and *La Nación* launched editorial campaigns in support of the rapid colonization of Neuquén and the neighboring territory of Chubut.[71] When several hundred of the Welsh colonists in Chubut,

---

[68] The population estimate first appeared in *El Mercurio*, February 13, 1895, p. 4; see also *La Prensa*, April 18, 1895, p. 3, and November 21, 1897, p. 4.

[69] Roberto J. Payró, *La Australia argentina*, p. 24.

[70] Gabriel Carrasco, *De Buenos Aires al Neuquén*, pp. 40–50, 71.

[71] For example, *La Nación*, November 4, 1901, p. 5, January 26, 1902, p. 5; *La Prensa*, April 7, 1901, p. 6, December 14, 1901, p. 5.

whose settlement dated from 1865, left in 1902 for other homes in Canada, the newspapers attacked the government strongly. Editorialists had at various times criticized the colonists' reluctance to assimilate, but *La Prensa* equated their exodus with "the failure of colonization in Patagonia," and *La Nación* evinced "profound sadness" as they departed.[72]

Much of northern and western Argentina suffered the same backwardness and lack of population affecting the south. After a visit to Cartamarca, one of the most underdeveloped provinces, Payró reported that only the foreign settler could break the stranglehold that tradition, laziness, and fatalism held over the area. Other voices, particularly *La Prensa*, demanded prompt government action to direct a current of immigration toward Misiones Territory, whose loss to Brazil many feared. The newspaper noted in 1898 that only about nine thousand out of a potential three million arable hectares were under cultivation in the territory.[73]

The national government, however, was interested in directing immigration toward the flourishing agricultural provinces of the littoral, not in settling the remote interior. Consequently, the state did little to solve problems of poor transportation and inadequate rural credit, nor did it set up a system by which immigrants could easily gain title to tracts of government land in the territories. Corruption and maladministration had made existing land legislation almost inoperative. Discouraged by those obstacles, few foreigners ventured into Patagonia or the far north. In 1909 *La Prensa* noted with dismay that, of the 200,000 immigrants who arrived the previous year, only 110 settled in Misiones, 76 in the Chaco and 35 in Formosa, two other territories in northern Argentina.[74]

Perhaps the most common theme of the pro-immigration ideology was that rapid economic development required vast numbers of foreign laborers. Increased population, economists in both nations repeated,

---

[72] John E. Baur, "The Welsh in Patagonia: An Example of Nationalistic Migration," *Hispanic American Historical Review*, XXXIV (November, 1954), 487; *La Prensa*, October 18, 1901; *La Nación*, May 15, 1902, p. 4.

[73] Roberto J. Payró, *En las tierras de Inti*, pp. 50–51, 55–56.

[74] *La Prensa*, October 17, 1898, p. 4; January 17, 1909, p. 5.

would stimulate expansion of the export industries, whose growth was often made synonymous with economic development. Argentine writers cited the contribution that foreigners were making to the country's rapid rise as a leading agricultural exporter.[75] *La Nación* praised the immigrant farmers as "heroes of labor" while Leopoldo Lugones in his poem "To the Cattle and the Harvests" celebrated "the blond European youth," who produces "a wealth of golden wheat."[76] Lugones and the future political scientist Horacio Rivarola also called attention to the immigrant as a factor of progress in the cattle industry, traditionally regarded as the stronghold of the Argentine creole. Both writers praised the English stock breeders in Argentina as progressive innovators.[77]

Inspired by the rapid growth of Argentine population and wealth after 1900, intellectuals began to praise the impact of immigration in adulatory terms. In one outburst of patriotic pride, Manuel Gálvez exulted that the immigrants were helping native-born Argentines form "a new nation, the nation of tomorrow, while Europe represents the agonizing past."[78] In like vein, the respected former president, Carlos Pelligrini, testified that immigration and foreign capital were making Argentina "one of the greatest nations of the earth."[79] The greatest in power and wealth was not quite enough for Juan Alsina, the government's director of immigration, who predicted that the millions of foreigners would "realize here the CHRISTIAN REPUBLIC, perfect and durable, long desired by philosophers."[80]

These enthusiasts of immigration sometimes claimed that Argentina

[75] Juan A. Alsina, *La inmigración en el primer siglo de la independencia*, pp. 141–145.

[76] *La Nación*, February 17, 1893, p. 1; Leopoldo Lugones, "A los ganados y a las mieses," in *Obras poéticas completas*, p. 438.

[77] Lugones, *Obras poéticas completas*, p. 448; Horacio C. Rivarola, *Las transformaciones de la sociedad argentina y sus consecuencias institutionales (1853 á 1910)*, p. 117.

[78] Manuel Gálvez, "Los himnos de la nueva energía," *El Monitor de la Educación Común*, XXXIX (October 31, 1911), 71.

[79] Carlos Pelligrini, in his Introduction to Albert E. Martínez and Maurice Lewandowsky, *The Argentine in the Twentieth Century*, trans. Bernard Miall, p. xliii.

[80] Juan A. Alsina, *La inmigración europea en la República Argentina*, p. 350.

would regenerate and give new hope to the world's poor and dis-
possessed. The penniless European could hope to find economic re-
wards in Argentina, the land that, in the words of novelist Carlos M.
Ocantos, "does not hide its treasures, but offers and delivers them to
the strong, the laborious and the audacious." Argentina, repeated a
chorus of authors, was a "land of promise."[81] This was a promise not
only of economic opportunity but also of fraternalism and brother-
hood. Gálvez, for example, exclaimed,

> Here we are all brothers
> And we give to those who come from abroad
> The friendship of our hearts and a place
> In this land of promise and of love.[82]

Chilean intellectuals did not share this optimistic and fraternal rheto-
ric, perhaps because immigration never succeeded in promoting rapid
economic growth in Chile.

Immigrant contributions to agriculture received less intellectual attention in Chile, although travelers to the German colonies of the south
frequently pointed to the flourishing state of agriculture there. After
visiting Llanquihue, the engineer Santiago Marín Vicuña praised the
German farmers as "extremely hardworking, economical, and orderly."
El Mercurio echoed this theme, but the strongest support of the immigrant farmer was Alejandro Venegas, a well-known social essayist.
Because Chilean farmers hated foreign innovations, he wrote, they
gathered no forage and built no stables, even for milch cows. In general, Venegas concluded, the most backward sectors of Chilean agriculture were the least foreign.[83]

By 1914 a few economic thinkers in both republics were beginning
to question the wisdom of an export economy and to support the de-

---

[81] Two works that developed this theme were Carlos María Ocantos, *Promisión*, p. 208, and Manuel C. Chueco, *La República Argentina en su primer
centenario*, I, 484.

[82] Gálvez, "Los himnos de la nueva energía," pp. 70–71.

[83] Santiago Marín Vicuña, *Al través de la Patagonia*, p. 29; Alejandro
Venegas (pseud. J. E. Valdes Cange), *Sinceridad: Chile íntimo en 1910*, pp.
18, 21. Newspaper comments include *El Mercurio*, September 30, 1910, p. 3,
and *El Porvenir*, October 4, 1893, p. 1.

velopment of national industry. The immigrant, however, was still essential to the more self-sufficient industrial economy these writers envisioned. For one thing, massive immigration would create the large internal market needed to support manufacturing industries.[84] Furthermore, according to economists in both Argentina and Chile, foreign skilled laborers would promote industrial growth, while other immigrants would bring capital to start whole new industries.[85]

By the first decade of the twentieth century, industrialization was gaining some support in Chile, which was not prospering under the classical liberal model of international free trade, as was its neighbor across the Andes. While world demand for Argentine beef and wheat seemed to grow insatiably, a decline in Chilean nitrate exports during the 1890's had produced a national economic slump by 1896.[86] Perhaps because of these fluctuations in the world market for raw materials, *El Mercurio* wrote in 1896 that "the future of Chile is essentially industrial," and that the national interest required a steady immigration of skilled workers and consumers. This newspaper, along with the middle-class Radical party's *La Lei*, supported industrial immigration through most of the pre-1914 period. The latter paper hoped at one point to witness 500,000 "English, German, Belgian, Norwegian, and BOER" industrial workers arrive in Chile.[87] The strong currents of racism pervading the Chilean intellectual climate inclined Chileans who envisioned an industrial economy to rely on immigration to supply the required workers. Nicolás Palacios' *Raza chilena* of 1904 was the first important Chilean book to suggest that a wiser course would be to establish vocational schools and technical institutes to train native-born Chileans for industrial jobs. But the conviction that the European

[84] Carlos Saavedra Lamas, *Economía colonial*, p. 55.

[85] Argentine economists who employed these arguments included Francisco Rodríguez del Busto, *Problemas económicos y financieros*, p. 544, and Francisco Latzina, *Diccionario geográfico argentino*, second edition, p. 281. Similar Chilean arguments are in *El Mercurio*, April 14, 1910, p. 5, and del Campo N., *La inmigración europea*, pp. 15–17.

[86] Jaime Eyzaguirre, *Chile durante el gobierno de Errázuriz Echaurren, 1896–1901*, second edition, pp. 83–84.

[87] *El Mercurio*, April 24, 1896, p. 2; *La Lei*, February 14, 1902, p. 2.

would be a better industrial worker than the Chilean lingered on during the decade preceding World War I.

As part of their theory that the foreigner was the key to prosperity, economists in both countries tried to compute the value of immigration in monetary terms. An Argentine scholar, Francisco Latzina, calculated that each immigrant brought with him capital amounting to 20 gold pesos and that the muscle power of an agricultural laborer was worth 1,500 pesos annually. Thus, net immigration of 70,000 workers per year would contribute 102,000,000 gold pesos annually to the national stock of capital. Similarly, an editorialist in *El Mercurio* computed the value of immigration in terms of the resources the nation would save with the arrival of each foreign worker. Assuming that the education of one laborer cost the nation 3,500 francs, while the government had to spend only 150 francs to transport an immigrant to Chile, the writer calculated that the nation would save 335,000,000 francs through the immigration of the 100,000 workers he thought Chile required.[88] The lack of nationalism and of concern for the welfare of the native born that such statements evidence may startle today's reader but raised few eyebrows in the cosmopolitan intellectual climate of Argentina and Chile in 1900.

Although intellectual opinion regarded immigration's contribution to economic development as extremely important, writers in both countries predicted that the foreigners would make the equally significant impact of spreading modern European civilization throughout Argentina and Chile. The intellectual climate at the turn of the century was hostile to traditional creole culture. As heirs of positivism and of the Enlightenment, most writers before about 1905 believed that Argentina and Chile had inherited fanaticism, superstition and ignorance from three centuries of Spanish clerical and reactionary rule. These traits were assumed to be so deeply rooted in the national character that the only hope for rapid improvement was the massive introduction of Europeans to spread what was purportedly the reason and light of contemporary Western civilization.

[88] Latzina, *Diccionario geográfico*, p. 282; *El Mercurio*, September 26, 1899, p. 2.

Agustín Álvarez Suárez, an Argentine philosopher and educator, was well known for his conviction that the important contribution of immigration was not material progress but new European ideas to combat the allegedly reactionary heritage of the Spanish regime. Álvarez Suárez, however, feared that the influence of creole culture was so powerful that the second or third generation immigrant would gradually forget his heritage of civilization and adopt old creole ways. Few writers who supported immigration shared this pessimism. Most of them, like Payró, were content to praise the contribution of the foreigner to the development of liberalism and the suppression of clericalism.[89]

Chilean intellectuals were similarly convinced that immigration would raise their country's cultural level. *El Sur*, the principal newspaper of Concepción, noted that as a "young nation without any culture, we must assimilate from other nations their most important contributions." Chile, the article went on to boast, was the most advanced of the Latin American nations because of "the liberal welcome we have always given to foreign culture without stupid pride and foolish patriotism." Valentín Letelier, a leading Chilean educator, typified the views of the cosmopolitan intellectuals when he proclaimed that Chile welcomed any foreigner who might contribute his "intelligence, industry, art, science, or simple muscular force," and that the country "asks of each nation the best of what it has to offer."[90]

These writers, in their urge to Europeanize Latin American culture, welcomed the foreigner not only because he was presumably a general civilizing element but also because he would disseminate European arts and letters. Instead of decrying the lack of an Argentine tradition of painting, Horacio Rivarola seemed content to report that among prominent Buenos Aires artists during the 1825–1875 period, there were eight Frenchmen, eight Italians, one German, and one Uruguayan, but no Argentine creoles. Other authors praised the strong Italian influ-

[89] Agustín Álvarez Suárez, *¿Adónde vamos?*, pp. 323–324, 344; Roberto J. Payró, *Los italianos en la Argentina*, p. 6.

[90] *El Sur* of Concepción, October 7, 1896, quoted in *El Mercurio*, October 9, 1896, p. 2; Valentín Letelier, *La lucha por la cultura*, p. 440.

ence in the architecture and sculpture of the rapidly expanding city of Buenos Aires.[91] Similarly, Chilean liberals emphasized the contributions foreign intellectual immigrants had made during the nineteenth century. Frequently praised were the French naturalist Claudio Gay, the German scholar R. Armando Philippi, the Polish astronomer Ignacio Domeyko, and the Venezuelan poet, educator, and legal scholar Andrés Bello.[92] El Mercurio in 1898 was sure that "almost all of our intellectual culture" was a product of European university and secondary-school teachers.[93]

At least until 1912, when the foreign born began to challenge the creole oligarchy's traditional control of politics, many Argentine intellectuals regarded the European as a civilizing political influence. Immigration's impact on politics was seldom mentioned in Chile, which had long enjoyed relative stability and order under the rule of a strong central government. But in Argentina caudillismo and violence had marred politics for generations. Lucas Ayarragaray argued that nothing better could be expected from a mestizo population and that only a more advanced race composed largely of immigrants would be able to replace caudillismo with a rational and mature political order. Unlike Ayarragaray, some political writers did not emphasize race but simply maintained that immigrants would bring responsible, orderly, and peaceful habits to transform Argentine politics.[94] This was a frequent assertion even though many immigrants originated in parts of Europe lacking democratic political traditions.

The support that intellectuals gave immigration reached its high point around 1905 and then began to decline. This shift in opinion, during which many authors who once had justified immigration began to reject it for nationalistic social philosophies, paralleled rapid social

---

[91] Rivarola, Las transformaciones de la sociedad argentina, p. 47; "Los italianos en Buenos Aires," Caras y Caretas, II (September 23, 1899), n.p.

[92] An example of such praise is in Alejandro Venegas (pseud. J. E. Valdes Cange), Cartas al excelentísimo señor Don Pedro Montt, second edition, p. 36.

[93] El Mercurio, February 2, 1898, p. 2.

[94] Ayarragaray, La anarquía argentina, pp. 258–288; Lucio V. Mansilla, Un país sin ciudadanos.

and economic change in Argentina and Chile. Aspects of this change, which alarmed many Argentine and Chilean creoles and forced them to re-examine the cosmopolitan ideology, included foreigners' sudden accumulation of vast economic power and their rapid ascent into the middle class of society.

CHAPTER TWO

The Economic and Social Impacts of Immigration

➤➤➤

THE PROPONENTS OF IMMIGRATION had assumed that the vast majority of the newcomers would be content to remain agricultural workers or laborers in the seaports, factories, and mines. Particularly in Argentina, the foreign born did in fact supply much of the muscle power that the rapidly expanding economy required. What Argentines and Chileans who backed immigration had not foreseen was that along with European laborers would come thousands of ambitious businessmen and entrepreneurs, determined to succeed and enrich themselves. By 1914 they were becoming affluent property owners and were seizing control of commerce and industry in both nations. These immigrants moved into the middle classes of society with remarkable rapidity. The most significant impact of immigration upon Argentine and Chilean social structure was the rapid emergence of urban middle groups composed largely of the foreign born and their descendants.

Between 1890 and 1914 Argentina became one of the great nations of immigration in the modern world. Over 4,000,000 foreigners poured into the country during this period, but many returned home after a brief stay, leaving about 2,400,000 to settle permanently (Table 1). By the eve of World War I, 29.9 per cent of the popula-

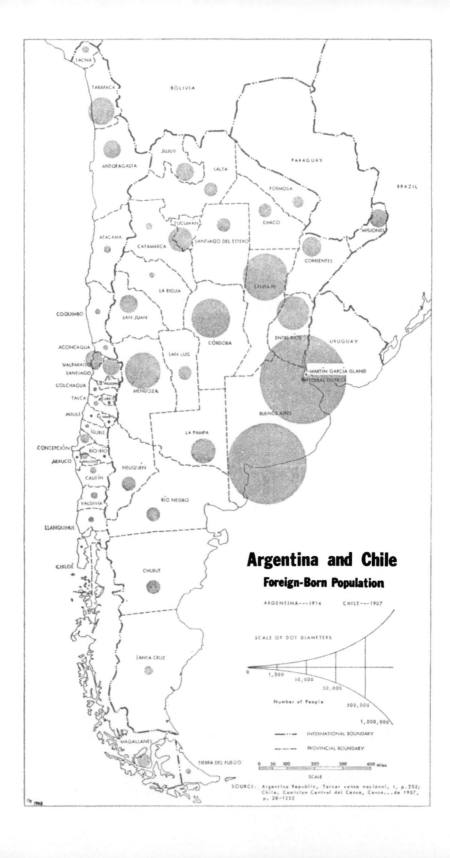

Argentina and Chile

Foreign-Born Population

ARGENTINA---1914   CHILE---1907

SCALE OF DOT DIAMETERS

0   1,000
      10,000
           50,000
Number of People   500,000
                 1,000,000

────·── INTERNATIONAL BOUNDARY

────── PROVINCIAL BOUNDARY

0 50 100   200   300   400 Miles

SCALE

SOURCE: Argentina Republic, Tercer censo nacional, t., p.202;
Chile, Comisión Central del Censo, Censo...de 1907,
p. 28-1252

TABLE 1

Net Immigration to Argentina and Chile, 1889–1914*

Year	Argentina	Chile
1889	220,260	10,413
1890	30,375	11,001
1891	−29,835	818
1892	29,441	286
1893	35,626	405
1894	39,272	395
1895	44,169	665
1896	89,282	1,114
1897	47,686	870
1898	41,654	564
1899	48,842	548
1900	50,485	936
1901	45,700	1,149
1902	16,653	864
1903	37,895	N.A.
1904	94,841	N.A.
1905	138,850	293
1906	198,397	1,442
1907	119,861	8,462
1908	176,080	5,484
1909	140,640	3,098
1910	208,870	2,561
1911	109,581	863
1912	206,121	1,839
1913	172,628	1,142
1914	38,349	360
TOTALS	2,351,715	55,572

Sources: Argentine Republic, *Tercer censo nacional, levantado el 1° de junio de 1914*, X, 399; Chile, Oficina Central de Estadística, *Anuario estadístico de la República de Chile*, I, ix.

*Immigration statistics used in this study are usually drawn from official government sources. Since these tend to be inaccurate, they can be used safely only to illustrate general trends. The Chilean statistics on immigration are not as complete as the Argentine; the Chileans at times simply did not trouble to collect meaningful data about arriving foreigners. In the tables, N.A. indicates data not available; the symbol − means negative net immigration, i.e., more foreigners left than arrived.

tion had been born abroad, which gave Argentina the distinction of a higher proportion of immigrants to total population than any other major country.[1]

Fewer Europeans risked the passage to Chile. Before the Panama Canal opened, the trip was long and expensive, and once the immigrant arrived he encountered less opportunity than in Argentina, Brazil, the United States, or Canada. A steady trickle of Europeans continued to emigrate to Chile, but the foreign-born proportion of the nation's population rose from only 2.9 per cent in 1895 to 4.1 per cent in 1907 (Table 2). The proportion of the European born in Chile was smaller because the two largest foreign groups enumerated in the census were Peruvians and Bolivians. Nearly all of them served as unskilled labor in Chile's northern nitrate mines, while very few became property owners or achieved middle-class status. Since the category of

TABLE 2

Total Populations and Proportion of Foreign Born
in the Argentine and Chilean Populations

	Total Population	Foreign Born	% Foreign Born
1895			
Argentina	3,954,911	1,004,527	25.4
Chile	2,687,985	79,056	2.9
1907			
Argentina	N.A.	N.A.	N.A.
Chile	3,114,755	134,524	4.1
1914			
Argentina	7,885,237	2,357,952	29.9
Chile	N.A.	N.A.	N.A.

Sources: Argentine Republic, *Tercer censo nacional*, I, 205–206; Chile, Oficina Central de Estadística, *Sétimo censo jeneral de población de Chile*; *levantado el 28 de noviembre de 1895*, IV, 463; and Chile, Comisión Central del Censo, *Censo de la República de Chile levantado el 28 de noviembre de 1907*, p. xix.

[1] Gino Germani, *Política y sociedad en una época de transición*, p. 197. Only 14.4 per cent of the population of the United States was foreign born in 1910.

foreign born in the census always included these Peruvian and Bolivian miners, the relative impact the European immigrants were making in activities like commerce and industry was even greater than the statistics indicated. The power and influence that the 85,000 Europeans and Orientals in Chile held was tremendous and bore little relationship to their sparse numbers.

Most European immigrants in both Argentina and Chile came from Italy and Spain (Table 3). The muscle power of the Italians, more of whom went to Argentina than to any other country except the United States, produced the bulk of Argentina's huge and rapidly growing agricultural and pastoral exports. By 1900 hundreds of thousands of northern Italians had become agricultural laborers and tenant farmers in the provinces of Buenos Aires, Córdoba, and Santa Fe. After the turn of the century, most Italian immigrants originated in the homeland's depressed south. Many southern Italians came to settle permanently, but thousands of others took advantage of low steerage-class steamship fares to migrate back and forth between Italy and Argentina, working in the harvests of each country. Called *golondrinas*, after the swallows their migration resembled, their labor made possible the record Argentine wheat crops of the early twentieth century.[2]

While many Italians labored in agriculture, thousands of others entered urban occupations. One out of four Italian immigrants settled in the city of Buenos Aires, where they became skilled artisans of all sorts and formed a large part of the urban working class. Italian laborers and entrepreneurs also built the wine industry of Mendoza, while their compatriots provided most of the manpower to construct the Argentine railroads. In the smallest provincial towns, as well as in the great cities, Italian businessmen opened all types of shops and light industries.[3] Aside from their contribution to economic development, the Italians made a strong impact upon Argentine culture. Argentines, for example, enthusiastically adopted Italian cuisine into the national diet, incor-

---

[2] James R. Scobie, *Revolution on the Pampas: A Social History of Argentine Wheat, 1860–1910*, pp. 29, 55–56; Anna Maria Ratti, "Italian Migration Movements, 1876 to 1926," in Walter F. Willcox, ed., *International Migrations*, II, 446.

[3] Robert F. Foerster, *The Italian Emigration of Our Times*, pp. 261–262.

TABLE 3

Nationality of Foreigners in Argentina (1914) and Chile (1907)

Nation of Origin	Total in Argentina	% of Argentine Immigrants	Total in Chile	% of Chilean Immigrants
Argentina	—	—	6,952	5.17
Austria-Hungary	38,123	1.62	3,813	2.83
Bolivia	17,993	0.76	21,968	16.33
Brazil	36,442	1.46	x	x
Chile	34,217	1.45	—	—
China	x	x	1,920	1.42
France	79,491	3.37	9,800	7.28
Germany	26,995	1.14	10,724	7.97
Great Britain	27,692	1.17	9,845	7.32
Italy	929,863	39.43	13,023	9.68
Japan	x	x	209	0.15
Ottoman Empire	64,369	2.73	1,729	1.28
Paraguay	28,049	1.19	x	x
Peru	x	x	27,740	20.62
Russia	93,634	4.10	660	0.49
Spain	829,701	35.19	18,755	13.94
Switzerland	14,345	0.61	2,080	1.55
Uruguay	86,428	3.66	x	x
Others	50,610	2.11	5,306	3.94
	2,357,052	100.00	134,524	100.00

x=included in Others
Sources: Argentine Republic, *Tercer censo nacional*, I, 205–206; Chile, Comisión Central del Censo, *Censo . . . de 1907*, p. 1282.

porated scores of Italian expressions into the vernacular, and began to substitute the Italian accordion for the traditional Spanish guitar.

The typical Italian immigrant in Chile inhabited one of the larger cities and owned some small business, probably a shop devoted, as one observer put it, to the inner man. The Italian was "above all a cook and confectioner and refreshment-house keeper; he runs general stores, and manufactures soap and candles."[4] Whatever their business, Italians prospered sufficiently to construct new stores and dwellings. As a re-

[4] "Cosas de Chile—The Gringo," *The Saturday Review of Politics, Literature, Science, and Art*, LXXII (October 3, 1891), 388.

sult, the architecture of Valparaíso, one of the centers of this immigration, took on a definite Italian cast.

Spanish immigrants made nearly as powerful an impact upon the two republics as the Italians. Most of the Spaniards who came to Argentina originated in Galicia, the extreme northwestern region of the Iberian peninsula. The Gallegos, as the Argentines call all new Spanish arrivals, composed the second largest nationality among Argentine immigrants.[5] At least one-third of them remained in Buenos Aires, where they frequently entered the most menial occupations. Gallegos collected the capital's garbage, swept its streets, and toiled on its docks. Thousands of others became unskilled agricultural laborers, especially in the province of Buenos Aires. Although the majority of the Spaniards started at the bottom of Argentina's occupational ladder, several thousand soon entered retail commerce. In Chile the Spanish concentrated on business. They opened small shops and stores of all types, and by 1914 they were among the largest commercial groups in Antofagasta, Santiago, Valparaíso, and Punta Arenas. Spanish artisans and skilled workers also trickled in, along with small groups of farmers who toiled in Chile's southern frontier provinces of Malleco and Cautín.

The Russians, who formed the third largest national group among Argentine immigrants, were primarily Jews fleeing pogroms in the Russian Empire. Few Israelitas, as they were called in both Argentina and Chile, arrived until 1891, when the wealthy Jewish philanthropist Baron Maurice Hirsch began to transport immigrants from Russia's Black Sea ports to the agricultural colonies he was establishing in Santa Fe and Entre Ríos. By 1914 the Hirsch scheme had settled about 25,000 Jews in the nine large Argentine colonies that the Baron's representatives controlled.[6] About 25,000 other Jews, most of them Rus-

---

[5] About 60 per cent of all Spanish emigrants in 1911 came from Galicia, long an overpopulated region. Jaime Vicens Vives, ed., *Historia social y económica de España y América*, V, 28.

[6] Morton D. Winsberg, *Colonia Baron Hirsch: A Jewish Agricultural Colony in Argentina*, pp. 5–6; Luis Gudiño Kramer, "Colonización judía en el litoral," *Davar*, No. 14 (November, 1947), 5; Ernst Schwarz and Johan C. Te Velde, "Jewish Agricultural Settlement in Argentina: The ICA Experiment," *Hispanic American Historical Review*, XIX (May, 1939), 185–193.

sian, emigrated on their own initiative by 1914 and settled in Buenos Aires, where they prospered in small retail commerce and the trades.

Aside from the Jews, the Russian immigrants to Argentina comprised mostly the Volga Germans, German-speaking people who long had lived within the Russian Empire. Since many of these Russo-Germans belonged to small millenialist Protestant groups, they often were happy to isolate themselves in tiny agricultural colonies scattered over the provinces of Entre Ríos and Buenos Aires, and over La Pampa Territory.[7] Very few Russians or Russian Jews migrated to Chile before World War I. The large Jewish commercial community flourishing today in Santiago did not arrive in significant numbers until the Nazi persecutions of the 1930's.

At the same time that Jews and Volga Germans were fleeing the Russian Empire, Syrian and Lebanese immigrants were leaving another oppressive empire, the Ottoman. A few of these Turcos, as they were derisively called, were Moslems, but most were Marionite Christians. Whatever their religion, they invariably avoided agriculture and turned toward business. In Argentina or Chile the typical Levantine immigrant arrived penniless and soon began to work as a sidewalk vendor peddling trinkets. An ambitious and indefatigable salesman, he would save to establish his own store. By 1914 many Syrian and Lebanese businessmen in both countries were becoming wealthy. Vendors shouting ¡cosa tienda! ("trinkets for sale!") still walked Argentine and Chilean city streets, but the Levantines also owned large and prosperous stores and were entering the field of textile manufacturing.

While the Syrians and Lebanese avoided agriculture, German immigrants turned toward farming with delight, particularly in Chile. Attracted by generous land grants, Germans began to colonize the southern provinces of Valdivia and Llanquihue during the late 1840's. Within a few decades, these hardworking immigrants transformed a near-wilderness avoided by Chileans into one of the showplaces of South America. The Germans' lush farms, sleek cattle, carefully tended flower gardens, and Teutonic-style houses gave parts of the southern provinces an atmosphere more of Bavaria or Switzerland than of Chile.

[7] Winsberg, *Colonia Baron Hirsch*, p. 18.

In the prosperous towns of Valdivia and Osorno ambitious German entrepreneurs opened breweries, tanneries, and furniture factories. Some of these immigrants also settled in Santiago and Valparaíso, where they prospered in commerce. In contrast, the Germans made only a slight impact in Argentina before 1914. The German population inhabiting the Buenos Aires area today arrived primarily during the 1930's and after World War II.

Like the Germans, the influence that English immigrants possessed was disproportionate to their number. This is because they often worked for firms financed by British capital, which controlled large portions of mining, banking, and transportation in both republics. In Chile the largest British investments were in nitrate mining, which brought thousands of English engineers, managers, and foremen to the far north. They became so numerous and powerful in the region that one traveler could refer to the Chilean inhabitants of Iquique as the "Chilean colony."[8] Argentina's English community, much of which lived in prim Buenos Aires suburbs like Hurlingham and Temperley, generally maintained an attitude of aloof superiority toward the native born. Nonetheless, upper-class Argentines admired the English and assiduously imitated their fashions, architecture, and sports.

The Serbo-Croatians (classified in the censuses as Austro-Hungarians) were another immigrant group small in numbers but highly successful economically. At least in Chile, they ranked among the richest and most respected national groups. Many Serbo-Croatians settled in rapidly developing Magallanes Territory, which lines both sides of the Strait of Magellan. By 1914 they had become the largest and the second wealthiest national group in the flourishing territorial capital of Punta Arenas. No large Serbo-Croatian population centers existed in Argentina, but by World War I an enterprising Dalmatian named Nicolás Mihanovich had monopolized the Argentine maritime transportation industry and had become one of the nation's richest men.

A few Chinese and Japanese immigrants were making their way to Argentina and Chile by 1914, but Orientals did not enter in significant numbers until World War I ended. The Chinese in prewar Chile lived

[8] Andre Bellesort, *La jeune Amerique: Chili et Bolivie*, p. 58.

mainly in the far north, where they labored in mining and construction or engaged in commerce, particularly in Iquique. Fewer Chinese went to Argentina, but in 1909, a steady immigration of Japanese and Okinawans began to enter that country. They engaged in commerce or the trades in Buenos Aires and in truck gardening on the city's fringes. Only ten Japanese inhabited Argentina in 1910, but nearly two thousand had arrived by 1920. Japanese and Okinawan immigrants shunned Chile, perhaps because other immigrant nationalities had preempted the trades and truck-gardening activities that they might have entered.[9]

All the immigrant nationalities considered here shared an extraordinary reluctance to become citizens, either in Argentina or Chile. In 1914 only 33,219 Argentine immigrants, or about 2.25 per cent of the total male foreign-born population, were naturalized. An even smaller proportion, about 1.8 per cent in 1895, of Chilean immigrants were citizens.[10] Legally, the immigrant in both republics remained a foreigner. The vernacular, which generally referred to the European immigrant as an *extranjero* ("foreigner") rather than an *inmigrante*, underscored this fact. The low rate of naturalization reflected, for one thing, the closed political systems that prevailed in the two republics. Since small upper-class cliques still controlled national politics, a meaningful choice in the selection of candidates was seldom possible, and political participation appeared futile to prospective citizens unless they wished to sell their votes, which was not hard to do. After an electoral reform in 1912 cleared the way for honest elections in Argentina, the rate of immigrant naturalization began to increase in that republic.

The intense desire for material advancement that motivated many immigrants further contributed to their lack of interest in becoming citizens. Comparatively few persons emigrated to Argentina and Chile

[9] James L. Tigner, "The Okinawans in Latin America," pp. 533–534, 643; idem, "The Ryukyuans in Argentina," *Hispanic American Historical Review*, XLVII (May, 1967), 205.

[10] The Chilean census of 1907 gave no statistics on naturalization. For the 1895 data, see Chile, Oficina Central de Estadística, *Sétimo censo jeneral de la población de Chile: Levantado el 28 de noviembre de 1895*, IV, 499–500; Argentine Republic, *Tercer censo nacional, levantado el 1° de junio de 1914*, II, 403–417.

for other than economic reasons. Many of the Jewish settlers of Baron Hirsch's agricultural colonies fled religious intolerance in eastern Europe, while, in Chile, some German immigrants had come because of political persecution following the revolutions of 1848. A few other individuals emigrated to avoid the military conscription that awaited them at home. But the vast majority came with the hope of bettering themselves economically.[11]

The many immigrants who came to try their luck in Argentina and Chile and who did not intend to remain more than a few years naturally hesitated to become citizens. If the immigrant decided to stay permanently, retaining his European citizenship was still to his advantage, particularly if he happened to be a property owner or businessman. Citizens of foreign countries not only enjoyed all the protection of the Argentine and Chilean civil codes, which applied equally to foreigners and nationals, but also could call upon the diplomatic protection of the mother country, usually anxious to maintain its ties with the immigrants.

Since they emigrated in order to work, the foreigners naturally concentrated in the most important economic regions of the two republics. In Argentina millions of immigrants after 1880 went to the rapidly developing agricultural provinces of the littoral (Table 4). As a result the population of this region (including the city of Buenos Aires) grew so rapidly that by 1914 it held clear numerical predominance over the rest of the country. The foreign population was particularly numerous in large towns of the littoral like Rosario, the metropolis of Santa Fe Province, whose 1910 municipal census revealed that 46.6 per cent of the population had been born in Europe.[12] The most cos-

[11] Carleton J. H. Hayes, *A Generation of Materialism*, pp. 104–105, discusses the factors motivating emigration from Europe. The economic motive is examined in José Luis Romero, *A History of Argentine Political Thought*, third edition, trans. Thomas F. McGann, pp. 174–175, and in Gino Germani, "Las repercusiones de la inmigración en la estructura social de los paises. El ejemplo de un país sud-americano," *Inmigración*, No. 7 (1963), 23. Roberto Saráh, in his novel *"Los turcos,"* second edition, p. 41, mentions that fantastic tales of easily obtainable South American wealth circulated as far as rural Palestine.

[12] Rosario de Santa Fe, *Tercer censo municipal: Levantado el 26 de abril de 1910*, p. 71.

mopolitan portion of Argentina was the Federal District, comprising the city of Buenos Aires. By 1914, 49.4 per cent of its 1,500,000 people were foreign born, as were nearly 80 per cent of the male inhabitants over the age of twenty.[13]

The foreign born in Chile similarly gathered in newly developing regions that were producing most of the nation's export wealth (Table 4). Immigrants, in fact, composed nearly 40 per cent of the population of Tarapacá, the province producing the bulk of Chilean nitrates. In Chile's far south immigrants made up 37.5 per cent of the population of Magallanes Territory, a crucial region containing valuable grazing lands as well as a principal avenue of world shipping. German immigrants and their descendants dominated political and economic life in two other important southern provinces, Valdivia and Llanquihue. Very few foreigners went to the most conservative and tradition-bound part of Chile, the rural provinces of the central valley.

Aside from altering the geographical distribution of population, immigration increased the size of the working class, particularly in Argentina. More than 70 per cent of that country's immigrants were between thirteen and forty years old, at the prime age of life for productive labor.[14] Consequently, by 1914 over one million foreigners had become laborers providing the brawn that Argentina's expanding economy required. At least 40 per cent of the agricultural laborers who planted, tended, and harvested the republic's huge volume of wheat and beef exports were foreign born.[15] Furthermore, about 60 per cent of the urban proletariat were immigrants. They were concentrated in Buenos Aires and included railroad workers, draymen, longshoremen, and others who transported and handled the rich produce of Argentine farm and pasture. Argentina's spectacular rise as one of the world's great agricultural nations rested squarely upon the European laborers.[16]

[13] Gino Germani, "La movilidad social en la Argentina," in Seymour Martin Lipset and Reinhard Bendix, *Movilidad social en la sociedad industrial*, p. 320.
[14] G. Beyhaut, R. Cortes Conde, H. Gorostegui, and S. Torrado, *Inmigración y desarrollo económico*, pp. 15, 18.
[15] Argentine Republic, *Tercer censo nacional*, IV, 383–395.
[16] A careful assessment of the impact of immigration on the rise of Argentine agriculture is Scobie, *Revolution on the Pampas*, pp. 27–38; statistics on the nationalities of the Buenos Aires urban proletariat appear in Buenos Aires

In sharp contrast to Argentina, European immigrants in Chile did not greatly enlarge the urban working class. Argentina, huge and virtually unpopulated, suffered a much more severe shortage of muscle power than Chile, which cried out for foreign unskilled labor only during brief economic booms. During much of the 1890–1914 period,

TABLE 4

Distribution of Foreigners by Provinces and Territories
(in Order of Rank)

	ARGENTINA (1914)		
Province or Territory	*Total Population*	*Foreign Population*	*% Foreign Population*
1. Santa Cruz	9,948	6,701	67.4
2. Tierra del Fuego	2,504	1,577	63.0
3. Federal District	1,575,814	777,845	49.4
4. Neuquén	28,866	13,319	46.1
5. Chubut	23,065	10,584	45.9
6. Formosa	19,281	8,774	45.5
7. Misiones	53,563	20,358	38.1
8. La Pampa	101,338	36,932	36.4
9. Río Negro	42,242	14,873	35.2
10. Santa Fe	899,640	315,941	35.1
11. Buenos Aires	2,066,165	703,931	34.1
12. Mendoza	277,535	88,354	31.8
13. Martín García Island	783	199	25.4
14. Jujuy	76,631	17,077	22.3
15. Chaco	46,274	9,858	21.3
16. Córdoba	735,472	150,420	20.4
17. Entre Ríos	425,373	72,501	17.0
18. San Juan	119,252	16,422	13.8
19. Tucumán	332,933	33,005	10.9
20. San Luis	116,266	9,962	8.6
21. Salta	140,927	11,830	8.4
22. Corrientes	347,055	24,462	7.0
23. Santiago del Estero	261,678	9,496	3.6
24. Catamarca	100,391	2,281	2.3
25. La Rioja	79,754	1,605	2.0
National Average			29.9%

(Continued on following page)

(City), *Censo general de población, edificación, comercio e industrias de la Ciudad de Buenos Aires . . . levantado en . . . octubre de 1909,* I, 53–60.

CHILE (1907)

1.	Tarapacá	110,036	43,774	39.8
2.	Magallanes	17,330	6,499	37.5
3.	Antofagasta	113,323	17,800	15.7
4.	Tacna	28,748	4,166	14.5
5.	Valparaíso	281,385	15,968	5.7
6.	Atacama	63,968	3,430	5.4
7.	Santiago	516,870	19,896	3.8
8.	Malleco	109,775	3,402	3.1
9.	Concepción	216,994	4,813	2.2
10.	Valdivia	118,277	2,529	2.1
11.	Cautín	139,553	2,311	1.6
12.	Llanquihue	105,043	1,259	1.2
13.	Aconcagua	128,486	1,432	1.1
14.	O'Higgins	92,339	751	0.8
15.	Coquimbo	175,021	1,512	0.9
16.	Talca	131,957	963	0.7
17.	Arauco	61,538	354	0.6
18.	Bío-Bío	97,968	495	0.5
19.	Colchagua	159,030	741	0.5
20.	Curicó	107,095	537	0.5
21.	Ñuble	166,245	728	0.4
22.	Linares	109,363	494	0.4
23.	Chiloé	88,619	392	0.4
24.	Maule	110,316	278	0.2

National Average 4.1%

Sources: Argentine Republic, *Tercer censo nacional*, I, 202; Chile, Comisión Central del Censo, *Censo . . . de 1907*, pp. 28–1252.

Chile actually exported labor to countries as diverse as Peru, where Chileans built railroads, and Panama, where they helped dig the Canal.[17] Foreigners constituted only about 1 per cent of Chile's rural laborers, 5 per cent of its skilled tradesmen, and 3.8 per cent of its industrial workers.[18]

[17] Francisco A. Encina, *Nuestra inferioridad económica*, p. 139; Watt Stewart. "El trabajador chileno y los ferrocarriles del Perú," *Revista Chilena de Historia y Geografía*, LXXXV (July–December, 1938), 128–171; Francisco de Bezé, *Tarapacá en sus aspectos físico, social y económico*, pp. 187–188.

[18] Chile, Comisión Central del Censo, *Censo de la República de Chile levantado el 28 de noviembre de 1907*, pp. 1299–1300; Chile, Oficina Central de Estadística, *Anuario estadístico de la República de Chile* (1914), VIII, 30.

Economic opportunity in Argentina and Chile attracted, in addition to laborers, many businessmen and entrepreneurs, a type of immigration that the elites had not foreseen and that they did not particularly desire. These ambitious European businessmen were determined to succeed in their new environments. Many of them sacrificed, saved, invested, and devoted their entire energies to their work. Some who succeeded paused late in life to write memoirs or autobiographies recounting their years of hard work and privation. One of the most interesting of these accounts is by Benedicto Chuaqui, who emigrated from Syria to Chile in 1908 and eventually built a large hosiery factory in Santiago. His book, *Memorias de un emigrante*, narrates the painful early years when he struggled to make a living as an itinerant peddler. After much sacrifice he was able to establish a small dry-goods shop, on whose single counter he slept at night. Similarly eager to rise was Enrique Dickmann, a Russian Jew whose family migrated to rural Argentina when he was still a boy and who became a distinguished physician as well as one of the first leaders of the Argentine Socialist party. He proudly recalled that, while a young agricultural worker in Entre Ríos province, "two or three ordinary peons would have been needed to equal my work." Through such summer agricultural labor, Dickmann financed his medical education at the University of Buenos Aires.[19]

Like the Syrians and the Russian Jews, Italian immigrants worked feverishly to attain economic success. In his classic study of Italian population movements, Robert J. Foerster has emphasized that wherever they migrated, the passion to earn and save "colors the details of the Italians' lives." Nowhere was this more true than in Argentina, where, as one Italian wrote, "in the struggle for a quick fortune . . . no fatigue is too great, no privation is too important." This is true, he continued somewhat erroneously, because in Argentina "the only real nobility consists of those who labor. Everyone has a right to advance . . . to earn a fortune." Another Italian, Pablo Guglieri, who went to Argentina in the 1880's and became a wealthy rural and urban property owner by 1910, wrote in a brief autobiography that he had been

---

[19] Benedicto Chuaqui, *Memorias de un emigrante*, second edition; Enrique Dickmann, *Recuerdos de un militante socialista*, p. 44.

searching only for "a good atmosphere in which to work and earn more." He recalled that as a young immigrant, he had "strong arms, a very firm will, and a great deal of confidence in my abilities. Accustomed to little, the idea of the privations I might encounter did not worry me."[20]

Spanish immigrant businessmen similarly threw their energies into their work. Francisco Grandmontagne, a novelist who came from Spain, described the Spanish merchants in rural Argentina as "gladiators in a struggle of small transactions. Their activity resembled a sort of vertigo." All immigrant businessmen, he continued, shared "one religion, which is that of commerce," and one motive, "the aspiration to accumulate material goods." Across the Andes in Chile, German businessmen repeated the same pattern of sacrifice, saving, hard work, and investment. In their businesses, "work began at the crack of dawn and did not end before nightfall, all week long," recalled one German in 1910.[21] Evidently, foreign businessmen in Chile were not immune to the pressures and tensions that often afflict men of affairs. In Valparaíso, for example, the Chilean poet Carlos Pezoa Véliz observed:

> Excited, the foreigners rush by
> With their sleeves rolled up,
> Smoking a cigar for their spleen,
> Preoccupied with their profits
> (or their losses)
> In Magallanes or in Cautín.[22]

Immigrants determined to make a fortune in Argentine or Chilean business found that cultural values typical of paternalistic, aristocratic societies often prevailed in both republics. In a statement of creole cultural standards, the "Eulogy to Laziness" by the Argentine journalist

[20] Foerster, *The Italian Emigration of Our Times*, p. 423; Francisco Scardín, *La Argentina y el trabajo*, pp. 18, 36; Pablo Guglieri, *Las memorias de un hombre de campo*, p. 13.

[21] Francisco Grandmontagne, *Teodoro Foronda*, I, 79, 145; Alberto Hoerll, "La colonización alemana en Chile," in Alberto Hoerll, et al., *Los alemanes en Chile*, p. 28.

[22] Carlos Pezoa Véliz, "Vida del puerto," in Raúl Silva Castro, *Carlos Pezoa Véliz (1879–1908)*, pp. 268–269.

Emilio Becher emphasized that work and useful activity was "madness."[23] Social prestige usually derived from the ownership of large rural estates. The aristocratic ideal in Argentina or Chile was to enjoy the leisure that the income from one's land made possible. The idea of the dignity of labor, which the European cultural heritage of many immigrants emphasized, was weak.[24]

Argentine and Chilean culture conferred slight social prestige on commercial or industrial entrepreneurship. These were not considered activities suitable for gentlemen. Commerce, proclaimed the Chilean essayist Alejandro Venegas, is "a second-rank industry, which considered morally and economically is an occupation of intermediaries, always of unproductive men, and often of scoundrels."[25] Chileans, the novelist Luis Orrego Luco observed, "could hardly imagine that a descendant of Spanish *hidalgos* might become a businessman." Young men who entered industrial work, complained Santiago's *La Lei*, had to "contend with social prejudice that marks them, humiliates them, and suffocates them with oppressive insolence."[26] The thought of a civic figure running a machine shop, as did the mayor of the Argentine immigrant settlement of Esperanza, was entirely alien to the creole mentality.[27]

Nor did creole culture emphasize saving. "*We don't know how to save*," cried one Argentine writer, an observation that many European visitors confirmed. An Italian traveling in Argentina was shocked to discover, "Our principles of economy, of saving, . . . the parsimony that for us is a point of honor, all those moral rules that oblige us to regulate our lives in provision for the future, are unknown in America."[28] The Buenos Aires municipal census taken in 1887 bore out

[23] Emilio Becher, "Elogio de la pereza," in Emilio Becher, *Diálogo de las sombras y otras páginas*, p. 117.

[24] Seymour Martin Lipset and Aldo Solari, eds., *Elites in Latin America*, pp. 7–15.

[25] Alejandro Venegas, *Sinceridad: Chile íntimo en 1910*, p. 267.

[26] Luis Orrego Luco, *Casa grande*, p. 199; *La Lei*, May 25, 1902, p. 1.

[27] Mark Jefferson, *Peopling the Argentine Pampa*, p. 71.

[28] Alejandro Calzada, "Enseñanza de la crisis," *Revista Argentina de Ciencias Políticas*, VIII (August 12, 1914), 493; Cesarina Lupati Guelfi, *Vida argentina*, trans. Augusto Riera, p. 71.

these observations. It revealed that of the 36,507 depositors in the Banco de la Provincia de Buenos Aires, one of the nation's largest financial institutions, only 7,565 were Argentine citizens, while 16,132 were Italians and 5,831 were Spaniards. Likewise, only about one-fourth of the total deposits belonged to Argentines.[29]

Frequently lacking interest in entrepreneurship, creoles tended to leave the business world to ambitious foreigners, who rushed to take advantage of the many opportunities awaiting them. During the late nineteenth and early twentieth centuries, the rapid growth of mining in Chile and of agricultural and pastoral activities in Argentina stimulated economic activity and created new opportunities in domestic commerce. Furthermore, in both countries virgin regions were opening to settlement for the first time. In remote towns of the Chilean frontier or of the steaming Argentine jungle province of Misiones, as well as in teeming cities like Santiago, Valparaíso, Buenos Aires and Rosario, immigrants opened stores and warehouses of all kinds. They formed banks, insurance companies, and export-import houses. Introducing the techniques of modern European industrial and commercial life, they developed branches of production and distribution previously unknown, as for example the production of butter.[30] According to one North American observer, this product was commercially unobtainable in Córdoba, Argentina, until enterprising Italians, Basques, and Galicians developed the industry during the late nineteenth century.[31]

Immigrant businessmen were, as Seymour Martin Lipset has put it, "marginal men," individuals who found themselves at odds with the prevailing values of Argentine and Chilean culture. They rejected the traditional elites' ways of doing things. Instead, they were innovators and modernizers who dared to promote economic enterprises into which few upper-class gentlemen would have ventured.[32] They were spectacularly successful. In Argentina, European-born businessmen

[29] Buenos Aires (City), *Censo general de población, edificación, comercio, e industrias de la Ciudad de Buenos Aires*, August-September, 1887, II, p. 185.

[30] Guido Di Tella and Manuel Zymelman. "Etapas del desarrollo económico argentino," in Torcuato S. Di Tella, et al., *Argentina, sociedad de masas*, p. 185.

[31] Jefferson, *Peopling the Argentine Pampa*, p. 74.

[32] Lipset, *Elites in Latin America*, p. 26.

TABLE 5

Nationality of Ownership of Commerce in Argentina and Chile, 1914

Country	National Owners	Foreign Owners	Both National and Foreign Owned	Total Owners	% Foreign Owned	% Foreigners in Population
Argentina	24,313	65,183	1,294	90,740	72.0	29.9
Chile	13,282	6,180		19,462	31.7	4.1

Sources: Argentine Republic, *Tercer censo nacional*, VIII, 141–207; Chile, *Anuario estadístico* (1914), IX, 131.

seized practically complete control of commerce by 1914 (Table 5). Foreigners, who composed 29.9 per cent of Argentina's population in that year, owned 72 per cent of the nation's commercial firms. Their pre-eminence was increasing, for in 1895 they had owned only 65 per cent. Immigrants dominated wholesale and retail commerce in every region of the country, with the exception of the most underdeveloped interior provinces—Corrientes, Santiago del Estero, San Juan, La Rioja, Catamarca, and Salta.[33] In some areas like the city of Buenos Aires, where foreigners owned 82 per cent of commercial establishments, and the province of Santa Fe, where they owned 78 per cent, native-born Argentines found themselves practically excluded from commerce.[34]

Most Argentine censuses did not report the amount of commercial capital owned by various nationalities. One exception was the 1913 municipal census of Tucumán, largest city of Argentina's northwest and center of the nation's sugar industry. This census revealed that Argentine citizens owned 27 per cent of the commercial establishments, but that these nationally owned firms accounted for only 19.8 per cent of the total capital invested in Tucumán commerce. In other words, not only did relatively few Argentines own commercial firms, but also the largest and wealthiest businesses were likely to be controlled by immigrants.[35]

[33] Argentine Republic, *Segundo censo de la República Argentina: Mayo 10 de 1895*, III, 362–411; idem, *Tercer censo nacional*, VIII, 141–207.
[34] Argentine Republic, *Tercer censo nacional*, VIII, 141–207.
[35] Tucumán (City), *Censo de la capital de Tucumán, 1913*, p. 87.

The same striking imbalance between national and immigrant ownership occurred in Chile. The miniscule 4.1 per cent of the total population that was foreign born owned nearly one-third of the nation's
commercial houses (Table 5). European pre-eminence was particularly
striking in the southernmost provinces. At Puerto Montt, capital of
Llanquihue, a French traveler observed that "the commerce of the city
is in German hands. There are only two Chilean businessmen. The
native population is miserable and lazy."[36] Further south at booming
Punta Arenas on the Strait of Magellan, Chilean citizens owned only
5.1 per cent of the total commercial capital in 1914. Germans, however, controlled 23.5 per cent and Serbo-Croatians an additional 21.5
per cent of the total.[37]

Other ambitious European entrepreneurs were devoting their energies to industrial development. By 1914 they owned approximately 65
per cent of Argentine and 49 per cent of Chilean industrial establishments (Table 6). Europeans were particularly active in industries like
construction, furniture, and metal products that required specialized
artisan skills traditionally scarce in both republics. Since industrialization was just beginning, most of these plants were only small work-
shops employing a few laborers. But in both countries it was the European, not the native-born citizen, who laid the foundations for later
industrial development.[38]

Agriculture and stock raising were the only major economic activities that Argentine and Chilean citizens still dominated by 1914.
Compared to their huge investments in industry and commerce, ownership of rural land by foreigners was slight. In Argentina about 29,000
of the republic's 72,000 rural owner-operators were immigrants
(Table 7). Furthermore, the *estancieros*, the great landlords who in-

[36] Jules Huret, *La Argentina de Buenos Aires al Gran Chaco*, trans. E. Gómez Carillo, II, 282.

[37] Agustín Gómez García, *Viaje de un chileno a Magallanes en 1914*, p. 81.

[38] For a study of the impact of immigration on Argentine industrial development, see Oscar Cornblit, "European Immigrants in Argentine Industry and
Politics," in Claudio Veliz, ed., *The Politics of Conformity in Latin America*,
especially p. 227. An evaluation of the relationship between immigration and
industrialization in both Argentina and Chile is Alcira Leiserson, *Notes on the
Process of Industrialization in Argentina, Chile, and Peru*, pp. 61–67.

TABLE 6

Foreign Owners of Industry in Argentina and Chile, 1914*

ARGENTINA

Industry	Total Producers	National Producers	Foreign Producers	Mixed Ownership	% Foreign Owned
Food Products	18,983	7,196	10,998	789	57.9
Clothing	7,081	1,060	5,918	103	83.6
Construction & Materials	8,582	2,211	6,162	209	71.8
Furniture	4,441	1,046	3,288	107	74.0
Artistic & Decorative Products	996	253	725	18	72.8
Metals & Metal Products	3,275	668	2,510	97	76.6
Chemical Products	567	137	375	55	66.1
Printing & Graphic Arts	1,439	567	813	59	56.5
Textiles	2,458	2,246	196	16	7.97
Wood & Products (included in other)					
Other	957	379	498	80	52.0
Totals	48,779	15,763	31,483	1,533	64.5%

(Continued on next page)

Source: Argentine Republic, *Tercer censo nacional*, VII, 195–246.

* Foreign control over Argentine industry would have been still greater had not the census counted as industrialists 2,100 semi-independent textile producers in the remote provinces of Salta and Catamarca. Almost all of them were domestic producers who wove small amounts of cloth under commission for large entrepreneurs. Immigrants composed the majority of owners in every branch of Argentine industry, excluding textiles.

(Table 6, continued)

CHILE

Industry	Total Producers	National Producers	Foreign Producers	Mixed Ownership	Not Specified	% Foreign Owned
Food Products	735	303	383	32	17	52.1
Clothing	146	49	94	3	—	64.4
Construction & Materials	30	8	19	2	1	63.3
Furniture	20	5	14	—	1	70.0
Artistic & Decorative Products	180	61	113	4	2	62.8
Metals & Metal Products	121	45	58	13	5	47.9
Chemical Products	75	42	28	4	1	37.3
Printing & Graphic Arts	93	51	36	4	2	38.7
Textiles	16	10	6	—	—	37.5
Wood & Products	163	94	55	11	3	33.7
Other	168	92	57	14	5	33.9
Totals	1,742	760	863	87	37	49%

Source: Chile, *Annuario estadístico* (1914), VII, 10.

TABLE 7

Rural Landowners in Argentina (1914) and Chile (1907)

	Nationals	Foreigners	Total
Argentina			
Owner-operators	42,993	29,436	72,429
Estancieros	23,940	3,344	27,284
Renters	20,899	54,615	75,514
Chile			
Rural landowners	65,575	3,204	68,799

Sources: Argentine Republic, *Tercer censo nacional*, IV, 383; V, 837. Chile, Comisión Central del Censo, *Censo . . . de 1907*, p. 1299.

dividually held title to thousands of hectares, were overwhelmingly native-born Argentines. Hundreds of thousands of immigrants went to rural Argentina, but the lack of opportunity to purchase land forced nearly all to work as *peones* ("day laborers"), *medeiros* ("sharecroppers"), or *arrendatarios* ("renters").[39] The foreign born by 1914 controlled only a few specialized branches of Argentine agriculture, the most important of which was winegrowing. About 62 per cent of the vineyard owners in the nation and 79 per cent in the key wine-producing province of Mendoza were foreigners.[40]

In Chile the upper class continued to monopolize ownership of most of the nation's best lands, and immigrants made up only 4.4 per cent of rural landholders. But foreigners who had made their fortunes in commerce, industry, or the professions were quietly and gradually buying up good land. By 1908 they owned nearly 20 per cent of the republic's 554 most valuable estates.[41] In the southern provinces Germans or the descendants of early German settlers owned a vast amount

[39] Foerster, *The Italian Emigration of Our Times*, pp. 242–243; Scobie, *Revolution on the Pampas*, pp. 57–60; Argentine Republic, *Tercer censo nacional*, IV, 227, and V, 837.

[40] Argentine Republic, Ministerio de Agricultura, Dirección de Comercio e Industria, *Censo industrial y comercial de la República Argentina, 1908–1914*, Part IX, 6.

[41] Luis Thayer Ojeda, *Elementos étnicos que han intervenido en la población de Chile*, p. 142.

of land; 98 of the 193 Valdivia estates valued at more than ten thousand pesos in 1907 belonged to this immigrant group.[42] Similarly, in Magallanes a relatively small group of foreign-born sheep ranchers controlled huge expanses of land, either through direct ownership or through long-term rental contracts with the national government. An official report of 1894 listing the 50 largest ranches of Magallanes revealed that thirty-six operators had foreign names and controlled 680,000 of the total of 820,000 hectares.[43]

While wealthy foreigners were able to afford the large expenditures necessary to purchase good rural land, most immigrants were unable to become landowners. No workable policies existed in either Argentina or Chile to distribute small plots of good land to immigrants at reasonable prices. In Argentina, where the provinces had the constitutional right to determine their own land policies, Santa Fe, Córdoba, and Entre Ríos had granted land to immigrant colonists between the late 1850's and the 1880's, but the provincial governments lost interest in promoting immigrant ownership after 1890. Legislation also existed to grant plots of the federal government's land in the national territories to settlers, but graft and maladministration in the national colonization department slowed the system of distributing these lands to a crawl. In the richest agricultural area, the pampas of Buenos Aires and southern Santa Fe provinces, speculation had pushed land prices so high that the ordinary laborer almost never could purchase a plot. The Chilean government's land policy was almost as restrictive as Argentina's. From the late 1840's to the 1880's, several colonization schemes had granted immigrants land in the southern frontier provinces. But after 1900 the government's interest in such programs lagged, and the national colonization department became corrupt and inefficient, with the consequence that few immigrants were able to secure a land grant.

In both republics the huge amount of urban real estate owned by

[42] Ibid., p. 146; George M. McBride, *Chile: Land and Society*, p. 298; A report on the general extent of German dominance over landholding in the southern provinces is Bernardo Gotschlich, "Reseña de la colonización de las provincias australes," *Boletín de la Sociedad de Fomento Fabril*, XVIII (November 1, 1901), 404–405.

[43] Chile, Ministerio de Relaciones Exteriores, Culto i Colonización, *Memoria . . . presentada al congreso nacional en 1894*, pp. 133–135.

TABLE 8

National Origin of Owners of Real Estate in Argentina, 1895 and 1914

Country	1895			1914		
	Number of Owners	% of Nationality who Were Owners	% of All Property Owners	Number of Owners	% of Nationality who Were Owners	% of All Property Owners
Argentina	290,953	9.9	71.4	673,409	12.2	62.6
Austria-Hungary	1,954	15.3	0.5	8,666	22.8	0.8
France	11,502	12.2	2.8	22,105	27.8	2.6
Germany	2,526	14.8	0.6	4,711	17.4	0.4
Great Britain	2,825	13.0	0.7	4,344	15.6	0.4
Italy	62,975	12.8	15.4	203,500	21.8	18.9
Ottoman Empire	70	13.4	0.1	7,709	11.9	0.7
Russia	2,016	22.9	0.5	9,687	10.3	0.9
Spain	17,687	8.9	4.3	104,339	12.5	9.7
Switzerland	3,398		0.8	4,730	32.9	0.4
Uruguay	4,022	8.0	1.0	13,973	16.2	1.3
Others	7,575	8.3	1.9	17,791	10.6	1.7
Totals	407,503	—	100.00%	1,074,964	—	100.00%

Source: Argentine Republic, *Tercer censo nacional*, I, 261.

immigrants contrasted sharply with their relatively small holdings of rural property and furnished another index of their economic power. In the city of Buenos Aires, for instance, immigrants owned nearly two-thirds of all real estate, while in Rosario the foreign born composed 60 per cent of property owners.[44] Immigrant-owned urban properties in Argentina were so numerous that when all real estate, both rural and urban, was added together, a much higher proportion of foreigners than of nationals emerged as property owners. In Argentina 12.2 per cent of the citizens, but 17 per cent of the immigrants owned some type of real estate (Table 8). Moreover, the foreigners' holdings of real estate in Argentina were growing much faster than those of the native born. It should again be emphasized that the Europeans were

[44] Buenos Aires (City), *Censo general . . . de 1909*, I, 101; Rosario de Santa Fe, *Tercer censo municipal*, p. 97.

gaining control primarily of urban property and not of rural holdings. So many immigrants invested in urban real estate between 1895 and 1914 that foreign-owned properties increased 3.45 times while ownership by Argentine citizens increased only 2.31 times (Table 8). This trend occurred both in the great urban center of Buenos Aires and in smaller provincial cities. In Tucumán, for example, the provincial census of 1910 reported that 2,642 Argentines sold real estate worth about 6,700,000 pesos, while only 1,733 nationals purchased property, with a total value of 5,600,000 pesos. The same census revealed that most immigrant groups were buying much more property than they were selling. The French, for example, sold forty-eight holdings worth 352,395 pesos, but bought sixty-six valued at 442,692 pesos, while the Levantines sold fifteen properties worth 124,611 pesos and purchased forty valued at 200,172 pesos.[45]

In Chile the foreigner also was more likely to become a real estate owner than was the native-born citizen. Nationally, 8.5 per cent of the citizens, but 13 per cent of the foreigners held real estate (Table 9). The immigrants who inhabited several provinces, particularly Tarapacá, Antofagasta, Santiago, Cautín, and Valdivia, held much more property than their numerical strength might suggest. In Valdivia the 2.13 per cent of the foreigners in the province's population held 8 per cent of the total number of properties. As in Argentina, the foreigner in Chile more likely held urban real estate than rural property. Europeans in 1902 owned at least 50 per cent of the parcels of real estate in the city of Valdivia and 35 per cent in Concepción, the largest city in southern Chile. Europeans in Valparaíso, the nation's largest port, owned almost 60 per cent of the total number of properties, a level matching that of Buenos Aires and Rosario.[46]

The enterprising immigrants who became successful businessmen and property owners profoundly altered the Argentine and Chilean social structures. Traditionally, a rigid two-class social stratification had

[45] Tucumán (Province), *Anuario de estadística de la Provincia de Tucumán correspondiente al año de 1910*, p. 161; Buenos Aires (City), *Censo general* (1887), II, 105; and Buenos Aires (City), *Censo general . . . de 1909*, II, 192.
[46] Thayer Ojeda, *Elementos étnicos*, pp. 144, 147.

TABLE 9

Owners of Real Estate in Chile, 1907 (by Province*)

Province	National Owners	Foreign Owners	Total Owners	% of Foreigners in Population	% of Foreign Property Owners
Tacna	3,909	1,057	4,966	14.5	21.3
Tarapacá	4,969	5,516	10,485	39.8	52.6
Antofagasta	7,751	2,196	9,947	15.7	22.1
Atacama	4,808	227	5,035	5.4	4.5
Coquimbo	20,466	159	20,625	0.9	0.8
Aconcagua	10,480	138	10,618	1.1	1.3
Valparaíso	14,418	1,120	15,538	5.6	7.2
Santiago	34,394	2,631	37,025	3.8	7.1
O'Higgins	8,499	98	8,597	0.8	1.1
Colchagua	16,455	134	16,589	0.5	0.8
Curicó	6,403	81	6,484	0.5	1.2
Talca	14,218	104	14,322	0.7	0.7
Linares	9,587	122	9,709	0.4	1.3
Maule	11,076	66	11,142	0.2	0.6
Ñuble	15,908	120	16,028	0.4	0.7
Concepción	16,636	751	17,387	2.2	4.3
Bío-Bío	7,400	715	7,515	0.5	1.0
Arauco	4,387	90	4,477	0.6	2.0
Malleco	5,526	711	6,237	3.1	11.4
Cautín	9,590	665	10,255	1.6	6.5
Valdivia	8,227	713	8,940	2.1	8.0
Llanquihue	9,144	290	9,434	1.2	3.1
Chiloé	8,703	40	8,743	0.4	0.5
Magallanes	956	663	1,619	37.5	40.9
Totals:	253,910	17,807	271,717	4.1%	13.0%

Source: Chile, Comisión Central del Censo, *Censo . . . de 1907*, p. 1306.
*Since Chilean statistics before 1907 did not distinguish the nationality of property owners, it is unclear whether the foreign-owned holdings were increasing relatively faster than nationally-owned properties. The provinces are listed here in north-to-south order.

characterized both republics. The small middle class, which depended almost entirely on the patronage of the elites, had imitated their cultural values and followed their opinions on most questions. But the economic expansion of the late nineteenth and early twentieth centuries fostered the growth of a new urban middle class in both republics. Composed of such diverse groups as teachers, government bureaucrats, shopkeepers, clerks, and professionals, these middle groups were disunited and lacked class consciousness; yet they have been one of the prime forces behind political change and economic nationalism during the twentieth century.

The immigrant found it much easier to enter the urban middle class than did the native-born Argentine or Chilean. It was the immigrant, not the national, who took advantage of the new commercial and clerical opportunities that were opening up.[47] The Argentine sociologist Gino Germani has demonstrated that at least two-thirds of those counted among the Argentine middle class in 1914 had originally belonged to the working classes, and that about 26 per cent of the immigrant working class but only about 19 per cent of the native-born laborers succeeded in rising into the middle class between 1895 and 1914.[48] In Argentina immigrants filled (in 1914) over half the middle-class positions other than government bureaucratic posts, to which foreigners enjoyed limited access. Such dominance was hardly possible in Chile, where foreigners composed only 4.1 per cent of the total population. Nevertheless, this small group held 11.7 per cent of the total number of middle-class positions. Furthermore, a relatively higher proportion of immigrants was concentrated in the middle class in Chile. In that country, 29 per cent of the employed foreigners held middle-class jobs, while in Argentina only 15 per cent did so (Table 10).

Argentine immigrants were beginning to move rapidly up the social scale, but before 1914 few had succeeded in entering the elites. The native-born aristocracy still jealously excluded wealthy foreigners from its ranks, although some notable exceptions existed. Wealthy descendants of British, French, Italian, and Basque merchants who had arrived during the 1830's and 1840's occasionally were able to marry into the highest social strata. One such individual was Carlos Pelligrini, the son

[47] John J. Johnson, *Political Change in Latin America: The Emergence of the Middle Sectors*, pp. 30–31; José Luis Romero, *Argentina: Imágenes y perspectivas*, p. 49; Jaime Eyzaguirre, *Chile durante el gobierno de Errázuriz Echaurren*, p. 19.
[48] Germani, "La movilidad social en la Argentina," pp. 321–327.

TABLE 10

Urban Middle-Class Occupations, Argentina (1914) and Chile (1907)

	ARGENTINA				CHILE			
	Nationals	Foreigners	Total	% Foreigners	Nationals	Foreigners	Total	% Foreigners
Commercial proprietors	56,021	117,382	173,403	67.7	66,419	12,071	78,490	15.4
Journalists	1,174	667	1,841	36.2	354	20	374	5.3
Employees:								
of commerce	40,781	39,484	80,265	49.2	83,294	8,464	91,758	9.2
of government	85,649	18,502	104,151	17.8	6,074	118	6,192	1.9
Lawyers	7,912	1,166	9,078	12.8	1,913	34	1,947	1.8
Pharmacists	1,427	1,211	2,638	45.9	756	99	855	11.6
Physicians	2,611	931	3,542	26.3	897	104	1,001	10.4
Teachers	22,939	5,527	28,466	19.4	6,417	530	6,947	7.6
Architects	335	619	954	64.9	592	105	697	15.1
Engineers & Surveyors	2,047	2,432	4,479	51.8	1,442	706	2,148	32.9
Theater artists	678	2,173	2,851	76.2	199	104	303	34.3
Others*	5,943	9,080	15,023	60.4	3,506	532	4,038	13.1
Totals	227,517	199,174	426,691	46.7%	171,863	22,867	194,730	11.7%
Total employed in all occupations:	1,670,545	1,356,438	3,027,033		1,256,774	77,772	1,334,546	
% of foreigners employed in middle class:		15%					29%	

Sources: Argentine Republic, *Tercer censo nacional*, IV, 383–395; Chile, Comisión Central del Censo, *Censo . . . de 1907*, pp. 1299–1300.
*Others: For Argentina, includes contractors, distributors, bookkeepers, specialized teachers, and agronomists; for Chile, includes scientists, dentists, impresarios, and hotel owners.

of Italian immigrants, who became not only a rich landowner, but president of the nation between 1890 and 1893.[49] Pelligrini's case was not typical, for immigrants and their sons seldom held high political office. As late as 1916, only four men of foreign birth were serving in Congress, while an additional 12 per cent of the Chamber of Deputies and 4 per cent of the Senate were first-generation Argentines.[50] It was not until after World War I that the foreign born and their offspring rose into the Argentine upper class. When the sociologist José Luis de Imaz surveyed approximately 1,900 Buenos Aires upper-class families in 1962, he found that only 48 per cent had Spanish surnames, while about 12 per cent were Italian, 14 per cent Anglo-Saxon, and 6.7 per cent French.[51] In another study Imaz shows that first-generation immigrants moved rapidly into high positions in the church and the army. Of the Argentine bishops in 1964, 77 per cent were sons of foreigners while 44 per cent of the 247 Argentine army generals on the active list between 1936 and 1961 were sons of immigrants.[52]

The Chilean upper class, which had long been admitting foreigners, was by 1914 a more cosmopolitan group than its Argentine counterpart. Many first- or second-generation foreigners, particularly English and Scotch-Irish, belonged to the commercial and mining plutocracy that was merging with the old agricultural upper class after the War of the Pacific. Some of these Britishers had come by chance, like Enrique MacIver, who decided to try his fortune in Chile after the ship he captained was wrecked in Valparaíso in 1838.[53] The majority, however, were merchants who came when Chilean foreign trade expanded after independence from Spain. Such was the origin of some prominent upper-class family names, including Blest, Edwards, Ross, Walker, and Bunster. French merchants also founded several distinguished families,

[49] Huret, *La Argentina de Buenos Aires al Gran Chaco*, II, 9; José M. Salaverría, *Tierra argentina*, p. 165.

[50] Darío Cantón, "El parlamento argentino en épocas de cambio; 1889, 1916 y 1946," *Desarrollo Económico*, IV (April–June, 1964), 28, 31.

[51] José Luis de Imaz, *La clase alta de Buenos Aires*, p. 13.

[52] José Luis de Imaz, *Los que mandan*, second edition, pp. 56–57, 174.

[53] Agustín Venturino, *Grandes familias chilenas descendientes de ingleses, franceses, e italianos.*

including Letelier, Subercaseaux, Dublé and Zegers.[54] Some of these families assembled great economic power. The Edwardses, for example, not only had nitrate mines, banks, insurance companies, and estates, but also owned (and still own) *El Mercurio*, the nation's most influential newspaper, which for decades was the "decisive organ of public opinion."[55]

The rapid economic and social ascent of immigrants continued in Chile after World War I. According to a study in 1963, immigrants or their offspring own approximately three-fourths of the Santiago industrial establishments employing over one hundred people.[56] This socioeconomic rise took place rapidly, often within two generations. Most of the original Syrian and Lebanese immigrants, for example, arrived during the first decades of the twentieth century with neither financial resources nor social prestige. By 1941 a survey revealed that nearly every adult Levantine male had become a shop owner, small industrialist, or professional. Less than 5 per cent held working-class jobs.[57] During the 1940's and 1950's, Syrians and Lebanese continued to better their economic position, so that presently they own many of the nation's largest banks and almost completely control the textile industry. They are also beginning to hold political office and to penetrate the highest social circles, such as Santiago's exclusive Club de la Unión.[58] Participation in the most elevated levels of government provides further evidence of the prominence held by the immigrants'

[54] Guillermo Feliú Cruz, *Chile visto a través de Agustín Ross*, pp. 48, 51–52; Agustín Venturino, *Sociología chilena: Con comparaciones argentinas y mejicanas*, p. 272.

[55] Raúl Silva Castro, *Prensa y periodismo en Chile (1812–1956)*, p. 343.

[56] Lipset and Solari, *Elites in Latin America*, p. 24.

[57] Ahmad H. Mattar, ed., *Guía social de la colonia árabe en Chile (Siria-Palestina-Lebanesa)*, pp. 198–330.

[58] Several Levantines held ambassadorial and ministerial posts during the second administration of President Carlos Ibáñez (1952–1958). See Donald W. Bray, "The Political Emergence of Arab Chileans, 1952–1958," *Journal of Inter-American Studies*, IV (October, 1962), 557–562. For comments on the social rise of Syrian and Lebanese immigrants, see Kalman H. Silvert, *La sociedad problema: Reacción y revolución en América Latina*, trans. Noemí Rosenblat, p. 226.

descendants in contemporary Chilean life. High in the Christian Democratic regime that took office in 1964 were descendants of Swiss
(President Frei), of Englishmen (Minister of the Interior Leighton
and Minister of Labor Thayer), and of Yugoslavs (Ambassador to the
U.S. Tomič). Two other twentieth-century presidents of Chile, Arturo
and Jorge Alessandri, were descendants of an Italian sculptor who arrived in 1821 and built a fortune in commerce and coastal shipping.[59]

Although foreigners were only beginning to penetrate the upper
classes by 1914, it was already obvious that their economic and social
rise was much greater than most supporters of liberal immigration policies had expected or desired. In both Chile and Argentina immigrants
composed the majority of owners of industry, and in the latter nation
they controlled commerce as well. They owned comparatively little
rural property, but they held large and rapidly growing amounts of
urban real estate. Some immigrants were becoming very wealthy, and
many thousands more were filling middle-class positions.

[59] Ricardo Donoso, *Alessandri: Agitador y demolador*, I, 11–13, 23.

CHAPTER THREE

"Intermediaries and Parasites": Argentine and
Chilean Images of Middle-Class Immigration

>>

The Europeans' astounding conquest of wealth along with
their rapid rise into the middle social class cooled the ardor with which
many an Argentine and Chilean creole had long regarded immigration.
Indeed, shortly after 1900 a hostile reaction set in against the foreigners
who competed socially and economically with nationals. Since the ruling groups of both republics remained convinced that immigration
was essential to continued development and vital to the smooth func-
tioning of the international economic system, the reaction led not to
restriction of immigration, but to defamation. Unable to stop the
ascent many newcomers were making into the urban middle class, Argentines and Chileans who resented foreign-born businessmen and professionals began to denounce them. As World War I approached, such
diverse groups as journalists, politicians, and literary artists developed a
new image of the immigrant businessman as an unscrupulous, immoral
scoundrel.

Little of the pronounced hostility against immigrant businessmen
that began to arise in Chile originated among the upper classes, who
still accepted liberal and cosmopolitan economic theories and continued

to associate the immigrant with the European culture they so deeply admired. Furthermore, the Chilean elites for decades had admitted wealthy businessmen of immigrant background. Proud of their cosmopolitan orientation, the best circles of Santiago society extended a warm welcome to the foreigner of wealth and culture, to "Europeans who know how to dress and speak correctly," as the blue-blooded scholar Benjamín Vicuña Subercaseaux put it.[1] But perhaps the key factor explaining the lack of upper-class resentment was that the foreigners never constituted a threat to elite power. Middle-class immigrants formed a small group, which for the most part was more interested in making money than in altering the course of Chilean public affairs. Many foreigners in Chile symbolized their lack of concern for civic life by living in "social isolation" from Chileans, as one Englishman described it. Save for their commercial affairs, English and other foreign businessmen withdrew into tight little ethnic enclaves and remained aloof from Chilean culture.[2]

Almost alone among writers of upper-class background who enjoyed a national reputation, Francisco A. Encina warned against the dangers that middle-class immigration posed for Chile. Born into a wealthy and distinguished Talca landowning family in 1874, Encina served several congressional terms and later became a prolific, popular, and highly nationalistic historian. Before World War I his fame rested on two studies, *Nuestra inferioridad económica* and *La educación económica y el liceo*, published in 1911 and 1912 respectively. These penetrating analyses of Chilean society rejected liberal international economics in general and immigration in particular. Immigration was unwise, argued Encina, because numerous foreign-born businessmen would come to Chile, invest in mining or commerce, and eventually return to Europe laden with the profits they had garnered in Chile. As a consequence immigration would not help develop a dynamic, self-sufficient national economy.[3] Furthermore, Encina claimed, Chile would

---

[1] Benjamín Vicuña Subercaseaux, *Un país nuevo (cartas sobre Chile)*, p. 272.

[2] "Cosas de Chile—The Gringo," *The Saturday Review of Politics, Literature, Science, and Art*, LXXII (October 3, 1891), 388.

[3] Francisco A. Encina, *Nuestra inferioridad económica*, pp. 133, 144–145.

never attract many working-class immigrants, but only more business-men, whose principal impact would be to tie Chile more closely to the European economy.[4] This ready acceptance of the foreigner was sup-posedly weakening the nation's self-confidence and might eventually destroy its will to maintain political independence. From his seat in Congress, Encina strongly opposed government immigration subsidies, which helped bring these "intermediaries and parasites" to Chile.[5] Al-though his books gained wide renown, Encina failed to end the admira-tion with which the Chilean elites regarded middle-class foreigners. His impact was much greater among the national middle class, those who were becoming dismayed at the rise of the foreign born into many of the nation's most lucrative commercial, professional, and managerial positions. Chile's economy was not generating enough of these em-ployment opportunities to accommodate both the foreign born and the nationals who aspired to middle-class status. The Chilean middle groups, which had slowly emerged after the 1860's as a result of the commercialization of economic life and because of increased educa-tional opportunities, were in danger of losing out to foreigners. The reaction against immigrant businessmen and professionals originated almost entirely among these national middle groups.

Some of the republic's most influential young intellectuals had emerged from the middle class and expressed the antagonism this so-cial group held against immigration. Nicolás Palacios, a physician of modest background, well known at the time as an analyst of Chilean social and economic affairs, summarized in a 1908 essay the fears and frustrations that pervaded the middle class. Lack of nationally owned industry along with the foreign domination of commerce, he argued, were restricting the national middle class to the liberal professions and government jobs. This situation, Palacios warned, would bring "very grave social consequences," since the "ruin of the middle class is the first step in the general ruin of nations." Fernando Santiván, one of Chile's best young novelists, put forth similar ideas. In a 1914 article he gloomily noted, "The defeat of the Chilean in business is already

---

[4] Francisco A. Encina, *La educación económica y el liceo*, p. 169.
[5] *B.S.C.D.*, sesiones extraordinarias, January 27, 1908, p. 1322.

an established fact," and that "the newcomers are limiting the native to the most secondary positions."[6] In full agreement with such analyses were editorials in *La Lei*, a newspaper reflecting the views of the middle-class Radical party. Immigration, wrote one editorialist, "by snatching small commerce away from the natives, is taking from them one of the steps of the social ladder, thus interrupting the upward climb anyone who wants to better his economic and social condition must make." Since immigration tends to block upward social mobility for the native born, "it is taking from our people the indispensable stimulant they need to maintain a lively, powerful love of labor and of the nation."[7]

Not content with denouncing the victory of the foreigners in Chilean commerce, several writers attempted to villify and discredit the immigrant businessman. They portrayed him as a scoundrel who sacrificed ethics to his all-consuming aim of enrichment. "One can't be a saint and a businessman at the same time," a rich Italian shopkeeper tells a fellow countryman in one of Joaquín Díaz Garcés' short stories. "In order to make money you need to be shrewd, to shorten the measure, to skimp a little on weight now and then." According to *La Lei*, Italian businessmen followed this philosophy by adulterating foodstuffs and by marketing poor quality wines.[8] Another ruse unscrupulous immigrants allegedly employed was to burn down their business houses in order to collect insurance. Palacios charged, probably with considerable exaggeration, that 90 per cent of fires in foreign-owned commercial houses were set intentionally.[9]

Few foreign-born businessmen incurred as much wrath as the group of Spaniards who controlled approximately 80 per cent of capital invested in Chilean loan houses and pawnshops in 1914. *La Lei* protested

[6] Nicolás Palacios, *Nacionalización de la industria salitrera*, II, 16; F[ernando] S[antinbáñez], "El desalojamiento del nacional," *Pacífico Magazine*, III (June, 1914), 705; Julio César Jobet, "Notas sobre tres sociólogos nacionales," *Atenea*, LXXXIX (March, 1948), 240–241.

[7] *La Lei*, June 14, 1907, p. 1.

[8] Joaquín Díaz Garcés, *Páginas chilenas*, third edition, p. 280; *La Lei*, February 9, 1907, p. 2.

[9] Nicolás Palacios, *Raza chilena*, p. 467; Alejandro Venegas, *Sinceridad: Chile íntimo en 1910*, p. 269.

in a series of editorials that Spanish loan sharks exploited Chileans by charging interest rates as excessive as 4 per cent a month and by enforcing very strict regulations for recovering pawned articles. *La obra*, a brief novel of social protest by Tancredo Pinochet, contains one scene in which a skilled Chilean worker has to pawn his suit to pay medical expenses. He finds that the Spanish loan shark offers only eight pesos for a suit costing sixty, and that the interest rates are seven times those asked of a rich man mortgaging a house.[10] Since some of these Spaniards were becoming rich and then returning to the homeland to live in style, the newspapers thought the interest rates all the more detestable.[11]

Immigrant businessmen found themselves criticized for exploiting not only the Chilean consumer but also the native-born laborer. Hostility against foreign-born mine operators was particularly strong on this issue. According to one spokesman for the Radical party, foreign nitrate operators "are motivated exclusively by one factor . . . profit," and usually treat "as simple beasts of burden" the unhappy Chilean miners "who are expending their energies and their lives."[12] Baldomero Lillo, born in the bleak coal-mining village of Lota and one of Chile's greatest writers, presented a grim picture of a foreign mine boss in *Sub terra*. Lillo's Mr. Davis was a "hard and inflexible" boss "whose treatment of the workers was pitiless." "In his racial conceit he considered the lives of these beings unworthy of a gentleman's attention."[13]

But the criticism that Spanish or English businessmen received was slight compared to the stinging rebukes that Chilean writers hurled at Chinese, Jewish, and Levantine immigrants who had by now entered commerce. Because they were identified with races that Chilean opinion tended to consider inferior, these immigrants were highly vulnerable to defamation. The Chilean press and several intellectuals lapsed into denunciations of Syrian, Jewish, and Chinese businessmen not only

---

[10] See Chile, *Anuario estadístico* (1914), IX, 158. See also *La Lei*, February 9, 1907, p. 2, and March 8, 1907, p. 1; Tancredo Pinochet Le-Brun, *La obra*, pp. 142–143.

[11] *La Unión*, March 13, 1913, p. 9.

[12] Javier Díaz Lira, *Observaciones sobre la cuestión social en Chile*, p. 7.

[13] Baldomero Lillo, "Grisu," in *Sub terra*, twelfth edition, p. 24.

sharply criticizing their business methods but sometimes employing crude arguments that these immigrants were biologically inferior creatures who should be excluded from Chile.

Few foreign groups in Chile were prospering more than the Chinese, who by 1914 numbered only a few thousand, but who already owned 456 business houses, mostly in the nitrate provinces of Tarapacá and Antofagasta.[14] Chilean and European businessmen in the northern cities reacted against this strong competition by charging that the Chinese sold cheap and shoddy Oriental goods, cheated on weights and measures, and exploited their customers with usurious credit terms. According to the short-story writer Víctor Domingo Silva, most Chileans in Tarapacá believed that the Chinese prospered because "they are pirates who have gained all they possess through robbery."[15] The anti-Chinese argument continued that the Orientals came to Chile to make a quick fortune, which they invariably would take back to Asia. To strengthen their case against the Chinese, newspapers employed bitter racist arguments that Orientals were biologically decadent.[16]

Only a few hundred Jews inhabited Chile before 1914, but Chilean comments on the subject of Jewish immigration revealed deep hostility. An editorialist in *El Mercurio* wrote that such immigration was undesirable, for most Jews became "astute and untrustworthy" businessmen.[17] More bitter was the contention of novelist Joaquín Edwards Bello that commerce to the Jew meant "legal robbery, authorized theft." In his novel *El inútil*, Edwards Bello pointed to the presence in downtown Santiago of "Rubenstein, Klein, Schwastzenberg, and all the rest of these Jews who came only yesterday and who have become rich by practicing their devious arts of robbery on the careless Chile-

[14] The last pre–World War I count of Chinese immigrants, the census of 1907, found 1,920 Chinese nationals residing in Chile (see Table 3). See also Chile, *Anuario estadístico* (1914), IX, 131.

[15] Víctor Domingo Silva, *La pampa trágica*, p. 163; *La Unión*, November 16, 1911, p. 3.

[16] *El Pueblo Obrero*, June 13, 1907, p. 1; August 22, 1908, p. 1; October 30, 1909, p. 1.

[17] *El Mercurio*, August 10, 1905, p. 5.

ans."[18] Such defamation foreshadowed the resentment one encounters frequently today in Chile against the several thousand Jewish immigrants who came in the late 1930's and have profited in business.

The Levantines in Chile were experiencing commercial success so rapid that by 1914 they owned small stores and artisan shops in all parts of the republic. Syrians and Lebanese owed their success partly to their ambition and drive and partly to their modern business methods. While Chilean businessmen still operated with slow turnover and small volume, the Syrians and Lebanese kept overhead low, operated with a small profit margin, and sold large quantities of merchandise, especially in working-class and lower-middle-class neighborhoods.[19] The Chilean press seldom analyzed the reasons that accounted for the Levantines' commercial success and instead directed irrational and bitter attacks against the so-called Turcos. One columnist writing in *El Mercurio* not only condemned these immigrants as "dirtier than the dogs of Constantinople," but also claimed they were biologically highly susceptible to diseases like leprosy and the plague, which they allegedly were bringing to Chile.[20] Such remarks were not unusual among journalists and intellectuals who discussed Syrian and Lebanese immigration.

To counter Levantine competition, other businessmen in Santiago began to urge the government to prohibit or at least tax all street vendors. In May, 1911, the municipal government responded by placing a stiff levy on all ambulatory salesmen and by ordering them to prove "good conduct."[21] But the city soon repealed this tax, and the journalistic campaign against the Levantines resumed. *El Diario Ilustrado* in a 1913 editorial tried to convince the public to avoid "Turco" merchandise, which the newspaper claimed was filthy and unsanitary. Levantine immigration should be prohibited, argued this newspaper,

---

[18] Joaquín Edwards Bello, *El inútil*, p. 120.
[19] "Vendedores ambulantes," *Pacífico Magazine*, II (November, 1913), 668.
[20] *El Mercurio*, April 13, 1908, p. 1.
[21] Benedicto Chuaqui, *Memorias de un emigrante*, p. 230; *El Mercurio*, August 3, 1908, p. 3, April 13, 1911, p. 1, May 13, 1911, p. 17, July 28, 1911, p. 14.

for the "Turcos" were only "leeches who grow fat from the sap of the body" and would return to their homelands after making a fortune in Chile.[22] The hostility with which many Chileans regarded the "Turcos" was vividly demonstrated when Santiago city officials ordered the Levantine community to demolish a small monument built to honor the Chilean independence centennial in 1910. The city had welcomed the construction of elaborate monuments by the Italian and German communities, but the authorities arbitrarily destroyed the partly constructed "Turco" statue on the pretense that it was obstructing traffic. Only after bitter protest from the local Syrian and Lebanese leaders did the city permit erection of the monument, which finally was dedicated in 1912.[23]

Syrian and Lebanese immigrants usually entered commerce, but several other foreign groups were moving into clerical, managerial, and banking positions. The possibility that immigrants might eventually monopolize these occupations directly threatened the middle-class aspirations held by many Chileans and appalled a growing number of Chilean intellectuals. Searching for explanations, some writers singled out foreign-owned business firms for blame. Tancredo Pinochet revealed that at least one firm specifically advertised in the major newspapers for European employees. Pinochet claimed this practice was common and that, as a result, the large foreign business houses in Santiago employed few Chileans "other than the lawyer and the porter."[24] Even worse, reported *La Unión*, was the situation in Iquique, where the many English and German concerns supposedly avoided hiring Chileans for responsible positions. A Chilean could work in that northern city only as a laborer or a government employee, complained the newspapers.[25]

The majority of intellectuals who were seeking to explain the defeat

22 *El Diario Ilustrado*, August 31, 1913, p. 3; see also *La Unión*, October 21, 1911, p. 3.

23 *El Mercurio*, June 11, 1911, p. 26, July 23, 1911, p. 22; "El monumento sirio-otamano," *Zig Zag*, VIII (September 28, 1912), 45.

24 Tancredo Pinochet Le-Brun, *La conquista de Chile en el siglo XX*, pp. 134–135.

25 *La Unión*, June 24, 1911, p. 3.

of the Chilean in middle-class occupations blamed not the large foreign businesses but Chile's educational system. Francisco Encina, Luis Galdames, and Fernando Santiván, all young writers deeply concerned with social and economic questions, argued that the theoretical and humanistic orientation pervading Chilean secondary education gave students little training for business life and put them at a disadvantage when competing with practical-minded foreigners. These intellectuals contended that secondary education ought to teach the dignity of labor and to instill the practical spirit needed for commercial success. Furthermore, the government ought to create a system of technical institutes, industrial schools, and business colleges. Although Chilean educational groups, including the national Congress of Secondary Education, slowly began to accept these ideas, many deficiencies in the educational system that were pointed out by Encina, Galdames, and others half a century ago still persist.[26]

The professions were a final area in which immigrants were challenging the positions of the Chilean middle class. Numerous foreign-born professionals, including doctors, pharmacists, architects, and journalists, practiced in Chile (Table 10). But the national middle groups expressed particularly great concern over immigrant penetration of two fields—engineering and teaching. Foreigners composed about one-third of Chile's engineers in 1907 and directed many of the nation's principal public-works projects. The impact of these foreign technicians first became pronounced during the Balmaceda government (1886–1890), which had created a national Department of Public Works and contracted at least seventy foreign engineers to staff it. After their contracts expired, about half of these men remained in Chile.[27] Numerous other engineers also arrived from abroad, many

[26] Among the numerous works emphasizing the need for practical education to equip the Chilean to meet the immigrant's competition are Encina, *Nuestra inferioridad económica*, pp. 116–117, 119–120; idem, *La educación económica y el liceo*, p. 147; Luis Galdames, *Temas pedagójicos*, p. 6; idem, *Educación económica e intelectual*, pp. 25, 41; idem, "El espíritu de la enseñanza comercial," *Revista de Educación Nacional*, VIII (June, 1912), 187; and Santibáñez, "El desalojamiento del nacional," pp. 706–707. At least one novel touched on this theme: Senén Palacios, *Hogar chileno*, especially pp. 94–95.
[27] Ernesto Greve, *Historia de la injeniería en Chile*, IV, 261–263.

contracted by the government at high salaries to direct port, railroad, and irrigation construction.

Government favoritism toward foreign engineers became a hot public issue in 1907 when the Department of Public Works contracted an English engineer, at a generous salary of two thousand pounds sterling annually, to direct the various national port construction projects then under way. Led by the distinguished engineer and educator Domingo V. Santa María, the Chilean Institute of Engineers protested that the native born were fully as competent as the foreigners, and that many Chileans who had taken specialized training at government expense could have filled the position.[28] At least one prominent intellectual, Joaquín Díaz Garcés, came to the support of nationally trained engineers. He asserted in *El Mercurio*, "Engineering studies in Chile are magnificent," and that "our engineers are not inferior to the Europeans." Official favoritism toward foreign engineers, he continued, symptomized Chile's grave lack of self-confidence.[29] Another editorialist protested that the contracted foreigners received higher salaries than national engineers doing comparable government work. In Congress, Deputy Roberto E. Meeks called for an immediate investigation of the competence of Chilean engineers. If found able, he contended, all favoritism toward foreigners must end; if incompetent, scientific and technical education must be improved to end Chilean reliance on the outsiders.[30] But the government ignored this clamor and in 1911 awarded the contract for new Talcahuano port works to a French company, rejecting the proposal of a Chilean firm. A new spate of protests ensued, led by *La Unión*, which was "fed up with the worship of the foreigner." Government policy, argued the newspaper, unjustly discriminated against competent Chilean engineers, revealed national defense secrets to outsiders, and needlessly sent Chilean wealth out of the country.[31] Later the same year the English syndicate that held the con-

[28] *La Lei*, April 13, 1907, p. 1; Santiago Marín Vicuña, *Nuestros ingenieros*, p. 117; *El Mercurio*, September 30, 1907, p. 3.

[29] *El Mercurio*, January 10, 1908, p. 1.

[30] Ibid., September 30, 1907, p. 3; *B.S.C.D.*, sesiones ordinarias, July 6, 1907, p. 560.

[31] *La Unión*, October 19, 1910, p. 3; February 19, 1911, p. 6.

tract to extend the government's major north-south trunk railroad line replaced most of its Chilean engineers with foreigners. *El Mercurio* protested the dismissal in a lengthy editorial, but the government did nothing to aid the national engineers.[32]

The Chilean navy was another state agency that neglected to utilize or develop national engineering talent. Instead, naval authorities contracted European engineers to service the fleet, a policy the press criticized. In Talcahuano, the nation's principal navy port, the newspaper *La Justicia* cried that government favoritism of foreign naval engineers was "preventing the national worker from rising to a level commensurate with his aptitudes, intelligence, capacity, and sobriety."[33]

The government also contracted foreigners to direct the national railroads, Chile's largest state-owned enterprise. When a Prussian named Von Dörner was appointed director general in 1910, *La Unión* protested that a Chilean should have been chosen. Several nationals not only were highly capable, but also could understand "our customs, our administrative vices and corruption, our personnel, etc., etc., things foreigners cannot know." The paper's prophecy was borne out in 1911 when Von Dörner resigned in frustration, but the government continued to discriminate against nationals and appointed a Belgian, Omar Huet, to the post.[34]

While Chilean engineers were urging the government to end its favoritism of foreigners, a loud and protracted clamor was arising to protest the Ministry of Education's practice of discriminating against national teachers in favor of Europeans. Foreign-born educators, most of them German, had long enjoyed the Chilean government's support. Although, according to the 1907 census, only about 8 per cent of Chile's teachers were foreign citizens, this group occupied many of the country's key educational positions. Reliance on foreign teachers began in 1889, when the government contracted a group of German specialists in pedagogical theory to head the newly founded Instituto Peda-

[32] *El Mercurio*, September 20, 1911, p. 17.
[33] Ibid., March 9, 1896, p. 2; March 24, 1897, p. 2. The arrival of over fifty foreign engineers for the Chilean navy was reported in 1896 and 1897. *La Justicia*, quoted in *El Pueblo Obrero*, October 12, 1909, p. 1.
[34] *La Unión*, February 9, 1910, p. 3; *El Mercurio*, April 11, 1911, p. 14.

gógico at the University of Chile. Few Chileans possessed the technical competence to hold these posts during the Instituto's early years, but the government made no move to replace the Germans with qualified nationals when the latter became available. The Ministry of Education further discriminated against Chileans when hiring teachers for positions in the state secondary schools.[35] This reliance on Germans for important teaching posts reflected the prestige that positivist educational philosophy enjoyed in Chile. Pedagogy, it was assumed, is a body of universal principles, applicable in any environment. Furthermore, Chilean positivists were convinced that "the German nation indisputably holds the honor of converting education into a technical art founded on scientific principles of universal applicability," as *La Lei* put it.[36] Thus, it was assumed that German educators were the most qualified to reorganize Chilean education along so-called scientific lines.

The most influential supporter of the Germans was Valentín Letelier, prominent educator and rector of the university from 1906 to 1913. Letelier spent six years in Berlin as secretary of the Chilean legation, and during this time he became a fervent positivist and a strong admirer of German pedagogy.[37] In 1893, after his return to Chile, Letelier, along with other disciples of positivism, called for the recruitment of German teachers and persuaded the government to reorganize the secondary curriculum to conform to contemporary German practice.

But German teachers and positivist educational theories antagonized many Chileans, particularly the Roman Catholic clergy and some middle-class intellectuals. The church early attempted to use the issue of the German teachers to discredit an old enemy, namely, state-sponsored

[35] Amanda Labarca H., *Historia de la enseñanza en Chile*, pp. 199–200, 221; Raúl Silva Castro, *Don Eduardo de la Barra y la pedagogía alemana*, p. 6. Several French educators also held important teaching posts, especially at the National Agricultural School and the Plant Pathology Station. See E. M. Vega, ed., *Album de la colonie française au Chile*, pp. 83–84.

[36] *La Lei*, May 13, 1899, p. 1.

[37] Luis Galdames, *Valentín Letelier y su obra, 1852–1919*, pp. 71–72, 364–365; Labarca H., *Historia de la enseñanza*, p. 198.

higher education.[38] Soon after arriving in Chile in 1890, the German teachers contracted for the Instituto Pedagógico found themselves the object of sharp attacks made by the powerful Conservative party, the church's political spokesman. Conservative deputies in Congress charged that the Germans were replacing competent Chileans. "There are professors imported to teach history and geography, as if no Chileans existed who knew geography," exclaimed Julio Zegers in the Chamber of Deputies. Conservative leader Carlos Walker Martínez agreed, asking, "Is it true that no one in Chile knows and can teach philosophy, or physics, or chemistry, or English? Why, this is incredible, and it is enough to say it to reject it completely."[39] Another tactic the conservatives employed was to portray the Germans as dissolute and lazy. "One who enters certain Santiago beer halls will find three, four, or even five individuals playing dominoes, engaged in animated conversation, and occupied conscientiously in drinking beer; they are some of the German professors brought by the government," editorialized El Estandarte Católico, the voice of the Conservative party.[40]

A few years later, when the Instituto Pedagógico replaced its Chilean teachers of Spanish with Germans, the church's journalistic allies again attempted to turn public opinion against foreign professors. El Porvenir, which had assumed the role of Santiago's principal conservative newspaper, strongly protested the humiliation of the Chileans, many of whom supposedly were scholars of international reputation. The virtual monopoly held by the German professors was "as irritating as it is unjust. It is really embarrassing and humiliating. Furthermore, it is grotesque and absurd." If Chilean nationhood were to endure, "the mother tongue . . . must in no case be taught by foreigners."[41]

The Conservative party's initial defense of Chilean teachers failed to arouse much public hostility against the Germans. The issue did not begin to attract national attention until 1899, when the educator and philologist Eduardo de la Barra opened a journalistic campaign against

[38] Valentín Letelier, La lucha por la cultura, pp. 413–415.
[39] B.S.C.D., sesiones ordinarias, January 13, 1892, pp. 561, 566.
[40] El Estandarte Católico, March 1, 1890, p. 1.
[41] El Porvenir, January 22, 1895, p. 1; January 18, 1895, p. 2.

the "German bewitchment" that he claimed pervaded Chilean education. The incident provoking De la Barra's wrath involved the appointment of a director for a new girls' secondary school in Santiago. When the government appointed a Chilean woman who had graduated from the Instituto Pedagógico, Germanophile educators protested, claiming that many German women residing in Chile were better suited for the post. This was too much for De la Barra, who asked in the first of a series of newspaper articles, later published under the title of El embrujamiento alemán, "Is Chile for the Germans or for the Chileans?"[42] He bitterly observed that the German professors disdained the native born, although the foreigners were "not very wise, and had been little or nothing in their own country." Although De la Barra was an avowed anticlerical, El Porvenir supported him in the debate over education and proclaimed that Chile must "learn to rely on itself and not live like a foreign colony or factory."[43] El Mercurio, previously an enthusiast of the Germans, evidently was convinced by these arguments and began to support the national teachers. "We do not desire the complete delivery of the instruction of our people to the foreigners, with systematic exclusion of the native born," editorialized Chile's most influential newspaper.[44]

Continuing their attack, De la Barra and his allies asked why the contracted German professors were receiving their salaries in gold while Chileans doing comparable work were paid in paper money, which constantly depreciated in value. As a result, foreign teachers were able to become property owners, while the Chileans "have enjoyed a ration of hunger."[45] This salary differential was even more unjust, De la Barra contended, because the Germans were often indifferent scholars and poor teachers. Professor Lenz, who taught foreign languages in the Instituto Pedagógico, allegedly spoke French "like a waiter in a German beer hall."[46] Other defenders of the Chilean teach-

[42] Silva Castro, Don Eduardo de la Barra, p. 22.
[43] Eduardo de la Barra, La vida nacional: El embrujamiento alemán, p. 105; El Porvenir, May 5, 1899, p. 1.
[44] El Mercurio, January 20, 1899, p. 2.
[45] El Porvenir, June 26, 1895, p. 1; De la Barra, La vida nacional, p. 53.
[46] De la Barra, La vida nacional, pp. 37, 97.

ers pointed out that the policy of contracting foreigners wasted some of the nation's best talent. In Congress, one Senator discussed the case of a Chilean youth who had studied chemistry with a state fellowship at the Sorbonne. He made a brilliant record in France but was unable to find employment in Chile, since all the chemists at the University and the Instituto Nacional, Chile's leading secondary school, were foreigners.[47]

De la Barra died in late 1899, but other Chilean intellectuals continued his campaign to discredit foreign teachers. Joaquín Díaz Garcés, in one short story, stereotyped the German educators, using a character named Vildeter, a dissolute adventurer who had fought in the Boer War and in Ecuadorian revolutions and who spent more time in Chile drinking cognac than teaching school. Alejandro Venegas harshly criticized the Germans as "false pedagogues," who emphasized memorization, discouraged the experimental method, and displayed the cowardice and hypocrisy supposedly common to peoples governed by strong authority.[48] Zig Zag, a popular magazine founded in 1905, mercilessly satirized the German professor as a stolid, unimaginative fool.[49]

Chilean intellectuals and journalists who attacked the German professors urged the government to support the employment of native-born teachers. El Mercurio, for example, grew steadily more hostile to the foreigners and justified contracting them only in the rare cases when no qualified Chileans were available. In 1902 the Radical newspaper La Lei abandoned its earlier support of foreign teachers and began to argue that the government's responsibility was to support the employment of Chilean intellectuals. The government should recognize that "we are not savages, nor are our brains defective, nor are we ignorant."[50] Another call for nondiscrimination was made by Pedro Aguirre Cerda, a law student who was to serve as president of Chile between 1938 and 1941. In his dissertation he contended that foreign teachers not specifically contracted by the government should be forced to pass

---

[47] B.S.S., sesiones extraordinarias, November 10, 1904, p. 400.
[48] Díaz Garcés, Páginas chilenas, p. 157; Venegas, Sinceridad, p. 73.
[49] "Un pedagogo alemán," Zig Zag, I (June 11, 1905), 22.
[50] La Lei, October 11, 1902, p. 1; El Mercurio, March 10, 1902, p. 2.

state examinations in the subjects they were to teach in Chile. To prevent discrimination against nationals, he continued, the foreigners
should be permitted to begin teaching only in the smaller secondary
schools, and procedures for their promotion should be the same as for
Chilean teachers.[51] Congress enacted no such legislation before 1914,
but the Ministry of Education quietly shifted policy and contracted no
more foreign educators for important posts after 1906. The development of intellectual opposition to the German professors roughly coin-
cided with the gradual decline of positivist educational philosophy in
Chile. By 1911 Luis Galdames, among others, was arguing that pedagogical principles valid in Germany might be meaningless in Chile
because of differences in the two peoples' national characters. Foreign
professors would be useless, continued Galdames, unless they could
adapt their theories to Chilean culture.[52] *El Diario Ilustrado* agreed
that German theories were invalid because "the Chilean race is not the
German race, our mentality is not like the German, and so the German
ways of teaching cannot be followed in Chile."[53]

The strong antagonism encountered by prosperous bourgeois immigrants in Argentina did not originate primarily among the national
middle groups. Unlike the situation in Chile, where the middle class
protested loudly against immigrant businessmen and professionals, in
Argentina the middle class seldom voiced great concern over the success that immigrants were rapidly gaining in industry, commerce, and
the professions. Two factors may help explain this difference. Economic prosperity in Argentina was creating large numbers of clerical,
managerial, and professional positions, but in Chile economic growth
was slower, with the result that immigrants and nationals often competed for white-collar positions. The Argentine middle class, furthermore, was much more cosmopolitan in origin than the Chilean and
therefore less apt to resent the success of immigrants who achieved
wealth and status. Not until Argentina's export economy collapsed in

[51] Pedro Aguirre Cerda, *Estudio sobre instrucción pública*, pp. 95–96.
[52] Galdames, *Temas pedagójicos*, pp. 19–20; idem, *Educación económica e intelectual*, p. 211.
[53] Quoted in *La Unión*, January 13, 1912, p. 4.

the early 1930's did the middle class turn strongly against immigration. About the same time the Great Depression hit Argentina, the sons of many Europeans who had arrived before 1914 were reaching maturity and were replacing their fathers in the Argentine middle class. Fervently nationalistic and identifying strongly with traditional Argentine cultural values, this new generation now resented the competition of middle-class foreigners and applauded government moves to restrict immigration.

In pre-World War I Argentina antagonism against prosperous foreign-born businessmen and professionals originated largely among the upper class. The Argentine landed elite was confronting a massive and steadily growing middle class, potentially of great political strength and composed largely of recent immigrants. This social change the Argentine elites had neither expected nor desired. They wanted foreign-born farm laborers, railroad men, and stevedores, not shopkeepers, clerks, and entrepreneurs. Argentines who had supported massive immigration had envisioned populating the agricultural provinces, not creating teeming metropolitan centers like Buenos Aires. The elites had expected to continue monopolizing political power and social prestige, not to share them with immigrants or their descendants. By 1905 the Argentine upper class found itself in a dilemma. Recent Argentine history as well as the accepted economic canons indicated that continued prosperity required more immigration. But new immigrants undoubtedly would continue to enter the middle class and would accelerate the social changes already undermining elite power. Frustrated by this dilemma and unable to stop the tide of change, upper-class families discriminated against wealthy immigrants while those intellectuals who reflected upper-class views furiously denounced foreign-born business and professional men.

Unlike the Chilean upper class, many Argentine elite families excluded foreigners, refused to receive them socially, and emphasized that their status would remain inferior.[54] This social discrimination

---

[54] Ezequiel Gallo (hijo) and Silvia Sigal, "La formación de los partidos políticos contemporáneos: La U.C.R. (1890–1916)," in Torcuato S. Di Tella, et al., *Argentina, sociedad de masas*, p. 169; Marie-Anne (pseud.), "Buenos

took place in the smaller interior cities as well as in the capital. In Córdoba, according to the perceptive French traveler Jules Huret, the upper class scorned wealthy immigrants, while in Salta the aristocracy similarly basked in the glory of its ancient Castilian family names and disdained the upper class of nearby Tucumán, into which foreigners had penetrated.[55] To prevent *nouveaux riches* immigrants from mingling socially with the traditional elite, entrance to aristocratic gathering places like Buenos Aires' opulent Colón Opera House was carefully restricted. One had to present one's baptismal certificate to gain admittance, joked *Caras y Caretas*.[56]

In the same manner, upper-class student circles snubbed the sons of foreigners. Francisco Grandmontagne's novel *Teodoro Foronda* relates an incident in which Simón, the son of a Spanish immigrant, was ignored by aristocratic students of "historic surnames" until his friends successfully spread the rumor that he really was the grandson of the Venezuelan liberator, Simón Bolívar.[57] Some support existed among the elites for limiting immigrant social mobility by excluding the sons of foreigners from higher education. In 1904 Honorio Pueyrredón, a rich and influential landowner, petitioned the University of Buenos Aires Faculty of Law to restrict enrollment in order to prevent foreigners and their descendants from entering the legal profession.[58] The university apparently ignored the petition.

Excluded from aristocratic society, wealthy immigrants still attempted, through conspicuous consumption, to emulate the elites' manner of life. Successful foreigners built massive mansions on Buenos Aires' fashionable Avenida Alvear, imported fine European automobiles, and flaunted the latest French and English fashions. Such "fickle adoption of the most ordinary and vulgar vanities," as one Argentine

---

Aires Social," *Revista de Derecho, Historia y Letras*, XXXIV (September, 1909), 5.

[55] Jules Huret, *La Argentina de Buenos Aires al Gran Chaco*, trans. E. Gómez Carillo, I, 151, and II, 329.

[56] "Todos al Colón," *Caras y Caretas*, XVI (April 5, 1913), n.p.

[57] Francisco Grandmontagne, *Teodoro Foronda*, II, 79.

[58] Tulio Halperin Donghi, *Historia de la Universidad de Buenos Aires*, p. 118.

put it, failed to gain entree and gave the upper class additional pretexts to criticize the foreigners.[59]

Immigrant businessmen and professionals also encountered increasingly hostile intellectual criticism. Several Argentine writers, themselves of upper-class background, voiced deep concern about the challenge immigration was posing to Argentina's traditional hierarchical social organization. The landed oligarchy, they claimed, had governed Argentina in an enlightened fashion and was responsible for the peace and prosperity the nation was enjoying during the early twentieth century. But, said these intellectuals, foreign-born shopkeepers, professionals, clerks, and other members of what Lucio V. López called the "bastard family of the new rich"[60] espoused dangerous ideas, such as social equality and effective majority rule. The implementation of these theories, it was claimed, would weaken Argentina and disrupt its progress. To discredit the foreign born who threatened the traditional social structure, several well-known intellectuals prepared strong denunciations that stereotyped bourgeois immigrants as highly unsavory characters.

One author who was troubled by the emergence of the foreign-born middle class was Lucio V. Mansilla, a wealthy, aristocratic, and widely traveled nephew of former dictator Juan Manuel de Rosas. Mansilla acknowledged the contribution that immigrant laborers were making to Argentine prosperity but feared that middle-class foreigners eventually would take control of the nation.[61] He bitterly portrayed the successful immigrant businessman as a stolid, unimaginative being who knew no high aspirations and whose only "battles are with the rules of compound interest." Furthermore, the foreigner supposedly ignored patriotism and civic duty and occupied himself with cheating the public through "the best and cheapest means of adulterating food products."[62]

---

[59] Quoted in Huret, *La Argentina de Buenos Aires al Gran Chaco*, II, 13; see also José M. Salaverría, *Tierra argentina*, pp. 48, 89.

[60] Lucio V. López, "Discurso pronunciado por el Dr. Lucio V. López en la colación de grados de la Facultad de Derecho el 24 de Mayo de 1890," in Comisión de Homenaje, ed., *Lucio V. López: En el cincuentenario de su muerte*, p. 27.

[61] For example, Lucio V. Mansilla, *Un país sin ciudadanos*, p. 49.

[62] Lucio V. Mansilla, *Mis memorias: Infancia-adolescencia*, p. 124.

Mansilla, who had grown up in a house full of servants and who was accustomed to rigid social hierarchy, was also perturbed that the foreign "sellers of pork chops, sausages, or oranges," wanted to "be accepted as gentlemen," and that "today everyone wants to be . . . equal."[63] These immigrant middle groups, he asserted, lacked the education and cultural sophistication to govern Argentina with the wisdom that the traditional elite families had long provided.[64]

Miguel Cané, a prominent politician who had served as ambassador to Vienna, Berlin, Madrid, and Paris, was another upper-class intellectual who condemned bourgeois immigration. Like Mansilla, he realized that foreigners were populating the agricultural provinces,[65] but he saw little else good about immigration, whose impact was eroding the bases of the aristocratic society he admired. Mourning the lack of good servants in recent years, he cried, "Where, where are old and faithful servants like those I saw in my early youth in my parents' home?" He answered that "today a European servant attends us who robs us, who dresses better than we do, and who reminds us of his status as a free man if one scarcely reprimands him." The "democratic, cosmopolitan movement," he concluded, is the cause of this disturbing lack of "constant respect, of the veneration of subordinate men for their superiors."[66] The challenge to traditional social hierarchy likewise irritated Lucio V. López, scion of a distinguished family and one of the nation's most successful lawyers. As early as 1890, long before most writers became concerned about the problem, he questioned the value of immigration and condemned immigrant businessmen as immodest, pretentious, and ignorant. Aghast at the prospect that foreigners might gain ascendency over the "thinking element of the nation," he reminded them that democracy is "government of the intellectual classes, of the just and capable men of the republic."[67]

None of these writers expressed so clearly the frustration and resent-

---

[63] Ibid., p. 173; and speech in D.S.C.D., July 17, 1891, p. 315.
[64] Adolfo Prieto, La literatura autobiográfica argentina, p. 153.
[65] Miguel Cané, Discursos y conferencias, p. 132.
[66] Miguel Cané, Prosa ligera, p. 132.
[67] López, Discurso, p. 27.

ment that immigrant economic success was producing among the traditional Argentine elites as the psychologist and educator José María Ramos Mejía. Son of a prominent Buenos Aires landowning family, he attended medical school, specialized in neuropsychology, and became one of Argentina's most respected physicians. He also headed the powerful National Council of Education between 1908 and 1913. Besides several works of history, his literary efforts included a volume on psychological theory, *Los simuladores del talento*, and a sociological essay, *Las multitudes argentinas*, both of which bitterly criticized immigration. Most Argentine intellectuals acknowledged the contribution the foreign born were making to Argentine prosperity, but Ramos Mejía found no kind words for immigration. The newly arrived foreigner, he wrote, was a *guarango*, a gross person who "will represent one of those low beings that future scientists will study with curiosity in order to establish the linkage of the successive types of our evolution." With their cheap, sensual tastes and their love of bright colors, raucous music, and gaudy clothing, immigrants were culturally inferior to native Argentines, continued Ramos Mejía.[68] Physically, the foreigner was a poor and ugly specimen; at least two generations of intermarriage must elapse before his descendants could compare with the creoles.[69]

The "gilded, insupportable, and voracious" immigrants who became businessmen incurred Ramos Mejía's greatest wrath. He was convinced that their desire to profit and advance economically demonstrated mental illness.[70] Equally undesirable were foreign-born professionals. According to Ramos Mejía, "Even when you see him as a doctor, lawyer, engineer, or journalist, you will sense from afar a sharp odor of the stable."[71] The European-born businessman and professional both were likely to engage in conspicuous consumption, which Ramos Mejía hated. But these immigrants could not cover over their banal quality, for if one would "just scratch the varnish" that covers the foreigner's

[68] José M. Ramos Mejía, *Las multitudes argentinas*, pp. 257–258.
[69] Ibid., p. 255.
[70] Ramos Mejía, *Los simuladores del talento en las luchas por la personalidad y la vida*, pp. 234–235.
[71] Ramos Mejía, *Las multitudes argentinas*, pp. 258–259.

"blemished soul," one would "immediately see his baseness emerge, invalidating the amnesty that the tailor or the impunity that some pompous diploma has conferred upon him."[72]

Proud upper-class Argentine families who lacked the wealth many *nouveaux riches* immigrants were accumulating shared the wrath that Ramos Mejía expressed. This antagonism found vivid portrayal in the Argentine drama of the period, and particularly in plays by Vicente Martínez Cuitiño and Carlos María Pacheco. Martínez Cuitiño's *Los Colombinos* and Pacheco's *Los equilibristas* present proud but recently impoverished upper-class creole families who arrange marriages with newly rich Italian businessmen. Although the Argentines quickly turn to their newly acquired relatives for financial aid, members of the creole families in both plays strongly resent the Italians and consider their lowly social backgrounds malodorous.[73] While such playwrights were reflecting the hostility against wealthy immigrants that some upper-class families expressed, other authors were beginning to voice the resentment with which the national middle class regarded immigrant businessmen. Similar to the situation in Chile, several prominent Argentine intellectuals became concerned that foreigners might totally exclude nationals from business enterprise. In their concern over this apparently inexorable economic trend, these authors began to defame the foreign-born businessman. They attributed his success to an insatiable materialism together with a complete lack of ethics. He was, in other words, a scoundrel.

The rampant materialism of middle-class immigrants became a common theme in Argentine literature. The distinguished educator Enrique de Vedia proclaimed that immigrants came to Argentina "as if to a California waiting for conquest," with "voracious appetites" but without "moral culture."[74] In agreement was Manuel Gálvez, a man of conflicting moods, who occasionally lauded the foreigner's contribution to Argentine grandeur. But in his major books he emphasized a convic-

[72] Ibid., p. 260.
[73] Vicente Martínez Cuitiño, *Los Colombinos*, in Vicente Martínez Cuitiño, *Teatro*, III, 111–197; Carlos María Pacheco, *Los equilibristas*, in *Argentores*, III (June 11, 1936).
[74] Enrique de Vedia, *Educación secundaria*, p. 30.

tion that "the conquering immigrant has introduced in the nation a new concept of life," which was "exclusive respect for material values."[75] While in the past the "collective soul" of Argentina was "noble and lived in the pursuit of great ideals," massive immigration brought a "repugnant materialism" and a "veneration of money."[76] The novelist Pedro G. Morante agreed that "the neurosis of money" completely dominated the immigrants and their offspring. In his novel *Grandezas*, the daughter of an Italian businessman dreams of nothing but "honors, huge riches, and splendid palaces." Living by the philosophy that "there were no other just causes . . . than money," she ruins her Argentine husband but uses her beauty, charm, and feminine wiles to achieve wealth for herself and her children.[77]

Scholars and newspapers critical of immigrant materialism frequently singled out Jews for particular reprobation. As in Chile, irrationality sometimes replaced dispassionate analysis when Argentines discussed Jewish economic activity. The press would note with alarm that "it is very general to see the great stores empty, while the Jewish shops are becoming very popular, and are constantly crowded with customers."[78] But rather than attributing such commercial success to patient, hard labor, the Argentine writer would explain it by usury, which the race allegedly always practiced. It was claimed, for example, that the Jew would loan his small initial capital at interest rates up to 240 per cent annually, and that he acquired much of his property through foreclosures.[79]

Jewish economic activity formed the theme of one major Argentine novel, Julián Martel's *La Bolsa* (1890). Martel, a journalist for *La Nación*, set his work against the background of the feverish speculation

[75] Manuel Gálvez, *El solar de la raza*, p. 10.

[76] Manuel Gálvez, *El diario de Gabriel Quiroga: Opiniones sobre la vida argentina*, pp. 53, 63.

[77] Pedro G. Morante, *Grandezas*, pp. 77, 85.

[78] Arturo Reynal O'Connor, "Por las colonias," *Revista Nacional*, XXXIII (January, 1902), 49; Saúl M. Escobar, *Inmigración*, p. 71; Mark Jefferson, *Peopling the Argentine Pampa*, p. 155.

[79] This common argument is found, for example, in E. de Cires, "La inmigración en Buenos Aires," *Revista Argentina de Ciencias Políticas*, IV (September, 1912), 745, and Reynal O'Connor, "Por las colonias," p. 49.

and rampant corruption that gripped the nation during the late 1880's. By 1890 total financial collapse opened the way to a political revolution, which, although abortive, forced the resignation of President Miguel Juárez Celmán. Martel attempted to shift the responsibility for this crisis from the landed interests who had profited from rapid inflation to a more vulnerable scapegoat. Jewish financiers and businessmen, he proclaimed, were the basic cause of speculation and graft.[80] Furthermore, these vile and unethical "vampires of modern society"[81] were attempting to deliver complete control of the Argentine economy to international bankers. The Jewish characters who appear in La Bolsa are all sinister and amoral. Filiberto Mackser, the most despicable of all, not only deals in white slavery and stolen jewelry, but also is an agent whom the Rothschilds have charged with establishing Jewish control over the Argentine economy.[82] To end the alleged threat, Martel called for an end of the equal protection that Argentine laws gave Jews and for restrictions on immigration.[83] Rather than a novel of social realism, Martel's work was little more than crude repetition of anti-Semitic arguments he had encountered while reading the works of Maurice Joly, an obscure French anthropologist.[84] But La Bolsa became popular. Newspapers published it in serial form and intellectuals in later years often regarded it as an accurate picture of the Argentina of 1890. The novel's enduring popularity is perhaps an index of the hostility with which the Argentine middle class viewed the increasing economic success of foreigners.

Like the Russian Jews, Levantine immigrants in Argentina experienced spectacular economic success after 1900. By 1910 the so-called Turcos owned at least 6,900 businesses scattered throughout the republic and were, according to Caras y Caretas, "on many occasions replacing the creole during the struggle for life."[85] In Tucumán and other

[80] José Miró (pseud. Julián Martel), La Bolsa, p. 98.
[81] Ibid., p. 100.
[82] Ibid, p. 28.
[83] Ibid., p. 98.
[84] Sergio Bagú, Julián Martel y el realismo argentino, pp. 12–15.
[85] La Prensa, June 13, 1910, p. 10; "Los turcos en Buenos Aires," Caras y Caretas, V (March 1, 1902), n.p.

interior cities where "the number of Syrian businessmen is so great that competition is absolutely ruinous," the Levantines were challenging the Italians and Spaniards for control of petty commerce.[86] The "Turco" economic advance unsettled most Argentine authors who commented on the topic. One specialist claimed that "the small-scale ambulatory commerce to which they dedicate themselves fills no commercial need whatsoever, and brings only an excess of competition, driving many already established shopkeepers to poverty." Government immigration reports of 1899 and 1900 made the same point and went on to ridicule the Syrian salesmen as "dirty and ragged."[87] La Nación observed that the Levantine salesman's "miserable commerce of geegaws" was a national disgrace and that immigration of these groups ought to be restricted.[88]

Argentine writers could effectively appeal to racial prejudice when attacking Levantine or Russo-Jewish businessmen, but could hardly use this approach against other prosperous immigrant groups. To denigrate merchants and shopkeepers of western European origin, men of letters attempted to stereotype them as essentially dishonest. The Italian or Spanish businessman who appeared in the Argentine short story, novel, or drama typically would lend large amounts to creole farmers and then would either foreclose or cheat the Argentine out of his land title. European storekeepers furthermore would falsify weights, measures, and even customers' accounts.[89] If arrested for such malpractice, they might bribe the police for release.[90] The European who profited by these methods might also mistreat his native-born Argentine workers. In José González Castillo's El grillete, for example, an Italian boss stabs to death an Argentine worker whose only misdeed was to glance

[86] La Prensa, November 17, 1906, p. 5.
[87] Silviano Funes, Inmigración y colonización, pp. 33; Argentine Republic, Ministerio de Agricultura, Memoria presentada al Honorable Congreso, enero de 1899–octubre de 1900, p. 134.
[88] La Nación, February 27, 1910, p. 8.
[89] Miguel Roquendo, Los saguaypes, in Bambalinas, No. 163, (1921), pp. 10–11, 17; Arturo Reynal O'Connor, Paseos por las colonias, p. 27.
[90] Agustín Fontanella, El secreto de la virgin, in Bambalinas, No. 48 (1919), p. 19.

at the Italian's cousin.[91] In a study of labor conditions in the Argentine interior which he undertook for the national government in 1902 and 1903, Juan Bialet Massé also criticized foreign-born employers. In particular he noted that they were more reluctant than Argentine employers to support the passage of government labor and social welfare legislation.[92] The foreign employer in the literature of the time might not pay his creole worker an honest wage, or if he did so, he might pay in counterfeit money.[93] When queried about the ethics of such transactions, the immigrant in Argentine literature was likely to reply coldly, "Men in this world are either wolves or sheep, and there is but one problem, to eat or be eaten." A Spanish immigrant in Pedro Pico's play *Ganarse la vida* agrees. "If one's shame must be exposed, it does not matter! The question is to succeed, to become rich, is it not?"[94]

In contrast with the reaction of the Chilean middle class, the Argentine middle groups expressed little resentment against the many foreigners who were entering clerical or managerial occupations or the professions. The only significant outcry came from the teaching profession, but this protest was mild compared to the clamor that arose over the issue of foreign professors in Chile. Europeans never occupied the key educational posts in Argentina that they did in Chile, nor did German pedagogical theory attain the influence in Argentina that it enjoyed in the neighboring republic. Since the 1860's, however, the Argentine government had contracted European and North American educators to help organize the secondary and normal school systems. The government's reliance on these foreign specialists was gradually declining when in 1903 the Ministry of Education sent a special com-

[91] José González Castillo, *El grillete*, in *La escena*, II (March 20, 1919).

[92] Juan Bialet Masse, *Informe sobre el estado de las clases obreras en el interior de la república*, II, 64, and III, iv.

[93] Roberto J. Payró, *El casamiento de Laucha*, fourth edition, p. 15; Enrique M. Ruas, "Cuento para inmigrantes," *Caras y Caretas*, X (November 2, 1907), n.p.

[94] Roquendo, *Los saguaypes*, p. 11; Pedro Pico, *Ganarse la vida*, in *Bambalinas*, No. 183 (1921), p. 14.

mission to Europe and the United States to search for another contingent of secondary-school teachers. Projected recruitment of foreigners provoked a flurry of protest. The poet Leopoldo Lugones, at the time also a teacher, criticized the government's move and argued that a much wiser policy would be to send Argentine teachers abroad for advanced training.[95] When the commission finally returned without contracting new teachers, defenders of the Argentine profession felt vindicated. "We do have to bring in foreigners to work our soil," reasoned *La Prensa*, "but as for the great task of the education of our youth, we fortunately possess the necessary national talent to do a good job."[96]

Occasionally Argentine writers poked scorn at the foreign schoolteachers. Enrique de Vedia portrayed them as unstable adventurers who drifted around the world, studying "crystallography in Göttingen or ancient history in Peking," and teaching where an opportunity happened to arise. Such foreign instructors of mathematics, physics, chemistry, or other sciences "are inferior to any distinguished graduate of our university faculties."[97] Much like its counterpart *Zig Zag* in Chile, *Caras y Caretas* pictured the foreign teachers as ignorant and poorly informed. There was, for example, "the illustrious geographer, who, aside from his maps, brings along letters of recommendation to present to residents of Veracruz, Iquique, and Ilo-Ilo, cities he believes are near Buenos Aires."[98]

Immigrant teachers, along with foreign-born shopkeepers, artisans, and clerks, were creating an urban middle class whose potential power worried the ruling elites in Argentina and the national middle groups in Chile. But the upper classes of both Argentina and Chile became much more alarmed at another social change—the rise of a militant urban working-class movement. The threat posed by the immigrant middle class paled into insignificance in comparison with the goals of the organized urban proletariat. The middle class essentially desired

[95] Leopoldo Lugones, *La reforma educacional*, p. 48.
[96] *La Prensa*, February 27, 1903, p. 6.
[97] Enrique de Vedia, *La enquête Naón*, pp. 98, 103.
[98] "Los que vienan á ilustrarnos; ó los sabios golondrinos," *Caras y Caretas*, XV (June 22, 1912), n.p.

not social upheaval but a share of the power and prestige traditionally monopolized by the elites. But the leaders of the working-class movement envisioned radical social change and, in some cases, social revolution to destroy class privileges and end the exploitation of labor.

CHAPTER FOUR

Immigration: The Scapegoat for Urban Social Problems

>>

Argentine and Chilean cities began to grow with unprecedented speed after 1890. As late as 1884 Buenos Aires contained only about 300,000 inhabitants and resembled, as Lucio V. López put it, "a large village."[1] Three decades later the Argentine capital had become one of the world's largest cities with a population exceeding 1,500,000. The Chilean census of 1920 revealed that 45 per cent of the nation's people lived in towns of over 5,000 and that Santiago's population had more than doubled (to 507,000) since 1890. Life in these burgeoning cities would have dismayed mid-nineteenth-century liberals like Sarmiento who had predicted that urbanization would bring civil order and cultural progress. An alienated, restless, and increasingly militant proletariat was emerging. The anarchist movement, aiming to overturn the existing social order, attracted the loyalty of many of these workers. Furthermore, some of the social ills characterizing modern urban life—crime, alcoholism, white slavery—were appearing, along

---

[1] López gave this title to a novel set in Buenos Aires about the year 1880. Traditional, provincial patterns of life still prevail. See *La gran aldea*.

with sensationalist newspapers that magnified out of proportion the incidence of violence and disorder.

The journalists, intellectuals, and politicians who surveyed this seemingly degenerating urban scene during the early twentieth century soon found a convenient scapegoat—immigration. As in the United States, where Nathan Glazer has pointed out that all the ills of the cities were laid on the shoulders of the foreign born,[2] Argentine and Chilean observers quickly asserted that immigration was at the root of urban social problems. By the end of World War I both the Argentine and Chilean governments had accepted this explanation, at least in the cases of anarchism and labor unrest, and had officially reversed the old cosmopolitan traditions by passing laws regulating the entrance of labor "agitators."

The crowds of tired, dirty, and unemployed drifters and beggars who gathered in the major cities of both nations constituted an eminently visible urban problem. In Argentina, there was evidence to suggest that some of these unfortunates were immigrants. One author reported in 1910 that 73 per cent of the inmates in the Buenos Aires beggars' asylum were foreigners. Similarly, *La Nación* noted during an unemployment crisis in 1914 that when the city offered food and shelter to the indigent, over 90 per cent of those who asked for help had been born abroad.[3] Argentine journalists and sociologists were quick to use such data to support their contention that immigration was the prime cause of pauperism.[4] These writers tended to ignore the desire for a decent job motivating most immigrants and instead assumed that many foreigners were unprincipled parasites, able to work but preferring to beg.

[2] Nathan Glazer and Daniel Patrick Moynihan, *Beyond the Melting Pot*, p. 21.

[3] Cayetano Carbonell, *Orden y trabajo*, II, 3; *La Nación*, November 19, 1914, p. 7.

[4] A few examples include *La Nación*, May 20, 1907, p. 6; Emilio Zuccarini, "Los exponentes psicológicos del carácter argentino: Evolución del gaucho al atorrante," *Archivos de Psiquiatría y Criminología Aplicadas a las Ciencias Afines*, III (1904), 191, 193; E. de Cires, "La inmigración en Buenos Aires," *Revista Argentina de Ciencias Políticas*, IV (September, 1912), 737; Miguel Cané, *Expulsión de extranjeros (Apuntes)*, p. 112.

An example of such xenophobic slander occurs in the play *La pobre gente* by Florencio Sánchez. An Argentine woman asks a friend, "Do you remember the *turca* who used to live upstairs? . . . Well, now she is rich and is earning all she wants by . . . sending her children out to beg."[5] Writers like Sánchez who equated mendicancy with immigration failed to present a balanced analysis. Poverty, sickness, and ignorance had given rise to pauperism since colonial times in Argentina; immigration was only a contributing factor to a problem with complex social and economic roots.[6] Furthermore, according to travelers' accounts, many of Buenos Aires' beggars were not immigrants but obviously nationals. During the nineteenth century Argentina was known for its mestizo beggars on horseback, and, as late as 1910, a reliable observer pointed out that numerous Indians, mestizos, and Negroes were making a living by begging.[7]

In Chile, as in Argentina, poverty and poorly organized social services had combined since the colonial period to force many to beg for a livelihood. There is no evidence that many Chilean immigrants were among those who turned to mendicancy. Nonetheless, xenophobic journalists and politicians attempted to blame Chile's foreign-born population for the increasing number of beggars. These voices would claim, with slim factual substantiation, that numerous foreigners were of such low quality that they eschewed work, turned to begging, and made the problem of pauperism much worse than it otherwise would have been. According to Senator Vicente Reyes the beggars of Santiago and Valparaíso had been recruited by Chilean colonization agents in alleged centers of vice like Marseilles, "where the very scum of the emigrants . . . who live in caves and have neither notions of morality nor habits of labor, await passage."[8] Newspaper editorialists would add that immigration had brought to Chile hundreds of European

---

[5] Florencio Sánchez, *La pobre gente*, in *Teatro completo de Florencio Sánchez*, p. 215. Another popular literary work that emphasized the large number of immigrant paupers was José Miró (pseud.), *La Bolsa*, p. 11.

[6] Sergio Bagú, *Estructura social de la colonia*, p. 117.

[7] Jules Huret, *La Argentina de Buenos Aires al Gran Chaco*, I, 79.

[8] *B.S.S.*, sesiones extraordinarias, November 8, 1906, p. 196; *El Porvenir*, October 29, 1905, p. 1; *La Lei*, November 29, 1908, p. 1; *El Mercurio*, February 18, 1913, p. 3.

Gypsies, a people whom *El Mercurio* likened to "ants, rabbits, or locusts," so voracious was their alleged appetite for begging or for extracting money disreputably.[9]

In Argentina a problem more serious than mendicancy was the rapidly rising urban crime rate, particularly in the metropolis of Buenos Aires. Between 1887 and 1912 the city's population tripled, but the number of crimes reported increased seven times. Although crime in the Argentine capital had not achieved the notoriety it was to attain during the 1920's, when organized gangsterism flourished, by 1914 the city swarmed with professional thieves, pickpockets, racketeers, and pimps.[10] The sudden rise of Argentine crime was at least partially a product of rapid social change and urbanization, which were dissolving the traditional bonds of a stable society and leaving a great mass of rootless, atomistic individuals.[11]

The many intellectuals who attempted to explain the cause of urban crime seldom discussed these complex social forces and instead tended to blame immigration. This was an arbitrary and unjustified conclusion for which there was little statistical support. Argentine intellectuals cited statistics on crime in a biased manner and in an effort to portray immigration unfavorably. These writers usually mentioned the Buenos Aires census of 1909, which reported that immigrants accounted for slightly less than half the city's population but for 65.6 per cent of the criminals apprehended between 1900 and 1909.[12] But Argentine intellectuals did not mention other statistics that invalidated the conclusion they wished to draw. In the segment of the population most likely to commit crimes—males of age 20 and over—77.2 per cent (in 1914) were foreign born.[13] Thus nearly four-fifths of Buenos Aires'

[9] *El Mercurio*, May 21, 1912, p. 3; also, *La Lei*, November 29, 1908, p. 1; *El Mercurio*, March 18, 1912, p. 15.

[10] For comments on the extent of crime in Buenos Aires see Miguel A. Lancelotti, *La criminalidad en Buenos Aires*, p. 13. See also Domingo F. Casadevall, *El tema de la mala vida en el teatro nacional*, pp. 45, 89; Juan José Sebrelli, *Buenos Aires: Vida cotidiana y alienación*, fifth edition, p. 126.

[11] Thomas F. McGann, *Argentina, Estados Unidos y el sistema interamericano, 1880–1914*, trans. Germán O. Tjarks, p. 65.

[12] Buenos Aires (City), *Censo general . . . de 1909*, II, 300.

[13] Gino Germani, *Política y sociedad en una epoca de transición*, p. 199.

male adults were foreigners, but the evidence indicates that this group was committing only about two-thirds of the capital's crimes.

Aside from citing statistics, Argentine intellectuals who commented on the causes of crime invoked theories of biological determinism to fix the blame on immigration. Whereas writers of an earlier generation had relied on racial theories to prove that immigrants were ethnically superior and would improve the mestizo population, some sociologists during the decade before 1914 were asserting that many immigrant nationalities were biologically inferior to Argentines. These intellectuals argued that certain nationalities inherit stronger tendencies to commit crime. Biological determinism as interpreted by its Argentine exponents further claimed that Argentine creoles inherited less criminality than Italians and Spaniards, who allegedly transmitted to their offspring "the highest crime rates in the world." These national groups, it was added, conserved their native criminal tendencies after arriving in the New World. This theory was first and most explicitly formulated in Argentina by Cornelio Moyano Gacitúa, a University of Córdoba sociology professor. His *La delincuencia argentina* (1905), the first study devoted specifically to Argentine crime and heavily biased against immigrants, strongly influenced other Argentine scholars of the time. One of them, a criminologist named Eusebio Gómez who wrote several books on crime in Buenos Aires and who became director of the National Penitentiary, specifically acknowledged his intellectual debt to the Córdoba professor.[14] The most widely respected Argentine sociologist, José Ingenieros, strongly supported biological determinism in general, but did not mention the relationship between immigration and crime, perhaps because his own father was Italian.

None of the experts was so crude as to use immigration as the only

[14] Cornelio Moyano Gacitúa's ideas appeared in an article, "La delincuencia argentina ante algunas cifras y teorías," *Archivos de Psiquiatría y Criminología Aplicadas a las Ciencias Afines*, IV (1905), 162–181, and in his book *La delincuencia argentina ante algunas cifras y teorías*. For the influence of Moyano Gacitúa on Eusebio Gómez, see the latter's "La mala vida en Buenos Aires," *Archivos de Psiquiatría y Criminología Aplicadas a las Ciencias Afines*, VI (1907), 437. For an early statement of Argentine biological theories of crime, see Miguel A. Lancelotti, "La herencia en la criminalidad," *Revista Nacional*, XXV (June, 1898), 402

explanation for the rising crime rate. Among the contributing factors sociologists mentioned were the capital city's extraordinarily rapid growth, the poor family environment of many lower-class children, and the inadequate educational system.[15] At the same time, these scholars' basic reliance on the theory that criminal tendencies were biologically transmitted impeded research into the relationship between rapid social change and the rise of crime. Argentine writers repeatedly fell back on the easy explanation that immigration, which allegedly brought to Buenos Aires "the antisocial scum of the rest of the world," was permanently instilling in the Argentine population stronger criminal tendencies than otherwise would exist.[16] Stereotyped images of immigrant criminals appeared in many articles published in the *Archivos de Psiquiatría y Criminología*, the professional journal of Argentine criminologists. The typical Italian immigrant, wrote one contributor, bore "his inseparable steel knife," which he was quick to use because of his "volcanic temperament and his excitable, aggressive passions."[17]

Men of letters joined the sociologists in casting the foreigner as a criminal. Manuel Ugarte, whose literary efforts made him famous throughout Latin America by 1925, portrayed in his short story *La venganza del capataz* a sadistic immigrant named Luis. Enraged to discover that his wife is having an affair with another man, Luis diabolically hatches a plan to torture to death both spouse and lover. "His wild and turbulent blood, which united all the atavisms of the Mediterranean, could not be content with a brusque execution," commented Ugarte.[18] The Italians received equally cutting treatment in another genre, the *sainetes*, short plays that enjoyed popularity during the early twentieth century. Alberto Novión, whose several dozen *sainetes* made

---

[15] See, for example, Lancelotti, *La criminalidad en Buenos Aires*, p. 47.

[16] José Gregorio Rossi, "La criminalidad profesional en Buenos Aires," *Archivos de Psiquiatría y Criminología Aplicadas a las Ciencias Afines*, II (1903), 173; other criminologists who echoed this view included Eusebio Gómez, *Criminología argentina*, p. xiii; idem, "La mala vida en Buenos Aires," 436–437.

[17] Hector A. Taborda, "El clandestinismo en las prisiones," *Archivos de Psiquiatría y Criminología Aplicadas a las Ciencias Afines*, VII (1908), 708.

[18] Manuel Ugarte, "La venganza del capataz," in *Cuentos de la pampa*, p. 148.

him one of the best-known Argentine playwrights, presented the Italians of Buenos Aires' Boca waterfront area as drunken vagrants who constantly brandished huge daggers. After witnessing one of these Italians knife another to death, an Argentine army officer bitterly scoffs, "Look at him! . . . they say it is these men who bring progress and civilization."[19] Equally critical was José S. Álvarez, a short-story writer popular around 1910. His *Mundo lunfardo* presented a lurid description of foreign thieves in Buenos Aires, while his *En el Mar Austral* claimed that Argentine Patagonia was becoming a haven for escaped European criminals.[20]

Perhaps because of the middle-class character of Chilean immigration, fewer writers identified it as a principal cause of crime. But the Conservative party's newspaper *El Porvenir* nonetheless attempted to convince its readers that foreign-born thieves and vagrants were rapidly increasing Chile's criminal population. This was so, according to one editorialist, because immigration is "a safety valve the European countries use to release their undesirable social elements."[21] Nicolás Palacios, the most famed Chilean writer of his time, expressed his strong agreement with this indictment of immigration. Palacios, who claimed he followed Gustave Le Bon's racial principles, published in 1904 *Raza chilena*, a book that became immensely popular and that presented racial theories startling to the Chilean reading public. Rejecting nineteenth-century positivists who scorned the Chilean mestizo, he upheld the Chileans as a superior race. Palacios asserted that the early settlers of Chile were not Latins but a more advanced race, the descendants of the Gothic peoples who had arrived in northern Spain after the fall of Rome. In Chile, the theory continued, these Germanic conquistadores mixed with another allegedly superior race, the Araucanian Indians. Issuing from this mixture, Palacios continued, was the Chilean mestizo, a strong people who inherited less tendency toward criminality than Italians or Spaniards, the two largest European im-

---

[19] Alberto Novión, *La cantina*, in *Revista Teatral*, No. 29, pp. 2, 9.

[20] José S. Álvarez, *Mundo lunfardo*, in *Cuentos con policías*, p. 82; idem, *En el Mar Austral*, p. 194.

[21] *El Porvenir*, October 9, 1903, p. 3; also, March 19, 1898, p. 1; April 24, 1901, p. 1; October 20, 1905, p. 3.

migrant groups in Chile. To substantiate this theory of criminality Palacios presented only one set of statistical data, which counted (in 1896) one Chilean criminal per 107 national citizens but one foreign criminal per 35 foreign-born residents.[22] To indict the foreigners as the cause of Chilean criminality on the basis of these unverified statistics was not justified.

Closely related to the problem of crime were prostitution and the white-slave trade, both of which were particularly serious in Buenos Aires. Apparently disregarding the fact that prostitution had flourished in Buenos Aires before the arrival of massive immigration,[23] Argentine observers again made the newcomers into a scapegoat. The consensus was that, since white slaves, procurers, and prostitutes were predominantly foreign born, immigration must be the underlying cause of the problem. The white slaver allegedly would book first-class steamship passage to Buenos Aires in order to avoid the immigration inspectors, who examined only second-class and steerage passengers. Once in the Argentine capital, he would deliver his human cargo to some large entrepreneur or would himself enter business. Such was the theme of Pedro Pico's play, *Así empieza una historia,* in which a nefarious Spanish immigrant-placement agent sends an unsuspecting immigrant girl into a career of prostitution. After studying the white-slave problem in his law school dissertation, Manuel Gálvez charged that foreigners in Argentina were fostering the growth of a huge industry based on traffic in human flesh.[24] Similar complaints resounded in the newspapers and in Congress,[25] but no one provided factual substantiation for the identification of the immigrant with the prostitute or the white slaver. The only statistical source available was almost certainly incomplete. This was the Buenos Aires census of 1909,

[22] Nicolás Palacios, *Raza chilena,* pp. 48–52, 249.
[23] Bagú, *Estructura social de la colonia,* pp. 125–126.
[24] Pedro Pico, *Así empieza una historia,* in *Teatro Nacional,* No. 35; Gálvez, *El diario de Gabriel Quiroga,* p. 207.
[25] For example, *La Prensa,* August 24, 1911, p. 8; *La Nación,* September 1, 1913, p. 11; September 2, 1913, p. 11; speech of Alfredo L. Palacios in *D.S.C.D.,* May 29, 1907, p. 71; ibid., September 17, 1913, p. 324.

which reported that only 235 of the 773 prostitutes counted were citizens.[26]

At least one writer, the criminologist Eusebio Gómez, mourned the apparent replacement of the Argentine streetwalker by her European competitors. The native-born prostitute, Gómez noted, had "certain noble traits," often including the "passion of true love" for her customers. Her foreign counterpart allegedly was emotionless, dishonest, and a willing partner in the growth of organized vice.[27] Gómez, like other Argentine essayists, tended to use immigration as an easy explanation for prostitution rather than examine the manifold social and economic factors that might have caused the problem to flourish.

In Chile prostitution did not trouble the nation's intellectuals as much as the chronic alcoholism appearing in the nation's cities during the 1890's. "There is not a weekend when one-third of the men in Chile are not drunk," exclaimed General Estanislao del Canto, a military hero who was one of the first Chileans to publicize the problem of alcoholism. Rather than investigating the poverty and malnutrition that turned Chilean workers to drink,[28] several intellectuals argued that the immigrants who produced and sold beer and cheap wine were responsible for the steady rise of alcoholism. The Italians, exclaimed one editorialist, were hardly a civilizing influence, for "they have opened taverns on every corner in Santiago and the other important towns, certainly not to educate or regenerate the people, but to corrupt them, exploit them, and addict them to vice!"[29] German immigrants, who had introduced modern brewing techniques and who nearly monopolized the industry after 1890, were the targets of other writers.[30] According to one traveler, "well-informed people" in Chile ascribed the demoralization and decline of the Araucanian Indians of southern Chile to the

---

[26] Buenos Aires (City), *Censo general . . . de 1909*, I, 60.

[27] Eusebio Gómez, *La mala vida en Buenos Aires*, p. 132.

[28] Quoted in Frederick B. Pike, *Chile and the United States, 1880–1960*, p. 106. See also ibid., p. 278.

[29] *La Lei*, March 13, 1906, p. 2.

[30] Palacios, *Raza chilena*, pp. 250–251; Heriberto López, "El germanismo en Chile," *Revista Nacional*, XXIX (May, 1899), 445.

cheap alcoholic beverages that the flourishing German-owned businesses of Valdivia supplied.[31]

Intense labor unrest and the emergence of a militant anarchist movement deeply troubled many Argentines and Chileans during the quarter century preceding World War I. Bombings, assassinations, and endemic labor turbulence constantly reminded the upper classes that urban laborers were deeply dissatisfied. Troubled by the unrest and the mounting violence afflicting Argentine and Chilean cities, intellectuals cast about for explanations.

A few writers examined the poverty and the poor working conditions that at least partially underlay working-class discontent. Urban labor was not sharing in the prosperity that gave a veneer of opulence to Buenos Aires and Santiago. In Chile real wages of urban laborers declined between 1890 and 1914, while the evidence available for Argentina indicates that they rose only slightly.[32] As late as 1904 nearly 140,000 Buenos Aires residents, amounting to 14 per cent of the city's population, still lived in squalid *conventillos*, the Argentine version of the tenement house.[33] Eight years later, a survey sponsored by the government found that the average immigrant working-class family contained five persons, lived in one room averaging twelve feet by twelve, and shared a bath with other tenants of the building.[34] Living conditions for the urban workers were more dismal in Chile, whose cities were infamous for high rates of infant mortality and tuberculosis.[35]

---

[31] Ferdinand Gautier, *Chili et Bolivie*, p. 22.

[32] Information on real wages in Argentina is found in Luis V. Sommi, *La revolución del 90*, p. 65, and in Samuel L. Baily, *Labor, Nationalism, and Politics in Argentina*, p. 23. For data on real wages in Chile, see Julio César Jobet, *Precursores del pensamiento social de Chile*, II, 66–67.

[33] Sergio Bagú, *Evolución histórica de la estratificación social en la Argentina*, p. 37.

[34] Donald S. Castro, "The Development of Argentine Government Immigration Policy, 1862–1914," Chapter 8, p. 33. For extended comment on the living standards of the Buenos Aires working class, see José Panettieri, *Los trabajadores en tiempos de la inmigración masiva en la Argentina, 1870–1910*, pp. 58, 69–72.

[35] Julio César Jobet, *Ensayo crítico del desarrollo económico-social de Chile*, p. 228.

Little social or labor legislation existed in either nation before 1914 to improve the lot of urban workers. The only Chilean law of this type, which the government neglected to implement, was a 1906 measure providing for state-financed workers' housing. Argentine social legislation, sporadically enforced and applying only to the capital city and the federal territories, was limited to provisions requiring Sunday rest and to regulations on the hours and working conditions of women and children. Although a number of investigators were suggesting that the precarious economic situation faced by the urban masses might explain labor unrest, many politicians, journalists, and intellectuals in both countries continued to attribute it to immigration. They based this belief on inaccurate assumptions about the nature of Argentine and Chilean society, to the effect that social mobility and economic opportunity prevented the emergence of the European-style class struggle. According to this reasoning, the objective conditions for class conflict were not present, and thus urban social unrest could result only from foreign agitators determined to revolutionize Argentine and Chilean life.

Social mobility did exist, but not to the extent that intellectuals like Emilio Rodríguez Mendoza, a columnist in *El Mercurio*, believed. He argued that in Chile, "no one is hungry who wants to work . . . prosperity is within the reach and at the disposition of everyone. It is simply a question of work."[36] In Argentina no one developed this Horatio Alger theme more thoroughly than the prolific social commentator Lucas Ayarragaray. In a 1912 essay he contended, "The European social problem is absolutely unknown here; we have neither castes, privileges, feudal complexions, nor historical injustices." The class struggle, proclaimed Ayarragaray, can hardly exist "where classes do not exist."[37] Seemingly unaware that speculation had pushed land prices to prohibitive heights and that graft and maladministration were probably discrediting the colonization laws, Argentine intellectuals

[36] *El Mercurio*, June 29, 1910, p. 3.
[37] Lucas Ayarragaray, "Socialismo argentino y legislación obrera," *La Nación*, April 26, 1912, p. 7. For a similar statement by one of the nation's most respected intellectuals, see Joaquín V. González, *El juicio del siglo ó cien años de historia argentina*, p. 250.

claimed that a discontented worker could easily escape the city and become a small landowner.[38]

Inaccurate assumptions like these underlay most intellectual discussion of anarchism and labor unrest during the decade preceding World War I. Rare was the frankness of one Chilean journalist who admitted that "our anarchism has indigenous roots," and that "we ought to call attention to the national anarchists, whom the police, the press, and the public do not want to see." An influential Chilean group that also questioned the prevailing interpretation of anarchism was the middle-class Radical party. Its position, claimed an official history published in 1911, was that working-class unrest resulted from social tensions common to all rapidly-changing Western countries.[39] This note of realism was absent in the statements of the Argentine Radical party. In Argentina only a few intellectuals, generally of socialist or anarchist leanings, rejected the standard assumptions about the causes of working-class unrest. The one major newspaper that hesitated to condemn immigration was Buenos Aires' influential La Prensa, spokesman for large landowners of the littoral. At least until 1909, its editorials took the position that the anarchist threat did not justify shutting off the flow of foreign labor on which the economy rested.[40] Aside from these exceptions, the articulate classes of both countries stubbornly continued to associate the rise of anarchism with European immigration.

A factual basis existed to support this conviction, for European anarchosyndicalist and socialist labor organizers had been arriving in both republics throughout the 1890's. In Chile El Mercurio began to note with alarm the arrival of foreign anarchists as early as 1894. Anarchosyndicalism enjoyed little success during the next two decades, but several European labor organizers did arrive to help Valparaíso-born Luis Emilio Recabarren found the modern Chilean socialist movement.[41] After three bloody episodes of urban labor unrest shook Chile

---

[38] For example, La Prensa, April 11, 1910, p. 9.

[39] The quote is from "Nacionalismo y boxers," El Mercurio, November 22, 1913, p. 5; Anjel C. Espejo, El partido radical, sus obras y sus hombres, p. 21.

[40] See, for example, La Prensa, April 11, 1910, p. 9.

[41] El Mercurio, September 7, 1894, p. 2; Julio César Jobet, Recabarren: Los orígenes del movimiento obrero y del socialismo chilenos, pp. 102–105; Hernán

in the first years of the twentieth century, upper-class opinion directed its wrath against foreign labor organizers, terming them unscrupulous agitators who goaded the usually docile Chilean workers into strikes and protests. This argument first appeared in 1903 when Valparaíso's stevedores and draymen began a protracted strike. Several confrontations between the workers and the police occurred, mass violence ravaged Chile's principal seaport, and thirty-five died before the army restored order. The author who commented most extensively on this incident and on other outbreaks of working-class unrest in Chile before 1914 was Benjamín Vicuña Subercaseaux, the rich, well-traveled scion of two of the nation's principal families, and one of Chile's most respected writers. He claimed that the Valparaíso working class was well paid and had no reason to strike. Only "waves of human scum thrown upon our beaches by other countries," could have caused the turmoil.[42] Other Chileans writing about the affair agreed that the leaders of the Valparaíso strike were "drifters and adventurers" who had migrated from "the most rotten holes of the Old World."[43]

Two years after the Valparaíso bloodshed, organized labor in Santiago called a general strike to protest a new import duty on Argentine cattle that greatly increased meat prices. Again mass violence broke out; this time the turmoil did not subside until the police and a group of wealthy vigilantes had killed over sixty people and wounded several hundred more. According to El Porvenir, the voice of the agricultural interests that profited from the cattle tariff, the cause of this tragedy must have been professional revolutionary agitators expelled from Europe and Argentina. Vicuña Subercaseaux agreed and added that not the capitalists, but foreign agitators and labor organizers, who "profit . . . at the cost of the hunger and life of the people," were the real exploiters of the laboring class.[44]

Ramírez Necochea, Historia del movimiento obrero en Chile: Siglo XIX, p. 205.

[42] Benjamín Vicuña Subercaseaux, El socialismo revolucionario y la cuestión social en Europa y en Chile, p. 235.

[43] Florentino Abarca, La decadencia de Chile, p. 196. The casualties of the Valparaíso disorders are listed in El Mercurio, May 13, 1905, p. 5.

[44] Vicuña Subercaseaux, El socialismo revolucionario, p. 73; Oscar Álvarez

More tragic than this unrest in Santiago and Valparaíso was a massacre of unarmed workers that occurred during a general strike in the nitrate mining center of Iquique late in 1907. The principal demands of the workers included payment in gold instead of in Chile's rapidly depreciating paper currency, an end to the monopolies that company stores held in the nitrate towns, and improvements in working conditions. To achieve these goals, the miners of the entire Iquique region left their jobs and took over operation of the local railroads, on which they traveled to the city of Iquique to organize a mass protest. The government countered by sending a contingent of several hundred troops from central Chile to reinforce the Iquique garrison. Determined to prevent mass demonstrations, the commanding officer on December 21, 1907, ordered a crowd of strikers gathered in the main plaza to disperse. The crowd refused, the troops opened machine-gun fire, and hundreds fell dead or mortally wounded. Although the government officially announced the death of 267, the real figure was probably much higher.[45] News of this massacre shocked all Chile, but several congressmen and journalists tried to relieve the government of responsibility by throwing the blame on "professional agitators who do not belong to the working class, but who are known criminals" expelled from Europe.[46] After the 1907 tragedy newspapers began to argue that Chile should bar further immigration of urban workers and welcome only agricultural colonists, who presumably would promote development and prosperity, but who would not add to social unrest. The foreigner who became an urban laborer, editorialized *El Mercurio*, was unconcerned about Chile's progress and was too often only a source of labor agitation and social discontent.[47]

Troubled by the unrest and carnage of these years, Chilean intellec-

---

Andrews, *Historia del desarrollo industrial de Chile*, pp. 168–169; *El Porvenir*, October 29, 1905, p. 5.

[45] Álvarez Andrews, *Historia del desarrollo*, p. 169, 225; Guillermo Kaempffer Villagrán, *Así sucedió: Sangrientos episodios de la lucha obrera en Chile*, p. 122.

[46] Speech of Luis Izquierdo B.S.C.D., sesiones extraordinarias, January 4, 1908, p. 837; *El Mercurio*, December 26, 1907, p. 3; Vicuña Subercaseaux, *El socialismo revolucionario*, pp. 234–235.

[47] *El Mercurio*, April 22, 1909, p. 11.

tuals and journalists began to call for legislation to forbid entry of foreign labor agitators and to expel those already in the country. Backers of such a law had to combat not only the strong influence that liberal international economic theory retained in Chile but also the republic's long tradition of legal equality between foreigners and citizens. These guarantees were enshrined in the constitution and in the civil code.[48] Writers who used immigration as a scapegoat argued that this tradition was outmoded, since most European countries, as well as Argentina (in 1902) and Brazil, had enacted laws against foreign agitators. The argument continued that, without such a law, Chile was rapidly becoming "what England is in the Old World—the asylum of all those pursued by justice."[49] Newspapers supported the campaign for restrictive legislation by portraying the working-class immigrant in the most unflattering terms. One cartoon in the conservative La Unión presented a wild-eyed, grubby anarchist debarking in Valparaíso. A notice on his suitcase proclaims: "Graduate of the Old World anarchist university. Arriving to give lessons and courses in Chile."[50] But supporters of immigration limitation found that dominant economic theories and Chilean legal tradition were difficult obstacles to overcome. Not until December 12, 1918, perhaps as a result of the recent triumph of Bolshivism in Russia, did Congress enact antiforeign legislation. The so-called Residence Law of that date forbade the entry and enabled the government to expel foreigners who had been condemned abroad for crimes, who had no useful occupations, or who preached violent change in the social or political order.[51]

In Argentina, also, a movement was gathering momentum to quell working-class unrest through restrictions on immigration. And, as in Chile, there was some truth to allegations that unrestricted immigration

[48] Agustín Correa Bravo, Los extranjeros ante la ley chilena, pp. 6–7, 13, 25.

[49] El Mercurio, September 24, 1913, p. 3. Similar appeals for legislation against foreign agitators appeared in El Mercurio of March 6, 1907, p. 3, May 2, 1907, p. 3, May 26, 1908, p. 1, and June 27, 1909, p. 3; B.S.C.D., sesiones extraordinarias, November 19, 1909, p. 563, and sesiones ordinarias, July 25, 1910, p. 931; B.S.S., sesiones extraordinarias, October 29, 1907, p. 214.

[50] La Unión, August 22, 1912, p. 1.

[51] Chile, Boletín de las leyes i decretos del gobierno, 2 vols. (Santiago, 1918), II, 1558–1562.

was allowing European anarchists to proselytize. One of the most effective was Pedro Gori, a militant Italian who plunged into organizational activity upon his arrival in 1898. A follower of Georges Sorel, Gori urged anarchist workers to organize their power by forming syndicates and to utilize this power by means of the general strike when necessary. After founding two anarchosyndicalist newspapers in Buenos Aires (one printed in Italian) and attracting a devoted group of native-born anarchists to continue his efforts, Gori returned to Europe in 1902.[52] Since approximately 60 per cent of the Buenos Aires proletariat was foreign born, organizers had fertile ground to work.

Long accustomed to servile laborers, the Argentine ruling classes after 1890 suddenly had to confront militant urban workers determined to improve their economic position. Most skilled workers entered socialist-oriented unions, but the anarchists, who controlled much of Buenos Aires' unskilled laboring class, quickly became the most powerful element in the Argentine labor movement. Dedicated to direct action and especially to the general strike to gain benefits for their members, anarchist unions began to call work stoppages that often became bitter and protracted. Nineteen major strikes in 1895 and sixteen the following year afflicted the city of Buenos Aires. Not to be outdone, in 1896 twelve thousand socialist-affiliated railroad workers left their jobs for several weeks, snarling Argentine transportation.[53] These strikes hardly seem threatening by mid-twentieth-century standards, but they alarmed a paternalistic society that never before had witnessed widespread labor unrest.

Troubled by the emergence of labor problems, some Argentine intellectuals began to criticize the nation's traditional policies of unrestricted immigration. To convince the public that foreign anarchists were at the root of the problem, newspaper and magazine writers de-

---

[52] S. Fanny Simon, "Anarchism and Anarcho-Syndicalism in South America," *Hispanic American Historical Review*, XXVI (February, 1946), 39; Enrique Dickmann, *Recuerdos de un militante socialista*, p. 69; Sebastián Marotta, *El movimiento sindical argentino: Su génesis y desarrollo*, I, 107.

[53] Dickmann, *Recuerdos de un militante socialista*, p. 131; Jacinto Oddone, *Historia del socialismo argentino*, I, 108–110; background on Argentine anarchism and labor violence during the period is in Simon, "Anarchism and Anarcho-Syndicalism," pp. 38–48.

veloped stereotypes picturing the typical anarchist as a fat, swarthy, and ugly Italian or Spaniard who bristled with knives, bombs, and other lethal weapons. The anarchist was portrayed as an unprincipled, shiftless adventurer, eager only to make trouble wherever he chanced to land.[54] "Today I am in one place, tomorrow they'll throw me out and I'll be somewhere else," laments a Spanish immigrant anarchist in *Los fuertes*, a *sainete* by Carlos María Pacheco.[55] These men were "professionals of disorder," who dedicated themselves to stirring up endemic labor violence, editorialized *La Nación* in 1908.[56]

Similar accusations began to echo through the halls of Congress. The first legislator to suggest that the government should exclude suspected foreign anarchists was Senator Miguel Cané, recently returned from an ambassadorial post in Paris where French laws against foreign agitators had impressed him. In an 1897 essay Cané claimed that thousands of "criminals and . . . madmen" were arriving in Argentina and were "destined to fill our prisons or to be a slow poison for our society."[57] From his Senate seat and in a book he published in 1899, Cané reiterated that Argentina, defenseless in the face of the anarchist threat, must forbid the entry of undesirable immigrants and expel those already in the country. Proclaiming that national self-preservation ought to override liberal immigration policies, Cané introduced an immigrant restriction law in the Senate on June 8, 1899.[58] The government hesitated to change Argentina's half-century-old tradition of unlimited immigration, and no action was taken until a huge anarchist-led general strike of November, 1902, threatened total disruption of the national economy. Buenos Aires' dock workers and draymen, soon joined by most other unskilled laborers in the metropolitan area, timed the walkout to halt Argentine grain exports at the height of the harvest season.[59]

---

[54] For example, "Inmigración peligrosa," *Caras y Caretas*, XII (June 12, 1909), n.p.

[55] Carlos M. Pacheco, *Los fuertes*, in *Bambalinas*, No. 200, p. 6.

[56] *La Nación*, March 12, 1908, p. 9; also June 24, 1909, p. 7; April 1, 1911, p. 9.

[57] Miguel Cané, *Notas e impresiones*, p. 135.

[58] Ibid., pp. 133–134, 190; Cané, *Expulsión de extranjeros*, pp. 7, 125; *D.S.C.S.*, November 22, 1902, p. 664; *La Prensa*, November 21, 1902, p. 5.

[59] Diego Abad de Santillán, *La F.O.R.A. Ideología y trayectoria del movi-*

To prevent a serious loss in export earnings that might endanger Argentina's European credit standing, President Roca called Congress into special session on November 22, 1902.[60] The legislators declared a state of siege to end the strike and then, after brief debate, enacted the "Residence Law." Most speakers emphasized that sinister foreign agitators, determined to subvert Argentina's economy, were "the only cause of the present strife," as Joaquín V. González put it. Argentina, argued the backers of the proposal, had a perfect right to protect itself against foreign doctrines. The proposed law, it was held, would also defend the laboring classes from exploitation by labor agitators, "those veritable entrepreneurs of strikes," who supposedly pushed the workers into dangerous conflicts against their own best interests.[61] A few congressmen, notably former President Carlos Pelligrini (himself the son of an Italian immigrant), contended that such a law would discourage immigration and would conflict with the Argentine liberal tradition.[62] Nonetheless, both houses enthusiastically approved the proposal, whose principal provision enabled the executive to expel any immigrant condemned by a foreign criminal court or whose conduct the president believed "compromises national security or disturbs the public order." The executive also was empowered to prevent the entry of foreigners who might become troublemakers.[63]

The Residence Law of 1902 was Argentina's first legislation designed specifically to discriminate against the foreign born. It served as a foundation for antiforeign legislation enacted by later governments. Juan Perón included its provisions in his strongly nationalistic

miento obrero revolucionario en la Argentina, pp. 105–107; Alberto Belloni, *Del anarquismo al peronismo: Historia del movimiento obrero argentino*, p. 17; *La Prensa*, November 21, 1902, p. 5.

[60] *D.S.C.D.*, November 22, 1902, p. 415.

[61] Speech of Joaquín V. González, *D.S.C.D.*, November 22, 1902, p. 415; speech of Domingo Pérez, *D.S.C.S.*, November 22, 1902, p. 658; also *D.S.C.D.*, November 22, 1902, pp. 379, 427, and *D.S.C.S.*, November 22, 1902, pp. 657, 662–663.

[62] Speech of Carlos Pelligrini, *D.S.C.S.*, November 24, 1902, p. 678; see also *D.S.C.D.*, November 22, 1902, pp. 418–423, 429–430.

[63] *D.S.C.D.*, November 22, 1902, p. 415.

Constitution of 1949.[64] Many Argentines who agreed that immigration was the basic source of anarchism nonetheless strongly opposed the Residence Law. The editors of *La Nación*, for example, worried that the new legislation might discredit Argentina among prospective agricultural immigrants in Europe. Numerous editorials contended that agriculture's need for immigrant labor outweighed any desire to eliminate foreign-born agitators.[65] By July, 1904, such opposition was sufficiently strong to force Congress to consider repeal of the controversial law. Led by Alfredo L. Palacios, the one Socialist member of Congress, enemies of the law argued that it was a "constant threat against the foreigners, against our foreign brothers, who are the principal factor of our civilization."[66] *La Nación* and *La Prensa* strongly supported repeal; the latter paper editorialized at length that the Residence Law defeated its own purpose by further embittering immigrants against Argentina. But the Roca government's opposition and its tight control over Congress prevented any action.[67]

The provision of the Residence Law that most flagrantly violated Argentina's cosmopolitan tradition gave the executive branch authority to decree expulsion of foreigners, disregarding the judicial process that the national constitution guaranteed. In protest, Roberto J. Payró wrote his first play, *Marco Severi*, which enjoyed great success when it appeared in 1905. Payró portrayed an immigrant printer who had lived in Argentina many years since fleeing Italy to evade prosecution for a minor crime. In Argentina he had worked hard, led an honest life, and fathered a large family. The government eventually discovers his identity and orders his expulsion under the Residence Law. A last-minute pardon from the king of Italy avoids this tragedy, but Payró has plenty of opportunity to protest the injustice and harshness of a

[64] Carlos Sánchez Viamonte, *Biografía de una ley anti-argentina: Ley 4144*, pp. 12–13, 167–170.

[65] See, for example, *La Nación*, January 8, 1903, p. 5; February 18, 1903, p. 3; September 27, 1903, p. 5.

[66] Speech of Alfredo L. Palacios, *D.S.C.D.*, May 27, 1904, p. 198; see also *D.S.C.D.*, July 18, 1904, pp. 441–448, 515, 556–559.

[67] *La Nación*, April 26, 1904, p. 5, May 29, 1904, p. 7; *La Prensa*, January 26, 1904, p. 3, January 27, 1904, p. 4.

"narrowly conceived law that ignores the exalted concepts of what our country ought to become." The play's concluding sentence was, "The law must be amended."[68]

Supporters of the Residence Law presumably were disappointed, for after its passage labor agitation continued and the number of strikes spiraled. A general strike, during which 150,000 workers left their jobs for several days, took place in January, 1907. Severe violence occurred in May, 1909, when 200,000 Buenos Aires workers struck to protest the bloody manner in which the police had broken up a May Day anarchist meeting. Eight demonstrators died in this incident and 105 suffered wounds. The week-long general strike ended only after the government moved five thousand soldiers and armed police into the capital and arrested hundreds of strikers.[69] Growing class hatred in Buenos Aires precipitated more violence, which suddenly exploded on November 14, 1909, when a gunman assassinated the metropolitan police chief, Ramón L. Falcón, who was infamous among the workers for his fierce repression of strikes and demonstrations.

The assassin was a Russian worker named Radowitzky, and the deed gave the upper class of Buenos Aires an excuse to begin a xenophobic campaign. Soon after the murder, several socially prominent young men formed Argentina's first avowed anti-immigrant society, the Juventud Autonomista. Although short-lived, its intention "to openly combat the ideas of certain immigrant groups, which are causing our present social commotion,"[70] foreshadowed the rash of ultranationalist and xenophobic societies that began to spring up after World War I. At Falcón's funeral on November 17, distinguished citizens spoke against the immigrants, warned that "the exaggerated cosmopolitanism of our laws has brought us to the brink of social disorganization," and proclaimed that "we natives must unite in a movement of common

[68] Roberto J. Payró, *Marco Severi*, in *Teatro completo*, Roberto F. Giusti, ed., pp. 131–187, especially pp. 172, 187. See also Raúl Larra, *Payró: El novelista de la democracia*, p. 145.

[69] Oddone, *Historia del socialismo argentino*, II, 47–53; Santillán, *La F.O.R.A.*, pp. 163, 190–193; Belloni, *Del anarquismo al peronismo*, p. 25; *La Nación*, May 2, 1909, p. 8.

[70] *La Nación*, November 15, 1909, p. 9.

Caras y Caretas, VI (January 10, 1903), n.p.

THE RESIDENCE LAW

Argentina (man): I'm here to get immigrants, but from now on, you'll have to give me selected ones only, because I don't want agitators, revolutionaries, strikers, Communists, socialists, anarchists . . . .

Europe (woman): That's enough; I know what you want—an immigration composed purely of bankers and archbishops.

Caras y Caretas, XII (June 12, 1909), n.p.

DANGEROUS IMMIGRATION

First Policeman: The minister of agriculture is right. The immigrants must be well
selected, as in North America.

Second Policeman: Right! . . . And look at that one. We'd better ask him whether
he has been insane and whether he knows how to read and write.

defense."[71] By this time both major Buenos Aires newspapers had abandoned their opposition to restrictive immigration legislation and were responding to the assassination with strong attacks on foreign-born radicals. *La Nación* appealed for more effective repressive legislation and for careful inspection of arriving foreigners to eliminate potential troublemakers.[72]

The campaign against foreign anarchists and labor organizers culminated during the 1910 centennial celebrations of Argentine independence. Hoping to impress the world with Argentina's opulence and progress, the government organized elaborate festivities to which it invited foreign dignitaries, including President Montt of Chile and Princess Isabella of Spain. When the anarchists, still bitter over the repression they had suffered in 1909, announced plans for a general strike during the centennial celebration, the government reacted harshly.[73] Congress loudly applauded speakers who denounced foreign agitators as insane, vicious rabble engaged in "war and subversion . . . against Argentine civilization and history." On May 14, both houses declared a state of siege.[74] That night the Buenos Aires police, joined by numerous upper-class volunteers who formed a citizens militia, moved to eliminate the capital's anarchist and Socialist leadership. The vigilante mob, which included such distinguished upper-class figures as Juan Balestra, Pedro Luro, and Congressman Manuel Carlés, sacked and burned the offices and newspaper plants of both the Socialist and anarchist parties, while the police arrested several hundred working-class leaders, including the Socialist chief Juan B. Justo. Summary deportations followed for scores of foreigners active in the labor movement. The following night the citizen mob, unhindered by the police, struck at Buenos Aires' so-called Russian district and destroyed the property of several Russian Jews thought to be sympathetic to the

[71] Ibid., November 17, 1909, p. 6.

[72] Ibid., November 16, 1909, p. 6; *La Prensa*, November 15, 1909, p. 8.

[73] Santillán, *La F.O.R.A.*, pp. 213–215; Belloni, *Del anarquismo al peronismo*, p. 26; Dickmann, *Recuerdos de un militante socialista*, p. 185.

[74] Speech of Lucas Ayarragaray, *D.S.C.D.*, May 13, 1910, p. 60; see also *D.S.C.D.*, May 14, 1910, pp. 124–125, 133–134.

working-class movement.[75] A few days later the centennial celebrations took place peacefully, but in a grim city whose angry passions were repressed only by thousands of troops and police.

Violence next struck Buenos Aires on June 27, 1910, this time during a performance at the Colón Opera House, symbolic gathering place of Argentine high society. Someone exploded a bomb under a main floor seat, injuring several persons. The police, unable to identify the culprit, finally accused a Russian anarchist named Romanoff, who probably was innocent.[76] Frightened by this incident, the upper classes blamed the anarchists for the crime and demanded harsher legislation against foreign agitators. Congress responded the next day with new anti-immigrant legislation, the so-called Social Defense Law. The legislators were clearly using immigration as a scapegoat for Argentina's worsening social violence, for no proof existed that the foreign born had any connection with the Colón bombing. Nonetheless, most congressmen agreed with Deputy Manuel Carlés, who shouted during debate that "a dastardly, ignominious, and cruel foreign mind inspired the crime!" The Chamber of Deputies loudly applauded Carlés' concluding outburst: "If there are foreigners who insist on abusing our liberality to outrage our fatherland's honor, there are also patriotic gentlemen who will risk their lives in a war against barbarism, in order to save our civilization."[77] The new law specifically prohibited the entry of anarchists, criminals, and anyone who preached the use of force or assassination as political weapons. It also prohibited anarchist meetings and demonstrations, strictly regulated the manufacture and use of explosives, established fines and punishments for navigation lines that transported prohibited immigrants to Argentina, and authorized immediate expulsion of any foreigner the government thought was endangering public order.[78]

[75] *La Vanguardia*, September 30, 1910, p. 1; *La Prensa*, May 14, 1910, p. 10; Dickmann, *Recuerdos de un militante socialista*, p. 186; Marotta, *El movimiento sindical argentino*, II, 73–77.

[76] *La Prensa*, June 28, 1910, p. 11; Marotta, *El movimiento sindical argentino*, II, 81.

[77] Speech of Manuel Carlés, *D.S.C.D.*, June 27, 1910, p. 297; ibid., June 27, 1910, pp. 306–313, 315; *D.S.C.S.*, June 28, 1910, p. 204.

[78] *D.S.C.D.*, June 27, 1910, pp. 310–311.

Argentine upper-class opinion, which by this time agreed that stricter legislation was vital to prevent further violence, strongly supported the Social Defense Law. Journalists argued that Argentina must exercise its right of self-preservation against the "human scum" which allegedly formed a large part of immigration.[79] The essayist and educator Carlos O. Bunge agreed that laws for the expulsion of foreigners were society's foremost defense against anarchism. Writers who criticized the wide arbitrary powers the law gave the police sadly concluded that the anarchist threat made such provisions necessary.[80] Social violence in Buenos Aires led some Argentine writers to oppose further immigration to urban areas. They published articles, similar to those in Chile's El Mercurio at about the same time, urging the government to discourage urban immigrants and to welcome only agricultural laborers.[81] One scheme editorialists urged to prevent further agglomeration of the foreign born in the capital would have required immigrant ships to avoid Buenos Aires and to dock at Rosario or Bahía Blanca. Since these small cities offered relatively few employment possibilities, immigrants presumably would move quickly to the agricultural areas that needed labor. The government hastily rented an immigrant hostelry at Bahía Blanca, but after the first ship docked there in 1910 La Nación was dismayed to note that at least one-third of the foreigners refused agricultural jobs and promptly entrained for Buenos Aires.[82] The newspapers seemingly did not realize that immigrants would continue to seek employment in the capital until the government enacted more liberal land policies.[83]

[79] Alejandro M. Unsain, "La ley de defensa social," Renacimiento, VIII (May, 1911), 32.

[80] Carlos O. Bunge, "Cuestiones jurídicas: El anarquismo y su terapeútica social," Renacimiento, VII (April, 1911), 315; Juan Luis Ferrarotti, "Algunas reflexiones sobre la defensa social: La ley 7029," ibid., VII (April, 1911), 232; La Nación, October 19, 1910, p. 10.

[81] Luis A. Bachini, "El problema de la inmigración," Revista Nacional, XLVII (1910), 34.

[82] One journalist who suggested the Bahía Blanca hostelry was E. de Cires, "La criminalidad en Buenos Aires," Revista Argentina de Ciencias Políticas, IV (July, 1912), 501–502; see also La Nación, November 4, 1910, p. 11, March 8, 1911, p. 10.

[83] Enrique Dickmann, "Inmigración y latifundia," Revista Argentina de Ciencias Políticas, X (May, 1915), 163, 168.

The desire to reduce urban immigration reflected a widespread conviction among the Argentine upper class that the foreign-born residents of Buenos Aires were responsible for the capital city's social problems and labor unrest. The Chilean ruling groups, similarly troubled by working-class unrest, also established a pattern of blaming foreign-born agitators. Unrestricted immigration had allowed such individuals to enter both republics, but, in each case, the intellectuals and the state magnified out of proportion the impact of immigration on urban social problems. Assigning blame to the foreign born was especially inappropriate in Chile, where most European immigrants were respectable middle-class types. It was much simpler for the Argentine and Chilean elites to blame outsiders when unfamiliar social tensions began to arise than to admit that other and more complex causal factors—the rise of modern cities, the economic exploitation of the working classes, and the decay of traditional social and economic institutions—might have been responsible. So strong was the Argentine belief that immigration was at the root of social problems that the government enacted antiforeign legislation in 1902 and 1910. These laws controverted policies designed to encourage massive immigration that Argentine statesmen had painstakingly constructed during the previous half century. Similarly, enemies of the foreigners in Chile were able to overcome the nation's cosmopolitanism by enacting legislation in 1918 that resembled the earlier Argentine laws. But neither nation yet attempted to erect strong barriers against immigration in general.

CHAPTER FIVE

An Unwelcome Participant: The Immigrant
in Argentine and Chilean Politics

≻≻

E MBATTLED BY LABOR UNREST, the Argentine and Chilean elites
also had to face mounting political challenges. In both republics political changes begun during the early twentieth century eventually ended
upper-class control over the state. One significant area of change involved the political integration of the immigrants, a group that, for a
variety of reasons, had seldom participated in national politics. By
1914 a growing number of foreigners were voting, forming new
political parties, and seeking public office, particularly in Argentina.
Immigrant political control became a distinct possibility, and the Argentine ruling groups reacted vigorously by defaming foreign-born
politicians and by attempting to prevent the naturalization of the immigrant masses. Large-scale immigrant participation was impossible in
Chile, where the relatively few foreign-born residents restricted their
political activities to the municipal level. But Europeans who entered
local Chilean politics encountered the same strong hostility from the
ruling groups that faced the foreign born who ventured into Argentine
public life.

Although Argentina was in theory a constitutional republic in which
popular sovereignty prevailed, in practice the large landed interests of

the littoral provinces dominated the central government. Through its political organizations, particularly the powerful Partido Autonomista Nacional, the Argentine upper class had long controlled the national executive, by far the most powerful branch of the government. Informal alliances with local provincial bosses enabled the president to rig congressional elections and to maintain a tight rein over the national Congress.[1] In this oligarchic political system, the ordinary citizen's vote meant little.

Nonetheless, citizens who hoped eventually to substitute democratic politics for the prevailing system were organizing new political parties. The largest of these was the Radical party, in these years a heterogeneous group of middle-class creoles and small landholders, who made little effort to attract the votes of naturalized foreigners.[2] Emphasizing the need for political reforms to guarantee universal, free, and secret elections, the party before 1916 paid little attention to economic or social questions. This was the course plotted by the Radical party's inflexible leader, Hipólito Yrigoyen, who refused to let the party run candidates for office until meaningful electoral reforms were achieved. Since most Radicals considered the prevailing political system hopelessly corrupt and nonrepresentative, on several occasions they engaged in violent but unsuccessful attempts to topple the government. One of these abortive uprisings, which occurred in Santa Fe Province in 1893, marked the only occasion prior to World War I when immigrants took direct action to overthrow a constituted Argentine government.

Widespread political discontent smouldered among the immigrant farmers in Santa Fe Province during the summer months of 1893. Already suffering severe financial distress because of recent sharp declines in agricultural prices, the colonists bitterly protested a new provincial tax levied against each hundred kilos of wheat and linseed produced. In February, 1893, hundreds of immigrant farmers refused to pay this tax and began forceably to drive away the revenue

[1] Peter Snow, *Argentine Radicalism*, pp. 5–6.

[2] Challenging the common assertion that the Radicals before 1916 appealed mainly to the immigrants and their descendants is Ezequiel Gallo and Silvia Sigal, "La formación de los partidos políticos contemporáneos: La *U.C.R.* (1890–1916)," in Di Tella, *Argentina, sociedad de masas*, pp. 124–176.

agents. Several sharp clashes between foreigners and provincial police took place around the colonies of Humboldt and Esperanza.[3] Meanwhile, the Radical party, which had been plotting the violent overthrow of the Santa Fe government, appealed for the support of these disgruntled farmers. When a political revolution began late in September, 1893, hundreds of colonists came to aid the Radicals and took part in a march against the city of Santa Fe, defiantly flying the Swiss flag. The insurgents already had seized Rosario and probably would have taken control of the whole province had the federal government not intervened to save the regime.[4]

Participation of foreigners in this attempt to topple a provincial government shocked many Argentines. In Santa Fe itself retaliation came swiftly. Led by Governor Luciano Leiva, who proclaimed a "war against the gringos," the provincial police raided and plundered the agricultural colonies and jailed several hundred immigrants. To justify this repression Leiva claimed that the foreigners preached revolt, demanded special privileges, and disdained both the creole populace and the provincial authorities. There was no alternative, he concluded, than forceably to teach them to stay out of Santa Fe politics.[5] News of the rebellion also angered politicians in Buenos Aires. The Chamber of Deputies loudly applauded a denunciation of the foreigner made by José García González of Santa Fe. The immigrant, he cried, "must not interfere in political questions and especially not in revolutions!" La Nación agreed that the foreigner who takes part in politics is like the striker and the anarchist, . . . and this is not the kind of immigration that we want."[6] What the Argentine upper class did want was subservient and obedient immigrants who would provide cheap labor and leave politics to others.

The alliance between the Santa Fe colonists and the Radical party dissolved after 1893, but the resentment that the foreign settlers and

<hr />

[3] La Prensa, February 6, 1893, p. 5; February 7, 1893, p. 4.

[4] Juan Álvarez, Historia de Rosario, (1689–1939), pp. 502–509; Juan Schobinger, Inmigración y colonización suizas en el siglo XIX, pp. 169–170; La Prensa, October 5, 1893, p. 5, October 6, 1893, p. 4, October 8, 1893, p. 4.

[5] La Prensa, October 6, 1893, p. 4, October 10, 1893, p. 4, October 16, 1893, p. 3, October 18, 1893, p. 5, October 23, 1893, p. 4.

[6] D.S.C.D., August 15, 1893, p. 439; La Nación, October 6, 1893, p. 1.

their descendants harbored against the provincial regime remained. In 1908 a new political group, the Liga del Sur, emerged to represent the southern regions of Santa Fe. Like the Radicals, the Liga primarily emphasized political reform. But the new party went far beyond Radical demands when it called for the transfer of the provincial capital from the somnolent old city of Santa Fe to the robust new metropolis of Rosario. The proposal reflected the Liga's desire to end the tight control that creoles from the poor and sparsely settled northern half of Santa Fe held over the much richer and more populous south, where the great bulk of the province's 300,000 immigrants lived.[7]

While the Liga del Sur was beginning to organize foreign political strength in the Rosario region, the Socialist party was hard at work in Buenos Aires constructing a strong political base among immigrants and their descendants. The socialists did not attract the capital's unskilled laboring elements, which eschewed party politics and threw their weight behind the anarchist movement. Rather, the Argentine Socialist party since its foundation in 1894 had been attempting to form a political amalgam among the skilled workers and the lower middle class. In contrast with the anarchists, who used the general strike and direct action to gain their ends, Argentine socialists were nonviolent reformers who emphasized reason and education and who sought gradual social change. Nonetheless, elite opinion labeled them dangerous revolutionaries who, once in power, would overturn Argentine social and economic institutions.[8]

The appearance of the Radical and Socialist parties and of the Liga del Sur on the Argentine political scene alarmed the traditional ruling groups. Conservative political writers predicted that once the immigrants possessed effective suffrage, they would enable the new parties to triumph at the polls. Victory would produce a political crisis that might culminate in grave civil strife between foreigners and creoles. To prevent any such challenge to its political power, the oligarchy

    [7] Enrique Thedy, "Indole y propósitos de la Liga del Sur," *Revista Argentina de Ciencias Políticas,* I (1909), 76–79; H. García Ledesma, *Lisandro de la Torre y la pampa gringa,* p. 36.
    [8] Alfredo Galletti, *La política y los partidos,* pp. 63, 71; Samuel L. Baily, *Labor, Nationalism, and Politics in Argentina,* p. 16–18.

vigorously opposed movements that would encourage the immigrant masses to naturalize. Congress, for example, refused to consider the proposals that several intellectuals were making to reform the labyrinthine procedures an applicant for citizenship had to undergo.[9] Indeed, some conservative writers advocated new restrictions, such as a ten-year residence period before immigrants could apply for naturalization.[10]

Spokesmen for the ruling elites sought to justify the foreigner's political exclusion by portraying him as culturally inferior. As the journalist Augusto Belín Sarmiento put it, "To make citizenship obligatory for all foreigners is simply to degrade the title of citizen." Miguel Cané, long one of the immigrant's most bitter enemies, claimed that the newcomer possessed neither intellectual capacity nor preparation for public life sufficient to make him a responsible voter.[11] In agreement with Cané's assessment was *Caras y Caretas*, one of whose cartoons portrayed an Italian applicant for citizenship trying to demonstrate his knowledge of the Argentine constitution to a federal judge. The ignorant immigrant, confusing the fundamental charter with Buenos Aires' Constitution Square, assures the judge, "Why sure! I know that square and even the railroad station on it!"[12] In order to further discredit immigrant political participation, the oligarchy charged that many foreigners wished to naturalize only to promote their economic interests or to be eligible for government jobs. Some applicants, it was claimed, used false witnesses and bogus documents to obtain citizenship before the legal residence period of two years had elapsed.[13] Although Argentine creole politicians had long indulged in

9 Ezequiel Leguina, "A propósito de la nacionalización de extranjeros," *Renacimiento*, I (June, 1909), 61; Santiago Vaca Guzmán, *La naturalización de los extranjeros: Conversación familiar*, p. 101; Augusto Belín Sarmiento, *Una república muerta*, p. 149.

10 Juan Álvarez, *Estudio sobre las guerras civiles argentinas*, p. 198; Carlos Güiraldes (hijo), "La cuestión de la ciudadanía," in *Anales de la Facultad de Derecho y Ciencias Sociales*, III, second series, second part, 262.

11 Belín Sarmiento, *Una república muerta*, p. 162; Miguel Cané in *El Tiempo*, ed., *La naturalización de los extranjeros: Opiniones y proyectos*, p. 16.

12 "Buscando carta de ciudadanía," *Caras y Caretas*, XI (June 20, 1908), n.p.

13 *D.S.C.D.*, May 26, 1913, p. 484; Juan Álvarez, "Observaciones sobre el

vote buying, several upper-class writers singled out for denunciation foreigners who naturalized and then sold their votes. These authors pointed to the relationship between immigration and the growth of boss rule in the United States and argued that immigrant participation would only increase the corruption and immorality that afflicted Argentine political life.[14] The newspapers substantiated such charges when they revealed that foreign-born political bosses had long been purchasing immigrant votes, not to support reform candidates, but to back the ruling oligarchy. Cayetano Ganghi, the best known of these entrepreneurs of the vote, was a picturesque Neapolitan shopkeeper who barely spoke Spanish, but who shrewdly manipulated Italian-bloc ballots to support his political allies. Ganghi regularly delivered about 2,500 votes to President José Figueroa Alcorta (1906–1910), whom the Neapolitan brashly referred to as "Don Pepe."[15]

Conservative concern about the impact of immigration on politics intensified in 1912, when the Argentine Congress approved sweeping electoral reforms. Naturalization had posed no real threat to elite predominance as long as the ruling groups had been able to manipulate elections. But the so-called Sáenz Peña reforms of 1912 restructured Argentine political life by guaranteeing meaningful elections for the first time in the nation's history. The author of the new election laws, President Roque Sáenz Peña, was something of an anomaly. Proud, wealthy, and well educated, "the foremost gentleman of his generation," as his contemporary Juan Balestra described him,[16] he appeared to symbolize the Argentine oligarchy. But, unlike many elite politicians, Sáenz Peña sensed the magnitude of the social and economic transfor-

---

procedimiento para naturalización de extranjeros," *Revista Argentina de Ciencias Políticas*, V (October, 1913), 51.

[14] Leguina, "A propósito de la naturalización de extranjeros," p. 61; *La Nación*, April 28, 1900, p. 4.

[15] Alejandro N. Peralta, "El pueblo quiere principios," *Revista Argentina de Ciencias Políticas*, VI (May 12, 1913), 137; *La Vanguardia*, March 18, 1910, p. 1; June 16, 1911, 1; *D.S.C.S.*, April 29, 1913, pp. 45–46. For comments on the extent of Ganghi's influence, see Juan Abelardo Ramos, *Revolución y contrarrevolución en la Argentina*, II, 90–91.

[16] Quoted in Miguel Ángel Cárcano, *Sáenz Peña: La revolución por los comicos*, p. 173.

mation Argentina was undergoing and realized that the traditional political system no longer met the country's needs. He was convinced that electoral reform would integrate the powerful Radical party into the political system and end the Radicals' threats to overthrow the national government by force. Sáenz Peña undoubtedly realized that the Radical party was basically concerned with constitutional democracy, not with striking at the economic power of the Argentine upper class. With this in mind, the president made electoral reform practically the sole object of his administration. Within two years after his election in 1910, Sáenz Peña pushed through a reluctant Congress legislation providing for universal, obligatory, and secret adult male suffrage, as well as for honest elections.[17] Apparently, some congressmen voted for the bill only because they believed the traditional ruling groups would still be able to control the electorate through timeworn practices of corruption.[18]

Hardly had the Sáenz Peña reforms passed when the new parties began to win smashing electoral triumphs. Radical candidates were victorious in the 1912 congressional elections in Buenos Aires, but, when the Socialist party triumphed completely in by-elections the following year, immigrant political participation became a major national issue. The election of Nicolás Repetto and Mario Bravo to the Chamber of Deputies and of Spanish-born Enrique del Valle Iberlucea to the Senate shocked all Argentina and alarmed the elites, who had monopolized power for so long.[19] "Most of the country has been living in a state of strange terror for the last few days," commented the usually jocular *Caras y Caretas* a fortnight after the elections, while a scholar writing in the *Revista Argentina de Ciencias Políticas* reported the vote was "a stupefying surprise for the old governing class."[20] *La Nación* attempted to convince its readers that the foreign-born vote accounted for the Socialist victory, but calmer opinion analyzed the election sta-

[17] Ibid., pp. 207, 264; Galletti, *La política y los partidos*, p. 30.
[18] Nicolás Repetto, *Mi paso por la política (de Roca a Yrigoyen)*, pp. 119–120.
[19] *La Vanguardia*, April 5, 1913, p. 1.
[20] José M. Salaverría, "El miedo," *Caras y Caretas*, XVI (April 19, 1913), n.p.; Peralta, "El pueblo quiere principios," p. 140.

tistics and found that the total number of registered immigrants in Buenos Aires was smaller than the Socialist majority. Nonetheless, the influential newspaper continued to view the election as a gloomy portent of immigrant control over Argentine politics.[21]

Conservative writers assumed that an evil international conspiracy had enabled the Socialist party to triumph in Buenos Aires. It was claimed that hundreds of thousands of embittered European workers had brought their ancient class hatreds to Argentina, where the class struggle allegedly did not exist. The working classes had been led astray, according to this conspiracy theory, by European labor agitators who posed as immigrant laborers but who came to flood the nation with their pernicious doctrines.[22] Once they had accepted the assumption that socialism was an import, conservatives began to call for stricter naturalization requirements. On May 26, 1913, Deputy Gómez proposed to the Chamber a comprehensive revision of Argentine citizenship laws. Gómez' plan would not only have required an applicant for citizenship to prove to a federal judge his "good conduct and reverence for Argentine constitutional principles," but would also have forced the foreigner to insert at his own expense in the local newspaper a notice that anyone opposed to his prospective citizenship should state specific objections to the nearest federal judge. The proposed legislation also would have denied foreign-born citizens suffrage until four years after naturalization. These restrictions, Gómez told the Chamber, were vital to protect the Argentine people from foreign political ideologies.[23]

But the government did not need to enact stricter citizenship requirements, for national and local officials had long used a variety of informal and extralegal devices to discourage naturalization. Soon after the 1912 electoral reform, reporters for *La Prensa* and the Socialist newspaper *La Vanguardia* exposed the government's manipulation of naturalization procedures. The Argentine reading public learned

[21] *La Nación*, April 22, 1913, p. 10; August 14, 1913, p. 12.
[22] Baltazar D. Branca, *Al márgen de un problema: Nuestro partido socialista: Su cosmopolitismo ante la nacionalidad argentina*, pp. 7, 9, 11, 18; Lucas Ayarragaray, *Socialismo argentino y legislación obrera*, p. 34.
[23] *D.S.C.D.*, May 26, 1913, pp. 467–469, 471–474, 484–485.

that before an immigrant could apply for citizenship he had to undergo a thorough police investigation, which tended to disqualify immigrants active in working-class movements.[24] If he received police approval, the aspirant had to spend days or weeks in crowded reception rooms awaiting an interview with one of the federal judges, the only government officials authorized to grant citizenship. The judges, whose number had not kept pace with population growth, claimed that they were overworked and could allot only three or four hours a week to citizenship matters. Huge piles of paper work accompanied each application and so delayed the procedure that officials in Buenos Aires processed only thirty or forty cases each week. To correct these interminable delays, political reformers proposed, without success, the establishment of special judicial offices devoted exclusively to citizenship applications.[25]

Additional obstacles blocked the naturalization of foreigners who inhabited rural areas. They found it difficult if not impossible to make the frequently long and expensive journey to the urban centers where federal judges resided.[26] Lisandro de la Torre, then leader of the Liga del Sur, revealed in Congress that the minister of the interior had ordered the local rural police to examine the background and conduct of each applicant. The records were then sent to the Buenos Aires metropolitan police, who investigated the applicant's affiliation with urban labor or socialism. The whole process was insulting and excessively time consuming, De la Torre argued.[27]

Conservative politicians who were attempting to discredit and limit immigrant political participation received unexpected support from the Radical party after the 1913 elections. The Radicals, who had no effective political link with the immigrant masses, lashed out at the Socialists as a foreign, non-Argentine party. In a public statement, the

[24] For example, *La Vanguardia*, September 22, 1905, p. 1; May 6, 1906, p. 1; October 26, 1907, p. 2.

[25] *La Prensa*, May 13, 1912, p. 10; August 4, 1912, p. 13; December 26, 1912, p. 10. Comments of the Socialist deputies in Congress on this issue are found in *D.S.C.D.*, September 3, 1913, pp. 28–29; August 17, 1914, pp. 731–733.

[26] *La Prensa*, January 20, 1891, p. 6; August 9, 1891, p. 5.

[27] *D.S.C.D.*, August 1, 1913, pp. 706–707.

Radical National Committee claimed that "amoral scum of European civilization," who were "systematic enemies of all common welfare," composed the Argentine Socialist party.[28] The Radicals continued this defamation during a heated Senate debate over the seating of Enrique del Valle Iberlucea, the 1913 Socialist victor in Buenos Aires, who had become a citizen in 1901. Radical Senator José Crotto tried to convince his colleagues that Del Valle should not be seated, because he had expressed alleged antipatriotic views while editor of an international Socialist review and in some articles published in La Vanguardia. Crotto continued, "I do not believe that he is sufficiently saturated in Argentine nationalism, for if he were, he would not express ideas that tend to destroy nationhood itself." Although the legislators loudly applauded Crotto's peroration attacking the Socialists, "who have completely perverted the national soul and have proscribed the Argentine hymn," Del Valle's election was legal and the Senate had little choice but to seat him.[29]

The Radical party's xenophobic stance did not forestall another Socialist party victory when the voters chose a new congressional delegation in March, 1914. The Socialists won seven of the capital's ten seats and began to show impressive strength in Mar del Plata as well as other urban centers of Buenos Aires Province.[30] The results of the 1914 election reflected the increasing political power that immigrant voters wielded in the capital city, where they cast over 18,000 of the total of 45,000 ballots.[31] Reflecting on the allegiance that most of these foreign-born voters gave the Socialist party, La Nación forecast the end of traditional Argentine culture.[32] But the upper classes in general did not react against the 1914 election with the shocked hostility they had expressed a year earlier. Perhaps the moderate behavior

[28] The party statement was reprinted in La Nación, April 9, 1913, p. 9. For discussion of the Radical party's xenophobia, see Oscar Cornblit, "European Immigrants in Argentine Industry and Politics," in Claudio Veliz, ed., The Politics of Conformity in Latin America, pp. 242–243.

[29] D.S.C.S., April 29, 1913, pp. 18–24, 45–47.

[30] La Vanguardia, April 2, 1941, p. 1; Gallo and Sigal, "La formación de los partidos políticos contemporáneos," p. 161.

[31] Cárcano, Sáenz Peña, p. 219.

[32] La Nación, April 1, 1914, p. 12.

of the Socialist congressmen elected in 1913 had convinced the elite that the party posed no real threat to the established order. The Socialists may not have been threatening the elites but they did strike at the foundations of the power base the Radicals were attempting to form in the capital. As a result, Radical-inspired denunciation of foreign-born Argentines who voted Socialist continued after the 1914 election. Not content with speaking out against immigrant voters, some Radical leaders were beginning to demand restrictions on naturalization. In a move aimed clearly against working-class immigrants, Senator Crotto proposed to limit suffrage to those foreign-born citizens who had maintained at least ten years' residence in Argentina, who owned real estate, or who had fathered at least four Argentine children.[33]

Not content with their defamation of the Socialist party, Radicals employed xenophobic arguments against another political enemy, the Liga del Sur. Aware of the potential political strength that immigrants possessed in southern Santa Fe, the Liga strongly identified with their interests. "We do not fear the foreigner," said a party statement of 1910, "we ask him to collaborate, confident that we will assimilate him."[34] Statements like this enabled Radical propaganda to attack the Liga as "a party of the *gringos*," led by foreign storekeepers and landowners, who were none too popular among the rural masses.[35] The Radical propaganda campaign had its humorous side. During a Liga parade through the streets of Rosario in 1911, a young Radical hiding on a rooftop reportedly began to shout, "E' viva Garibaldi! E' viva Italia!" Most of the Italian participants in the parade joined the cheer heartily, and the local Radical press widely publicized the incident.[36] The close ties between the Liga and Santa Fe's foreign-born population may have induced the native-born masses to support the Radicals, who kept control of the provincial government during the remainder of the pre-World War I period.

[33] *La Vanguardia*, March 25, 1914, p. 1; March 28, 1914, p. 1.
[34] Quoted in Raúl Larra, *Lisandro de la Torre*, p. 126.
[35] Ricardo Caballero, "Primer ensayo de sufragio libre," in Roberto A. Ortelli, ed., *Discursos y documentos políticos del Dr. Ricardo Caballero*, p. 433; García Ledesma, *Lisandro de la Torre y la pampa gringa*, p. 36.
[36] Ricardo Caballero, *Yrigoyen: La conspiración civil y militar del 4 de febrero de 1905*, pp. 186–187.

While the Argentine oligarchy reluctantly had allowed political change to begin with the adoption of the electoral reform of 1912, the upper class in Chile stubbornly continued to dominate the nation's politics until the early 1920's. The Chilean oligarchy maintained this political power by controlling the municipal-level electoral machinery that selected the national Congress, by far the strongest branch of the central government. After decades of struggle for supremacy between the executive and legislative branches, Congress had defeated the forces of the president during the bloody Civil War of 1891. This victory firmly established congressional predominance over Chilean political life and vastly reduced the president's powers.

In sharp contrast with Argentina the political impact of the foreign born never became a major issue in Chile. The immigrant population lacked the motivation and the numerical strength necessary to challenge the national political order, although unnaturalized foreigners did attempt to take a role in municipal government. This was particularly true in Valparaíso, which contained a large and wealthy foreign-born population and many European businesses. In 1893 powerful Valparaíso foreigners who chafed at the city's inefficient government petitioned Congress for permission to hold municipal office, although not to vote in local elections. El Mercurio, which at this time placed considerably more faith in the political capabilities of foreigners than of natives, strongly supported the petition. In a characteristic demonstration of the intellectual elite's disdain for the abilities of the Chilean people, editorialists predicted that foreigners would administer Valparaíso more rationally and efficiently than nationals.[37]

But the participation of noncitizens in municipal office required a constitutional amendment, and Congress proved hostile to the whole idea.[38] For one thing, the proposal injured the pride of many legislators. "The intelligence of foreigners and of Chileans is equal," exclaimed Deputy Anjel Guarello. "I do not understand why an English head is better prepared for government than one of our countrymen."[39]

[37] El Mercurio, June 12, 1893, p. 2; July 24, 1899, p. 2.
[38] The original proposal for a constitutional amendment is in B.S.S., sesiones ordinarias, June 9, 1893, p. 56.
[39] B.S.C.D., sesiones extraordinarias, October 21, 1899, p. 175.

LOOKING FOR A CITIZENSHIP CARD

Judge: Do you swear faithfully to obey the national constitution?
Immigrant (in broken Spanish): But of course!
Judge: Are you acquainted with the constitution?
Immigrant: But of course! I know that square and even the railroad station on it!

THE JEWISH SCHOOLS OF ENTRE RÍOS

School Inspector (to student): How many letters are there in the Spanish alphabet?
Teacher (noting that the student remains quiet):
  Ask him in Russian if you want him to answer you.

But the principal objections reflected fear that foreigners might eventually be able to assume national political power.[40] A law of 1891 had granted extensive control over national elections to the municipalities, which assumed responsibility for registering voters, for appointing election officials, and generally for conducting elections. In practice the law often enabled powerful local interest groups to influence the outcome of national political contests. Since the proposed amendment theoretically would have enabled foreign-born residents to influence the outcome of congressional elections, Congress denied its assent.[41] After much debate the Senate approved the proposal in 1893, but the Chamber of Deputies shelved it until 1899 and then rejected it.

Similar congressional hostility greeted an executive proposal of 1893 to grant municipal self-rule to the city of Punta Arenas, capital of the national territory of Magallanes and traditionally governed by officials from Santiago. At least half the population of this rapidly growing community were citizens of foreign nations, and they had long desired a municipal council on which they might serve. But when President Montt asked Congress to approve such a body, the Senate refused its assent, fearing that the immigrants of Punta Arenas might establish a virtually independent state within Chile. Congress refused for five more years to consider the question; finally in 1898 President Errázuriz settled the issue by arranging a compromise. He decreed the establishment of a municipal council that remained subordinate to Chilean territorial officials, but on which foreigners were allowed to serve. Punta Arenas remained the only Chilean city where unnaturalized foreigners could hold municipal office.[42]

Protests against foreign participation in Chilean local government al-

---

[40] Ibid., sesiones extraordinarias, November 21, 1899, p. 417.

[41] Julio César Jobet, *Ensayo crítico del desarrollo económico-social de Chile,* p. 115; Robert E. Mansfield, *Progressive Chile,* p. 245; Luis Moya Figueroa, *Estudio comparativo de la lei de municipalidades de 22 de diciembre de 1891,* p. 21. See also *B.S.S.,* sesiones ordinarias, June 9, 1893, p. 66, for speech of José Gandarillas, and *B.S.C.D.,* sesiones extraordinarias, November 23, 1899, pp. 460–461, for speech of Daniel Feliú.

[42] *B.S.S.,* sesiones ordinarias, June 21, 1893, pp. 146–147; sesiones ordinarias, June 23, 1893, pp. 154–158; Briones Luco, *Glosario de colonización,* pp. 145–149.

so occurred in Valdivia and Llanquihue, provinces containing large German populations. Here a furor arose not over the participation of noncitizens, but of naturalized foreigners who attempted to hold municipal office. The strongest reaction occurred in Osorno, one of the largest German population centers. Most of the area's Germans were Protestant backers of the anticlerical Radical party, which in 1894 began to actively campaign in the region. During the elections of that year, the Radicals elected two Germans to the municipal council, which in turn chose one of them mayor against strong Conservative party opposition. This stirred the local Catholic priest, a Conservative zealot, to action. Waging a bitter campaign against the Germans, he proclaimed that no town populated mostly by Chileans should accept a government composed of immigrants. So intense was this clerical pressure that the council reversed its position and appointed a Chilean Conservative as mayor. When the German who occupied this position refused to renounce it, civil strife broke out and did not end until the Conservatives had destroyed or pillaged much of the German property in the area. Finally the central government intervened to arrest the Conservative mayor and to restore the German.[43]

The Osorno affair did not alter the fundamental stability that characterized Chilean politics during the 1890–1914 period. In general the ruling elites had no intention of relinquishing control of the government to immigrants or to other newly articulate elements. Only in a few southern centers of immigration, such as Punta Arenas and Osorno, were the foreign born able to assume power. Congress' decision to exclude unnaturalized foreigners from municipal office scuttled the whole issue of immigrant political participation during the rest of the prewar period. But across the border in Argentina rapid political change already was under way. New parties, which were attempting to seize political power from the oligarchic ruling cliques, appealed for immigrant support. Once foreigners began to vote for the Socialist

---

[43] Victor Sánchez Aguilera, *El pasado de Osorno, la gran ciudad del porvenir*, p. 226. A narrative of events in Osorno from the Radical and pro-German point of view is Honorio Ojeda, *Detalles completos de los sucesos de Osorno, 10 de noviembre de 1894*, especially pp. 23–24, 80, 91, 130–131. A Conservative discussion of the same events is Jil de Veras (pseud.), *Los incendiarios ó sea narración completa de los sucesos de Osorno*, especially p. 12.

party or the Liga del Sur, the long-latent, oligarchic fear of immigrant political power crystallized into open hostility. Perhaps the most xeno-phobic political group, however, was the Radical party, which was competing for votes with the new immigrant-based parties. In its enmity against the Socialists and the Liga, the Radical party began to co-operate with its old adversary, the oligarchy, in attempts to slow the naturalization of foreigners.

CHAPTER SIX

Nationalism: The Antidote for Immigration
in Argentine and Chilean Social Philosophy

➤➤➤

THE GLEAMING IMAGE that European immigration had once enjoyed among Argentines and Chileans was tarnished by 1914. Only a
quarter century earlier the elites of both republics had welcomed the
foreign influx with enthusiasm, but many of the changes wrought by
immigration dismayed powerful segments of the population. Foreign-
born businessmen and professionals controlled ever greater shares of
both nations' economies. Immigrant urban laborers organized, struck,
and became continually more militant. The spectre of anarchism, and,
some thought, of bloody social revolution, loomed. Particularly in
Argentina, new parties that appealed to the immigrant vote threatened
to wrest political control from the creole elites. Many intellectuals who
observed these unforeseen results of immigration began to question
the postulates upon which Argentine and Chilean social and economic
policies had been founded. After 1905 influential writers in both republics were rejecting the positivist and cosmopolitan-oriented ideologies invoked by the elites since the 1850's to justify liberal immigration
policies. In place of cosmopolitanism, these intellectuals began to
formulate nationalistic ideologies that lauded traditional creole social

and cultural values and stressed the belief that immigrants must adopt these values. Such a vindication of creole culture contrasted sharply with nineteenth-century Argentine and Chilean social thought, which had disdained the Spanish and indigenous heritages as barbaric while regarding the immigrant as the very symbol of civilization.

Those Argentines and Chileans who feared the impact of immigration were quick to seize the nationalistic doctrines that the intellectuals were propounding. By 1910 manifestations of the shift in ideology toward nationalism were appearing on every side. In Argentina this concern led the government to adopt new educational policies stressing the use of the classroom to inculcate national cultural values among immigrant children. Concern for immigrant assimilation and cultural nationalism was less pronounced in Chile, whose immigrant population, as has been noted, was too small to challenge the elites. But by 1914 Chilean writers had begun to back economic nationalism, and the Chilean government was already moving to protect nationals participating in economic activity against the competition of foreigners.

Intellectual criticism of immigrant cultural exclusiveness failed to mention that the Argentine and Chilean governments had made little attempt to integrate the foreigners and had not developed comprehensive programs of assimilation. The case of the Germans in southern Chile, who retained their cultural identity for generations, illustrates the difficulty of assigning responsibility for the lack of assimilation. The Germans strove to maintain their heritage, but the Chilean government in effect had encouraged their cultural isolation by its failure to construct railways and good roads to link Valdivia and Llanquihue with central Chile and by its failure to promote the use of the Spanish language among the colonists. Those who attacked German exclusiveness ignored the fact that Chileans shared the responsibility for this situation. Chilean nationalists nonetheless began to condemn German cultural isolationism in no uncertain terms. Once regarded as the harbinger of culture and progress, the German after about 1905 found himself portrayed as an unsavory imperialist. The weekly magazine *Zig Zag*, for example, mercilessly satirized a German immigrant named Don Federico von Pilsener. Evidently a devotee of Pilsen beer, this individual tipped the scales at 240 pounds. In its long series of editorial cartoons, *Zig Zag* was criticizing Chile's German population when it presented Von Pilsener as a pompous fool who made no attempt to understand national customs and who unfairly denounced Chile on every available occasion.[1]

Other writers exclaimed that Llanquihue and Valdivia had become virtual German colonies within Chilean territory. The immigrants of these two provinces, lamented the Catholic *El Porvenir* in 1898, "will always form a race apart, a people apart, a society apart, with separate churches, cemeteries, schools, and language." As the threat of German worldwide colonialism grew, some writers began to fear that the immigrants might prove more loyal to their homeland than to Chile. Eduardo de la Barra, for example, claimed that Germans in Valdivia were openly urging Berlin to seize Chile on the grounds that the native born were incapable of self-government.[2] The threat of German colonialism became a recurring theme in the Chilean press, which attacked German clannishness and expressed the fear that the cultural ties between the southern provinces and Germany were stronger than they were with the rest of Chile.[3] Even Chileans who deeply praised the German immigrants' development of the south objected to their isolationism. Santiago Marín Vicuña noted the shock he felt upon hearing a Chilean-born youth proclaim, "I am a German born in Valdivia."[4]

Although immigrant clannishness troubled some Chilean writers, it never became a major intellectual preoccupation. But in Argentina, which contained millions of foreigners, quite the opposite occurred, and assimilation became an important issue during the decade preceding the outbreak of World War I. Argentine nationalists expressed fears that the huge immigrant population not only threatened the

---

[1] "Un alemán en Chile," *Zig Zag*, II (June 24, 1906), 26, II (July 8, 1906), 10, II (September 2, 1906), n.p., II (September 16, 1906), n.p.; "En Pillanlelbum," *Zig Zag*, I (September 3, 1905), 39.

[2] *El Porvenir*, January 14, 1892, p. 1; Eduardo de la Barra, *La vida nacional: El embrujamiento alemán*, p. 46. For similar comments, see Tancredo Pinochet Le-Brun, *La conquista de Chile en el siglo XX*, p. 42.

[3] *La Unión*, May 1, 1912, p. 1; May 3, 1912, p. 1.

[4] Santiago Marín Vicuña, *Al través de la Patagonia*, p. 29.

destruction of traditional cultural standards but possibly heralded European colonial expansion. The Argentine nationalist could find abundant evidence of immigrant cultural exclusiveness. If he should visit any sizable Argentine town, he would likely encounter several foreign fraternal and mutual benefit societies, often housed in imposing edifices. By 1914 a total of 1,202 such groups with 507,636 members existed in Argentina. Of these, 463 were Italian with 166,006 members, 250 were Spanish with 110,040 members, and 92 were French with 12,311 members.[5] Some of these associations controlled huge amounts of capital and had branches in all major towns. After touring Argentina, the Spanish traveler Federico Rahola noted his surprise at the power and size of the Sociedad Española de Benificencia, which he found "wherever one goes in the Republic," and which served as the "cohesive center for our fellow citizens."[6] Immigrants banded together not only to form benefit societies but also to celebrate the patriotic holidays of their homelands. Each September 20, to commemorate Italy's seizure of Rome from the pope in 1870, Buenos Aires witnessed Italian-sponsored parades, elaborate balls, gala parties, and festive theatrical performances.[7] In a major display of their continued allegiance to Italy, nearly 100,000 former subjects of King Humberto I marched through the cold and rainy streets of Buenos Aires to express their grief after the monarch's assassination in 1900.[8]

Of more concern, perhaps, to Argentine cultural nationalists than immigrant patriotic celebrations was the exclusiveness of the foreign agricultural colonists, who lived isolated from the rest of the nation in small communities scattered across the pampas. Often singled out for particularly harsh criticism were the Jewish farmers of Entre Ríos. Juan Alsina, for almost twenty years the government's director of im-

---

[5] Sergio Bagú, "Estratificación social y estructura nacional del conocimiento en la Argentina (1880–1930)," *Revista de la Universidad Nacional de Córdoba*, second series, III (March–June, 1962), 17.

[6] Federico Rahola, *Sangre nueva: Impresiones de un viaje a la América del Sud*, p. 127.

[7] "Los italianos en Buenos Aires," *Caras y Caretas*, II (September 23, 1899), n.p.

[8] "Manifestaciones de duelo en Buenos Aires," *Caras y Caretas*, III (September 20, 1900), n.p.

migration, did much to turn Argentine opinion against them. A man of national influence, Alsina composed reports that were widely read and that were regularly cited in newspaper articles and editorials. He expressed deep concern that the Jewish colonists would never adopt Argentine culture, alleging that their "language, customs, religion, and notions of government are totally different from ours." Over twenty years later influential newspapers like La Nación were repeating similar comments. One editorialist in 1914 claimed that "as they do in the rest of the world, the Jews in our country live, die, and perpetuate in their children Jewish culture."[9] Italian agricultural colonists, many of whom also formed isolated ethnic communities, received similarly sharp criticism. One attack on Italian exclusiveness appeared in Florencio Sánchez' play La gringa, first performed in 1904. During a card game taking place in a village tavern, an Italian physician refuses to go to aid a dying Argentine peon. Also in the tavern and overhearing the conversation is the local priest, who becomes alarmed, thinking a fellow Italian is ill. When he learns that the infirm man is a creole, the priest sighs with relief, "Ah! . . . that is something else!"[10]

Alarmed by the rush of the colonial powers into Africa and Asia during the late nineteenth century, Argentine writers about 1905 began to express fear that unassimilated immigration was preparing the way for European colonial expansion in South America. From time to time journalists would publicize and quote out of context Italian writers who referred to "our Argentine colony,"[11] or who claimed that "Italy has two types of colonies: . . . the official ones like Eritrea and the unofficial ones like Argentina."[12] Ricardo Rojas feared that the Italians in Argentina, "who have become dangerous because of their

[9] La Nación, June 19, 1914, p. 11. Alsina's comments are in Argentina, Departamento General de Inmigración, Memoria del Departamento General de Inmigración correspondiente al año 1891, p. 15. He made substantially the same remarks in 1895 in Argentina, Departamento General de Inmigración, Memoria del Departamento General de Inmigración correspondiente al año 1895, p. 214.

[10] Florencio Sánchez, La gringa, in Teatro completo, p. 120.

[11] Quoted in M. Fantozzi, "La 'colonia' italiana en la Argentina, conversación con el Comendador Cittadini," Revista de Derecho, Historia y Letras, XXIV (June, 1906), 562.

[12] Quoted in Clodomiro Cordero, El problema nacional, p. 29.

excessive quantity," might try to seize power in the name of their homeland.[13] Those who argued that immigration might foreshadow European colonialism could point to the example of the Welsh colonists who inhabited Chubut Territory. Although praised for their development of Chubut, the Welsh received a barrage of criticism in 1901 when they appealed to Great Britain to protect their interests, allegedly because the Argentine government was intervening unjustly in local affairs. Enraged at this impertinence, *La Prensa* advised the government to emphasize to London that Argentine sovereignty over Chubut was absolute. *La Nación* told the Welsh to leave Argentina if they continued to appeal for British intervention.[14] When London sent a commissioner to investigate, *La Prensa* bitterly attacked the immigrants' "colonial" attitude and feared that similar incidents would threaten continued Argentine rule over the region.[15] Hostility against the Welsh, who formed "an English colony within the national territory," persisted throughout the remainder of the pre-1914 period.[16] The attitudes that the Italian and Spanish governments maintained toward their citizens abroad further aroused Argentine misgivings about the ultimate impact of immigration.[17] Both nations insisted that they would protect the interests of their citizens no matter where they resided.[18] Particularly alarming from the Argentine point of view was Italy's refusal until 1912 to exempt from military service children born in Argentina of Italian parents. Spain had exempted Argentine-born Spaniards in 1906, but continued to claim them as subjects.[19]

The possibility of European colonial expansion concerned Argentine nationalists far less than the impact immigration was making on what they called the "national character"—the traditional cultural norms

[13] Ricardo Rojas, *La restauración nacionalista*, pp. 469–471.

[14] *La Prensa*, February 26, 1899, p. 4; *La Nación*, October 19, 1901, p. 4.

[15] *La Prensa*, October 8, 1901, p. 4.

[16] *La Nación*, March 28, 1913, p. 11.

[17] M. E. Malbrán, "Los italianos en la República Argentina," *Revista de Derecho, Historia y Letras*, V (January, 1900), 406–412.

[18] See, for example, Baltazar Avalos, "Proyecto italiano de colonización: La nacionalidad y los extranjeros," *Revista de Derecho, Historia y Letras*, IV (October, 1899), 572.

[19] *La Prensa*, March 8, 1906, p. 7; November 19, 1912, p. 13.

Argentines had developed over the centuries. The problem first attracted public attention in 1897, when a group of Italian immigrants requested government permission to erect a statue honoring Garibaldi in a Buenos Aires park. The proposal offended the national pride of a large minority of congressmen who insisted that statues help form a people's character and that monuments to foreign heroes clearly were out of place when immigration already threatened the Argentine "national soul." Debate in the Chamber of Deputies grew bitter when Indalecio Gómez of Salta charged that Garibaldi was only an "opportunistic revolutionary," the perpetuation of whose memory would "bastardize the national spirit."[20] At this point, *La Prensa*, still a spokesman for the liberal, cosmopolitan viewpoint, took up the issue and printed strongly worded editorials in favor of erecting the monument. Congress finally approved the Italian petition,[21] but the affair demonstrated that cultural nationalism already was gathering support.

Shortly after 1900, men of letters began to voice concern over the threat that immigration presumably presented to the national character. *La gringa*, the play by Sánchez that portrayed so many of the relationships between immigrant and creole, represented this foreign threat in the person of an ambitious and unscrupulous Italian named Don Nicola. At one point this immigrant shows his disdain for Argentine culture by chopping down an *ombú*, a tree Argentines traditionally revere as a national symbol. Creole audiences might have been unsettled when they heard Don Nicola exclaim that "the *ombú* was only a worthless creole tree not even valuable for firewood . . . it ought to be on the ground."[22] Denunciation of the cultural impact of immigration appeared in the novel as well as in the drama. In his *Promisión*, published in 1897, Carlos M. Ocantos had emphasized that immigrants were rapidly assimilating into creole culture. A French couple, the main characters in the novel, "gradually adjusted to the new culture" until both eventually adopted Argentine customs like drinking mate (Para-

---

[20] *D.S.C.D.*, August 13, 1897, p. 532. See also speech of Lucas Ayarragaray, ibid., July 20, 1897, p. 430.

[21] *D.S.C.D.*, August 13, 1897, p. 519; *La Prensa*, July 21, 1897, p. 4, August 4, 1897, p. 4, August 14, 1897, p. 4, August 19, 1897, p. 4.

[22] Sánchez, *La gringa*, p. 135.

guayan tea). After several years in Argentina, they were "as acclimated as if they had been born in the country."[23] But by 1911, when he published *El peligro* (*The Danger*), Ocantos had decided that assimilation was taking place too slowly. Now he feared that immigration, particularly through the changes it was causing in the Argentine vernacular, might warp the national character into unrecognizable forms.[24]

The rapid transformation that the Spanish language spoken in Argentina was undergoing during the era of massive immigration symbolized the decay of the national character to many intellectuals besides Ocantos. Pronunciation and usage of Castilian Spanish had been changing rapidly since the mid-nineteenth century in Argentina, and today Argentine Spanish differs considerably from that spoken in South American countries that received few immigrants. In 1900, when a Frenchman named Luciano Abeille strongly applauded this transformation in his book *Idioma nacional de los argentinos*, lively intellectual controversy began over the impact immigration was making on the language. Abeille, who taught French in Buenos Aires' Colegio Nacional, predicted that the fusion of Argentine Spanish with the immigrants' many tongues would create a new language "of great richness, of suave harmony, and of incomparable beauty."[25] These conclusions riled many Argentine writers, and none more so than the influential sociologist Ernesto Quesada, who quickly published two books to refute Abeille. Since Quesada's basic contention was that language is the very "depository of the spirit of the race, of its inner genius," he viewed with dismay the rapid incorporation of Italian, French, German, English, and Russian words into Argentine Spanish. The use of this weird mixture, he feared, might spread "until everyone accepts it as if it were the correct language."[26] Argentines, he concluded, must protect their national character by keeping the language pure from immigrant contamination.[27] *Caras y Caretas* agreed with Quesada's

[23] Carlos María Ocantos, *Promisión*, pp. 11, 15.

[24] Carlos María Ocantos, *El peligro*, pp. 50–53.

[25] Luciano Abeille, *Idioma nacional de los argentinos*, pp. 35–37, 415, 422–423.

[26] Ernesto Quesada, *El problema del idioma nacional*; see also idem, *El 'criollismo' en la literatura argentina*, pp. 53–54.

[27] Quesada, *El 'criollismo,'* p. 131.

analysis and added that the confusion of the Tower of Babel was "nothing compared to what is taking place in our language."[28]

Also quick to attack Abeille was that inveterate xenophobe, Miguel Cané. Immigration was debasing the Argentine language, he contended, and upon this shaky foundation good national literature never could arise. The impact of immigration on the vernacular would retard Argentine development, because "on good literature depends culture, progress, and civilization." Conversely, argued the criminologist Eusebio Gómez, the use of bad language seemed to be associated with deviant members of society. Gómez pointed out that the professional criminals of Buenos Aires spoke a weird dialect called *lunfardo*, perhaps the most degenerate form of Argentine Spanish.[29] The debate that Abeille's book had precipitated continued during the period preceding World War I. The foreigners, exclaimed one exasperated journalist in 1913, "are trying to change with their disastrous jargon one of the richest and most expressive languages of the earth!"[30]

Concern over the possible mutilation of the Spanish language constituted one aspect of a growing intellectual movement that questioned the cultural impact of immigration. This movement gathered so much momentum that by 1910 several of the republic's most prominent social essayists, many of them once friendly to the foreigners, were condemning unassimilated immigration as a clear threat to the national cultural heritage. Carlos O. Bunge was one writer who dramatically changed his attitudes. His *Nuestra América* (1903) derided creole culture and regarded the immigrant as a desirable influence, but by 1908, Bunge was worrying that Argentina's increasingly heterogeneous population was making the national character "clearly chaotic." Roberto J. Payró, a staunch liberal who had long defended immigration as a

[28] Adolfo Paleró Escamilla, "Modificaciones al idioma," *Caras y Caretas*, III (May 12, 1900), n.p.

[29] Miguel Cané, "La cuestión del idioma," *La Nación*, October 5, 1900, p. 3; Eusebio Gómez, *La mala vida en Buenos Aires*, p. 110.

[30] Francisco Camón Gálvez, "Idioma nacional," *Revista de Educación (La Plata)*, LXIV (October–November, 1913), 1050; for another critique of the impact of immigration on the vernacular, see Saúl Escobar, "Orientación patriótica de la educación primaria," *El Monitor de la Educación Común*, XXXIV (September 30, 1910), especially pp. 502–503, 507.

progressive force, by 1909 also began to doubt his previous position. As a result of massive immigration, he complained, "Everything is anarchical, indecisive, nebulous, insecure. One cannot yet see nor determine the foundations of our future society . . . there is nothing to serve as a guide for our forward or backward evolution."[31]

Perhaps as a result of the labor unrest afflicting the Argentine capital in 1909 and 1910, the brilliant young author Manuel Gálvez, who had left his native city of Paraná to write in Buenos Aires, felt compelled to speak out about the effects of unassimilated immigration. His *Don Quijano de la pampa*, an analysis of Argentine society published in 1910, expressed Gálvez' deep concern that immigration was destroying the Argentine character and, with it, the people's traditional patriotism. Because of "the cosmopolitanism and the denationalization of the present era," he wrote, "few Argentines can understand the idea of the Fatherland and sense that we carry something of it within ourselves."[32] The rapidly rising popularity of foreign music was one of the many examples Gálvez used to demonstrate the impact of immigration on Argentine culture. The tango, which had originated among immigrants on the Buenos Aires waterfront and had become immensely popular by 1910, was "repugnant," "hybrid, unfortunate music," and a "lamentable symbol of our denationalization."[33] Gálvez belonged to a young generation of Argentine writers born in the interior provinces, who began to move to Buenos Aires shortly after 1900. Attracted by the capital's vigorous intellectual climate, they recoiled before the great city's European atmosphere, lavish display of wealth, and vigorous socialist and anarchist movements. Rejecting the cosmopolitanism of Buenos Aires, Gálvez, Ricardo Rojas, Leopoldo Lugones, and others evoked the traditional patterns of life in the interior, little touched by immigration. The values, traditions, and institutions that had developed in the interior towns over the centuries constituted for

[31] Carlos O. Bunge, "La enseñanza nacional," *Archivos de Pedagogía y Ciencias Afines*, IV (September, 1908), 358; Roberto J. Payró, *Crónicas*, p. 155.

[32] Manuel Gálvez, *El diario de Gabriel Quiroga: Opiniones sobre la vida argentina*, p. 54.

[33] Ibid., p. 129. Another writer who used changes in music to illustrate the triumph of foreign culture was Belisario Roldán, *Discursos completos*, p. 289.

these men the true Argentine cultural heritage, a tradition that they feared immigration was disrupting. The essays these writers published to defend the national cultural heritage influenced the reorientation of Argentine social thought away from the positivist social theories so long in vogue.

The most influential intellectual of this new generation was Ricardo Rojas, who left his native city of Santiago del Estero to write and teach in the capital. In 1909, at the age of twenty-seven, Rojas published *La restauración nacionalista*, his first major work and a sharp attack on the cultural impact of immigration. Argentine liberals in the tradition of Alberdi and Sarmiento, according to Rojas, had overemphasized rapid material progress and had forgotten that spiritual values make a nation truly great. Steeped in the philosophy of the German historian J. G. Herder, Rojas developed better than any other Argentine intellectual the idea that the nation possessed a unique "soul." *La restauración nacionalista* was hardly an objective analysis, for Rojas appeared convinced from the beginning that massive immigration threatened to destroy Argentina's cultural heritage and to subject Argentines to alien values and traditions.[34] The following year, in his book *Blasón del Plata*, he expanded his argument, identifying civilization with reverence for national cultural values and condemning cosmopolitanism as the antithesis of civilization.[35] Both books enjoyed immediate popularity and helped proselytize the idea that the foreigner endangered the "national soul."

Two influential foreign-born writers were among the few Argentine intellectuals who opposed the majority viewpoint by arguing that immigration posed no threat to the national character. One defender of the foreigner in this respect was Godofredo Daireaux, a wealthy merchant and cattleman who had come to Argentina in 1868 at the age of nineteen. In his autobiographical novel, *Las dos patrias*, which appeared in 1906, Daireaux emphasized that the Frenchman in Argentina "forms his family, becomes accustomed to the environment, and

[34] Rojas, *La restauración nacionalista*, pp. 41, 63–64, 91; see also Earl T. Glauert, "Ricardo Rojas and the Emergence of Argentine Cultural Nationalism," *Hispanic American Historical Review*, XLIII (February, 1963), 1–2.

[35] Ricardo Rojas, *Blasón del Plata*, pp. 150–152.

assimilates completely."[36] Similarly, the Russian-born Alberto Gerchunoff refuted the common argument that Jewish agricultural colonists never would assimilate. His first major novel, *Los gauchos judíos* (1910), passionately emphasized his conviction that the Entre Ríos farmers gradually were adopting Argentine ways of life while retaining their traditional religion.[37] Another defender of immigration was José Ingenieros, already one of the best-known social essayists in the Hispanic world. The son of an Italian, he may have been trying to demonstrate his own patriotism when he argued that the commotion about immigrant assimilation was needless. Foreigners' sons, Ingenieros pointed out quite correctly in his *Sociología argentina* of 1913, nearly always became fervent Argentine patriots.[38] But few Argentines by 1910 shared the optimism about the rapid acculturation of the immigrants that Daireaux, Gerchunoff, and Ingenieros were expressing.

Nationalism was the solution that Argentine writers were advocating to protect the creole cultural heritage against the alleged ravages of immigration. The intellectuals' conception of nationalism was essentially cultural and nostalgic; it demanded reverence for national traditions and cultural values handed down from centuries past, and it preached adoration of the patriotic symbols that represented these cultural values. Argentine nationalists generally emphasized that all the republic's inhabitants must learn to revere the *patria*, or fatherland, as a higher spiritual entity transcending the individuals composing it. Each foreigner must accept the *patria*'s cultural values as his own. Rojas summarized the determination of his generation to impose Argentine culture on the immigrants when he stated, "Our aim for now ought to be to create a community of national values among all Argentines."[39] Gálvez agreed that nationalism was necessary to combat "all

[36] Godofredo Daireaux, *Las dos patrias*, p. 313.
[37] Alberto Gerchunoff, *Los gauchos judíos*, p. 138.
[38] José Ingenieros, *Sociología argentina*, p. 98.
[39] Rojas, *La restauración nacionalista*, p. 352; for comments on nationalism among Argentine intellectuals at this time see José Luis Romero, "La realidad argentina y el análisis sociológico a comienzos del siglo," *Revista de la Universidad (La Plata)*, V (December, 1958), 56–57; Arthur P. Whitaker and David C. Jordan, *Nationalism in Contemporary Latin America*, pp. 54–56.

the ideas, all the institutions, and all the habits that might in any form contribute to the suppression of one atom of our Argentine national character."[40] The belief that the republic needed cultural nationalism to protect itself from immigration made a great impact on Argentine social thought by 1910.

Military conscription was one method suggested by some Argentines to inculcate national cultural values among the immigrants and especially their children. During congressional debate preceding the adoption of conscription for Argentine citizens in 1901, Minister of War Colonel Pablo M. Richieri argued at length that military service would fuse Argentina's diverse ethnic elements by teaching the soldiers patriotism and love for national institutions and traditions. Several years later President Roque Sáenz Peña praised the contribution that the Argentine military was making toward assimilating the foreigners.[41] Gálvez conjectured that an Argentine war with Brazil would be desirable because it would speed up assimilation of the first-generation immigrants. "War would convert the foreigners to Argentines and the cosmopolitan spirit would be destroyed beneath the vast patriotic fervor."[42]

But most intellectuals considered the public school a much more feasible instrument than the military for nationalizing the immigrants' children. The central idea of Argentine nationalistic education was that the elementary and secondary curricula should emphasize Argentine history and geography, national civic problems, and the Spanish language. Instruction in these subjects should not merely furnish factual information, but should stress patriotic traditions and legends that would stimulate the child's love for his country. The shift of emphasis in pedagogical theory away from fact toward myth illustrates the declining prestige that positivist educational theories in Argentina suffered. "Although I am a fervent partisan of scientific positivism," claimed Carlos O. Bunge in 1911, "I am most sincerely convinced of

---

[40] Gálvez, El diario de Gabriel Quiroga, p. 232. He repeated much the same arguments in his next book, El solar de la raza, p. 14.

[41] D.S.C.D., September 12, 1901, p. 723; Roque Sáenz Peña, Escritos y discursos, II, 15.

[42] Gálvez, El diario de Gabriel Quiroga, p. 78.

the importance of poetic fiction in the instruction of the child."[43] The issue of nationalistic education began to captivate the attention of Argentine intellectuals in 1908 when the government appointed José María Ramos Mejía as president of the National Council of Education. This dependency of the Ministry of Education supervised primary schools in the capital and the national territories. One of Argentina's most bitter xenophobes, Ramos Mejía used his position with single-minded determination to attack cultural heterogeneity. He was able to influence all Argentine schoolteachers, including those who taught in systems outside the federal government's control, by means of the council's monthly *El Monitor de la Educación Común*, a professional pedagogical journal that was distributed nationwide and enjoyed great prestige.

Soon after assuming leadership of the council, Ramos Mejía began to recruit Argentina's most respected educators, including Bunge and Enrique de Vedia, to write articles for *El Monitor* supporting nationalistic education. Bunge, who had advocated the idea as early as 1902, contended in a 1908 article that Argentina could not preserve its independence without a thorough program of nationalistic education.[44] De Vedia agreed and continued that Argentina ought to imitate Japan's emphasis on moral and patriotic studies. Noting with alarm that 49.2 per cent of the students in the school he headed had foreign-born parents, De Vedia argued that education must emphasize the duties and responsibilities the citizen owes the community. But he feared that nationalistic education on a scale sufficient to assimilate the foreigners' children was impossible without a constitutional amendment to give the central government control of primary education in the provinces.[45]

[43] Carlos O. Bunge, "La enseñanza de la tradición y la leyenda," *El Monitor de la Educación Común*, XXXVI (February 28, 1911), 265; see also Rojas, *La restauración nacionalista*, p. 43, and Hermosina Aguirre de Olivera, "La enseñanza de la historia," *El Monitor de la Educación Común*, XXXI (December 31, 1909), 698–709.

[44] Carlos O. Bunge, *La educación*, p. 175; idem, "La educación patriótica ante la sociología," *El Monitor de la Educación Común*, XXVII (August 31, 1908), 70.

[45] Enrique de Vedia, *Educación secundaria*, p. 56; idem, "Educación patriótica," *El Monitor de la Educación Común*, XXVII (September 30, 1908), 169–175; idem, "La escuela," *El Monitor de la Educación Común*, XXXV

The poet Leopoldo Lugones, who had served as inspector general of secondary education, also supported nationalistic education from the pages of *El Monitor*. In a 1912 article he wrote that only a determined effort to teach Argentine cultural values could counteract the exaggerated materialism that immigrants allegedly were disseminating.[46]

Not content with the testimony of these influential educators, *El Monitor* published a series of articles by less well-known Argentine teachers. They described how classroom experience had convinced them that nationalistic education was necessary to oppose the influence of the immigrants, "who perhaps have brought indifference to our once ardently patriotic people."[47] The Ministry of Education buttressed *El Monitor's* arguments by financing the research and publication of Rojas' *La restauración nacionalista*. Aside from eloquently attacking cosmopolitanism, this work provided a cogent theoretical justification for nationalistic education. Rojas journeyed abroad to analyze the comprehensive programs of patriotic education that several European countries were developing and concluded that only a similar scheme would preserve the Argentine soul.[48] A series of books and articles indicated that the Argentine educational profession was strongly supporting nationalistic education by 1910.[49] All this propaganda in favor of the study of national subjects encouraged at least two congressmen

---

(October 31, 1910), 28–29; idem, "La nueva tendencia," *El Monitor de la Educación Común*, XXXV (December 31, 1910), 587, 589. This prolific writer repeated his arguments for nationalistic education in another book, *La enquête Naón*, pp. 16, 50–58.

[46] Leopoldo Lugones, "Ciencia y moral práctica," *El Monitor de la Educación Común*, XLII (September 30, 1912), 187.

[47] Helena Irigoin, "Enseñanza patriótica," *El Monitor de la Educación Común*, XXXII (March 31, 1910), 848; see also Aguirre de Olivera, "La enseñanza de la historia," p. 707; Juan Beltrán, "La educación primaria en la República Argentina," *El Monitor de la Educación Común*, XXXVII (May 31, 1911), 346; and Escobar, "Orientación patriótica de la educación primaria, pp. 488–491.

[48] Rojas, *La restauración nacionalista*, especially pp. 16, 43, 87, 351, 359.

[49] Among the educators who declared support for nationalistic education were Enrique Hoyo, "Espíritu patriótico en la escuela," *Revista de Educación (La Plata)*, LXIV (October–November, 1913), 1028–1030; Ramón Melgar, *La nacionalización de la instrucción primaria*, p. 51; Juan R. Ramos, *Historia de la instrucción primaria en la República Argentina, 1810–1910*, I, 153.

to propose complete curriculum reforms. In 1908 Deputy Felipe Guash Leguizamón of Salta presented to the Chamber a plan for more thorough elementary-school study of Argentine history, geography, and civic problems in order, he said, to stimulate patriotism among children of socialist parents. A similar reform, proposed by Deputy Luis Agote in 1912, aimed to make secondary education "fundamentally moral and patriotic," in order to assimilate the children of the immigrants. Congress, however, approved no important change in study programs embodying these ideas.[50]

Apart from advocating curriculum reform, Ramos Mejía's council tried to foster patriotism in the schools it directly controlled through more extensive use of Argentine national symbols. The council ordered teachers to begin the day with an oath of allegiance to the Argentine flag, to praise a different national hero each day, and to lead the students in the song "Viva la patria" at the close of classes. Another decree set aside November 2 of each year as the Day of National Heroes, during which all schools were to hold special ceremonies in honor of Argentina's fallen patriots. The council organized a ceremony on July 8, 1909, during which all Buenos Aires elementary students publicly had to swear allegiance to the flag.[51] Emphasis on patriotic symbols became particularly pronounced during the annual May independence celebrations. During the 1910 festivities marking the centennial of Argentine independence, the council instructed all elementary schools to build an "altar to the Fatherland," on whose base the students were to strew flowers while intoning patriotic hymns.[52]

Backers of nationalistic education vehemently attacked the private educational systems maintained by many immigrant nationalities. "The foreign school . . . must not be tolerated, because it propagates in an alarming form clearly anti-Argentine tendencies," contended one writer

[50] *D.S.C.D.*, June 1, 1908, pp. 147–148, 152–153; June 21, 1912, pp. 324–327.

[51] Beltrán, "La educación primaria en la República Argentina," pp. 333–334, 339; "La jura de la bandera por las escuelas de los consejos escolares de la capital," *El Monitor de la Educación Común*, XXX (July 31, 1909), 102–173.

[52] Ernesto Bavio, "Instrucciones sobre la semana de Mayo," *El Monitor de la Educación Común*, XXIX (May 31, 1909), 326, 333; "La escuela en el centenario," ibid., XXXIII (June 30, 1910), 1040–1494.

in *El Monitor*.[53] The two great Buenos Aires dailies, as well as several writers on education, were in agreement. The schools that the Welsh maintained in Chubut and that the Russo-Germans built in their isolated farming villages frequently incurred the wrath of Argentine nationalists. The Russo-German schools, complained *La Prensa*, employed mostly foreign teachers and conducted classes in the immigrants' own languages. Furthermore, these schools were "destroying the child's sentiments of Argentine nationality," and "obstructing the nation's work of assimilation."[54] On another occasion, *La Prensa* harshly attacked the Russo-Germans of Lucas González village in Entre Ríos, who refused to permit their children to attend a new national school and who drove the recently arrived Argentine teachers out of town.[55]

But nationalists reserved their most virulent attacks for the Jewish schools of the Entre Ríos agricultural colonies. Controversy over these schools arose in 1908 when Ernesto A. Bavio, a national education inspector, purported to expose their anti-Argentine character in two *El Monitor* articles. According to Bavio the curriculum emphasized the Hebrew religion, most of the teachers were foreigners who despised Argentina, and Hebrew was usually the language of instruction.[56] The Entre Ríos government, which subsidized the Jewish schools, later revealed that Bavio had never visited them and that he had obtained most of his information from biased sources.[57] But in the meantime Buenos Aires newspapers and *Caras y Caretas* were using Bavio's reports to justify a full-scale journalistic campaign against the Jewish schools. *La Prensa* urged the government to close at once "those schools which have a Hebrew soul." *La Nación* agreed that they were "repug-

---

[53] Escobar, "Orientación patriótica de la educación primaria," p. 504.

[54] *La Prensa*, May 16, 1912, p. 12; Raúl B. Díaz, *La educación en los territorios y colonias federales. Propaganda. Educación y viajes*, p. 11; *La Prensa*, March 6, 1899, p. 4, April 19, 1899, p. 4.

[55] *La Prensa*, October 28, 1911, p. 10; April 19, 1914, p. 11.

[56] Ernesto A. Bavio, "Las escuelas extranjeras en Entre Ríos," *El Monitor de la Educación Común*, XXVII (November 30, 1908), 602; XXVIII (January 31, 1909), 16–17, 25–26.

[57] Manuel P. Antequeda, *Breve exposición sobre las escuelas ruso-alemanas é israelitas: Escuelas nacionales (ley Lainez) de la provincia de Entre Ríos*, pp. 25, 37–38.

nant to the development of the national spirit."[58] Others who literally
accepted Bavio's reports included Enrique de Vedia and Ricardo Rojas,
whose *La restauración nacionalista* repeated the inspector's charges.[59]
The controversy waned after 1909, but not until the press had stirred
up a good deal of hostility against Jewish immigrants. Another of the
National Council's inspectors, José B. Zubiaur, reported in 1910 that
the Jewish schools generally met minimum standards for teaching the
national language as well as Argentine history and civics, but the
papers gave his findings minimal attention.[60]

Cultural nationalists furthermore demanded that private immigrant
schools employ only the Spanish language in classroom situations. Agitation over this question began as early as 1894 when Congress learned
that many schools in the immigrant colonies and in the predominantly
foreign districts of the capital gave instruction in languages other than
Spanish. A group of congressmen led by Deputy Indalecio Gómez of
Salta, claiming that foreign languages in the schools insulted Argentine
sensibilities and hindered immigrant acculturation, introduced legislation to prohibit the use of foreign languages for instruction.[61] Congressional leaders, fearful of offending the immigrants, quickly shelved
the proposal, but Gómez revived it in 1896. While his earlier proposal
had included only schools in the capital and the national territories,
Gómez' new plan encompassed all schools in the nation. A long pro-
cession of congressional speakers together with the powerful voice of
La Prensa argued, "Language is the very basis of national unity," and
condemned the use of foreign languages in the schools.[62] The Prussia

58 *La Prensa*, December 26, 1908, p. 8; *La Nación*, December 14, 1908, p. 6.
See also *La Prensa*, November 25, 1908, p. 10, December 28, 1908, p. 8; *La
Nación*, December 11, 1908, p. 9; and "Las escuelas israelitas en Entre Ríos,"
Caras y Caretas, XI (December 5, 1908), n.p.
59 De Vedia, *La enquête Naón*, pp. 9, 18; Rojas, *La restauración nacionalista*, p. 341.
60 *La Nación*, December 30, 1910, p. 11.
61 Speech of Indalecio Gómez, *D.S.C.D.*, September 17, 1894, p. 812; speech
of Lucas Ayarragaray, ibid., September 17, 1894, p. 816.
62 Speech of Marcos M. Avellaneda, ibid., September 4, 1896, p. 755; speech
of Indalecio Gómez, ibid., September 4, 1896, p. 767; speech of Lucas Ayarragaray, ibid., September 7, 1896, p. 786. Two editorials in *La Prensa* strongly

of Frederick the Great, which imposed the king's language in all class-
rooms, ought to become Argentina's model, exclaimed Deputy Marcos
M. Avellaneda of Buenos Aires, upset at a report that some students
in private schools did not even realize they were Argentine citizens.[63]
Congressional clamor notwithstanding, the executive branch did not
wish to take action that prospective immigrants might interpret as un-
friendly. El Monitor pointed out that Article XIV of the Constitution
of 1853 guaranteed all inhabitants of Argentina the right to teach and
learn, but did not specify the language of instruction.[64] Other opponents of Gómez' proposal rejected language as a basis of national unity.
Attempts to impose nationalism by means of the school, continued
this argument, might create a superficial patriotism but would fail to
inculcate sincere love for Argentina and reverence for its institutions.
Since the administration influenced the votes of most congressmen, the
Chamber rejected the plan on September 9, 1896.[65]

When Ramos Mejía took over the National Council of Education,
he revived the issue of instruction in foreign languages. Claiming the
schoolchildren in the Russo-German and Jewish colonies often spoke
no Spanish, El Monitor in a 1909 article completely reversed its position of 1896 and argued that national survival required compulsory use
of Spanish in all schools. But the clamor for restrictive legislation never
grew loud enough to force Congress to act on the matter.[66]

The Argentine movement for nationalistic education also strongly
opposed the employment of foreign teachers, upon whom the schools
long had relied heavily. As late as 1887 foreign citizens composed almost 50 per cent of the teaching staff in the city of Buenos Aires.[67] The

supporting the proposal appeared on June 30, 1896, p. 3, and September 11,
1896, p. 3.
    [63] Speech of Marcos M. Avellaneda, D.S.C.D., September 4, 1896, p. 753.
    [64] "La enseñanza del idioma nacional," El Monitor de la Educación Común,
XIV (September 30, 1896), 817–818.
    [65] Speech of Francisco A. Barroetaveña, D.S.C.D., September 9, 1896, pp.
793–794, 803; speech of Emilio Gouchón, ibid., September 4, 1896, pp. 759–
760; La Prensa, September 10, 1896, p. 3.
    [66] Bavio, "Las escuelas extranjeras en Entre Ríos," pp. 597, 601; D. Guana,
"Enseñanza del castellano," El Monitor de la Educación Común, XXXI (October 31, 1909), 165–167.
    [67] Buenos Aires (City), Censo general de población (1889), II, 43.

issue of the cultural impact these teachers might be making first arose in 1894 when Congress debated the admission of foreign professors to a proposed Superior Council of Secondary Education. Led by Deputy Manuel Mantilla of Corrientes, enemies of the foreign teachers claimed that they failed to emphasize patriotism and respect for Argentine national values.[68] Liberal congressmen questioned the government's constitutional right to bar aliens from the proposed council, but the administration's position prevailed, and Congress voted to require Argentine citizenship.[69] Another step in the movement opposing foreign teachers was taken in March, 1899, when the Ministry of Education decreed that only Argentine citizens could teach the Spanish language as well as national history, geography, and civics in the public secondary schools. But the government did not enforce this decree, and many foreigners continued to teach these subjects, reported Ricardo Rojas in 1909.[70]

The National Council of Education after 1908 gradually restricted the employment of teachers in the schools it controlled to Argentine citizens and also began to regulate the employment of foreign teachers in private schools. After 1909 the council required all foreign teachers to pass comprehensive examinations in Argentine history and geography and in the Spanish language. The government rejected more extreme proposals, including one deputy's bill to permit only graduates of the state's pedagogical institutions to hold public or private teaching posts.[71] Many foreigners continued to teach in Argentine schools, especially in private institutions; the census of 1914 reported that

---

[68] *D.S.C.D.*, December 21, 1894, pp. 1208, 1211.

[69] Speech of minister of justice and education, in Argentine Republic, Congreso Nacional, *Debates parlamentarios sobre instrucción pública*, August 6, 1894, p. 1203. See also speech of Indalecio Gómez, ibid., August 6, 1894, p. 1199, December 21, 1894, p. 1357; speech of Agustín Álvarez Suárez, *D.S.C.D.*, December 21, 1894, p. 1214.

[70] *La Prensa*, March 21, 1899, p. 5; Rojas, *La restauración nacionalista*, p. 344.

[71] Beltrán, "La educación primaria en la República Argentina," p. 345; Bismark Lagos, "Escuelas particulares: La orientación de su enseñanza," *El Monitor de la Educación Común*, XXXI (November 30, 1909), 321; *D.S.C.D.*, August 18, 1909.

3,542 of the 26,449 elementary-grade teachers were foreign born.[72]
The Argentine campaign to promote nationalistic education produced few concrete results before the outbreak of World War I. The
government imposed no curriculum reform oriented toward national
subjects, most provincial schools remained outside the federal government's control, private immigrant schools continued to conduct classes
in the foreigners' native languages, and several thousand foreign-born
teachers still served in both public and private schools. The campaign
to impose nationalistic education was significant not because of its
immediate consequences but because it reflected a prevailing intellectual mood. The nearly unanimous support Argentine writers gave to
nationalistic education was perhaps the best measure of their rejection
of cosmopolitanism.

About the same time that this clamor in support of nationalistic
education was rising, cultural nationalists were beginning to rehabilitate
the image of the native-born Argentine, frequently a mestizo and long
scorned by positivist writers. This revisionist movement first began to
attract attention in 1903 when Juan Bialet Massé, under a commission
from the national government, published a three-volume report on the
performance of native-born and immigrant laborers. Although Argentine literature since the 1880's occasionally had proclaimed the virtues
of the national population, Bialet Massé was the first important social
scientist to vindicate the native born at the expense of the Europeans.
After praising the Argentines who labored in the Tucumán cane fields,
the Jujuy mines, and the wheat fields of the littoral, Bialet Massé concluded that the government had erred gravely by "paying attention
only to the foreign element," and by "leaving aside the creole, who
was much more effective and valuable." Throughout the report Bialet
Massé urged Argentines to end their sterile glorification of foreigners
and to learn to respect the native-born laboring classes.[73]

Historians and social essayists soon began to reassess the relative
contributions creoles and immigrants had made to Argentine development. Native-born Argentines, cultural nationalists claimed, had been

[72] Argentine Republic, *Tercer censo nacional*, IX, 207–216.
[73] Juan Bialet Massé, *Informe sobre el estado de las clases obreras en el
interior de la república*, I, v; see also I, 3; II, 37; III, 399, 401.

the real source of civilization and progress. Heroically, the creoles and gauchos had risked their lives to drive out Spanish colonial rule and to subdue the marauding pampas Indians. The immigrant in this revised view of history became only "an auxiliary factor," as Juan Alsina put it, a mere element of production who helped enrich Argentina, but who had done nothing to create the conditions that made prosperity possible.[74] By 1910 Ricardo Rojas, in *Blasón del Plata*, was urging his fellow citizens to venerate the Spanish and Indian heritage of the interior, along with the nation's geographical environment. From these sources sprang all that was good and noble in the Argentine character, Rojas proclaimed.[75] More extreme was the claim of essayist Emilio Becher that "Argentine writers and politicians have come exclusively from the Hispano-Argentine group."[76] Becher must have overlooked deliberately the contributions of men like José Ingenieros and former president Carlos Pelligrini, both sons of Italian immigrants.

While cultural nationalists were rehabilitating the creole's reputation, they were denigrating that of the foreigner. Enrique Larreta, whose novels celebrating the Hispanic cultural tradition made him famous during the 1920's, claimed as early as 1900, "True talent does not migrate. The wave washes up only the most insignificant fishes."[77] During the next decade, many intellectuals came to agree that Argentine immigrants were generally of low quality. Rejecting the foreigner's reputation as the enlightened agent of modern civilization, nationalist writers depicted him as illiterate, stupid, lazy, and dishonest. Typical was the comment of Alejandro E. Bunge, an economist, who wrote in 1914 that "our immigration barely possesses the minimum of capacity and knowledge that one might expect of civilized men."[78]

[74] Juan A. Alsina, *Población, tierras y producción*, p. 9. For similar comments, see Roldán, *Discursos completos*, p. 369; Leopoldo Lugones, *El payador*, p. 109; Rojas, *Blasón del Plata*, p. 147.

[75] Rojas, *Blasón del Plata*, pp. 94, 104–105.

[76] Emilio Becher, "La tradición y el patriotismo," in *Diálogo de las sombras y otras páginas*, p. 222.

[77] Enrique Larreta, *Discursos*, p. 15.

[78] Alejandro E. Bunge, "Los desocupados y la distribución del trabajo," *Estudios*, VII (October, 1914), 305. Similar comments include Reynal O'Connor, *Paseos por las colonias*, p. 14, and E. de Cires, "La inmigración en Buenos Aires," *Revista Argentina de Ciencias Políticas*, IV (September, 1912), p. 741.

Cosmopolitan writers had predicted that immigrants would disseminate the most advanced European agricultural skills in Argentina, but
by 1910 nationalists were arguing that the foreigner's cultural level was
so low that he probably would retard, not develop, rural areas. The
rural Argentine laborer was culturally more advanced than most immigrants, claimed Juan Álvarez.[70] Some agricultural colonists allegedly
knew so little about farming that "they do not even know how to yoke
a team of oxen,"[80] while at least one critic complained that the Spanish
immigrant farmer was so backward that "he makes a plow exactly like
the one the Romans used before Christ."[81] Roberto Campolieti, an
agronomist employed by the Ministry of Agriculture, agreed that the
average immigrant "knows nothing about agricultural life," and that
the government ought to begin a program of national agricultural education to train foreign colonists.[82]

By World War I, Argentine cultural nationalists had found a symbol, the gaucho, to represent the national cultural heritage and to
defend it from the threat posed by immigration. Although the legend-
ary horseman of the pampas had long figured prominently in folklore,
poetry, and drama, many Argentines ignored gauchesque literature,
including its most famous work, the epic poem *Martín Fierro*.[83] As
long as cosmopolitanism continued to dominate the intellectual climate,
Argentina's reading public disdained the gaucho, considering him to
represent the antithesis of civilization as well as the violence and civil
disorder characteristic of early nineteenth-century Argentina. But this
view of national history began to change as intellectuals became increasingly aware that immigration was altering the social and economic
patterns with which the upper class dominated Argentine life. Intellectuals who sympathized with the traditional social structure attempted to
use the gaucho as a symbol to convince the public that the cultural
values of the Argentine elites represented the true national character.
By the first decade of the century a few writers had begun to mourn

[70] Juan Álvarez, *Ensayo sobre la historia de Santa Fe*, p. 398.
[80] Bialet Massé, *Informe sobre el estado de las clases obreras*, I, 103, 120.
[81] Augusto Belín Sarmiento, *Una república muerta*, pp. 139–140.
[82] Roberto Campolieti, *La chacra argentina*, pp. 65, 69, 80.
[83] Guillermo Ara, *Leopoldo Lugones*, p. 197.

the passing of the gaucho,[84] but not until Leopoldo Lugones delivered a famed series of lectures in November, 1913, did an Argentine intellectual succeed both in idealizing the plainsman and in identifying him with the national character. Lugones' lectures, among the highlights of Buenos Aires' 1913 social season, filled the glittering Teatro Odeón to capacity. In the audience were many of the nation's most prominent figures, including President Sáenz Peña. Those who could not attend in person were able to read the lectures in *La Nación*, which reprinted them at once. Lugones then edited his comments and published them in 1916 under the title of *El payador*. The gaucho, Lugones emphasized, was the source of the basic traits of Argentina's national character —compassion, elegance, honor, loyalty, and generosity. "We are not gauchos, of course," he admitted, but the "Argentine of today, though racial mixture has changed his physical appearance, still bears the gaucho's heritage. When racial fusion ends, the characteristics of the gaucho still will dominate."[85] Lugones added that *Martín Fierro* expressed the national character better than any other work of Argentine literature.[86]

The revision of the gaucho's image that Lugones did much to promote received a boost from another prominent Argentine writer, Carlos O. Bunge. As late as 1903 he had gloomily catalogued the basic characteristics of the Spanish American mestizo as arrogance, laziness, and sadness. But, only eight years later, the prominent educator and essayist was exclaiming, "We must conserve [the gaucho's] memory, since he was the first symbolic type of the Argentine nationality!" Not to be outdone by Lugones, Bunge in 1914 celebrated the gaucho as loyal, courageous, strong of spirit, and patriotic.[87] Both Lugones and Bunge

[84] For example, Quesada, *El 'criollismo,'* p. 34; Francisco Aníbal Río, "Alma gaucha," *Caras y Caretas*, X (October 19, 1907), n.p.

[85] Lugones, *El payador*, pp. 79, 83–84. Lugones anticipated the ideas he expressed in his 1913 lectures in an article, "A campo y cielo," *Nosotros*, VII (May, 1913), 225–235. For other comments on the myth of the gaucho, see Madaline W. Nichols, *The Gaucho: Cattlehunter, Cavalryman, Ideal of Romance*, and Samuel Schneider, *Proyección histórica del gaucho*, p. 107.

[86] Lugones, *El payador*, p. 338.

[87] Bunge, "La enseñanza de la tradición y la leyenda," p. 274; idem, "El derecho en la literatura gauchesca," *Anales de la Academia de Filosofía y Letras*, II (1914), 13.

were attempting to define the Argentine character to include polite, elegant, and heroic characteristics found in aristocratic, hierarchical, paternalistic societies. Defined in this manner and symbolized by the gaucho, the Argentine character was not akin to the ideals of social and political democracy that immigrants were introducing. Argentine intellectuals rapidly accepted the idealized gaucho as the national symbol. To determine the impact that the concept was making, the literary review *Nosotros* conducted an inquiry among the nation's best-known writers asking, "What is the value of *Martín Fierro?*" Enrique de Vedia, Manuel Gálvez, Martiniano Leguizamón, Manuel Ugarte, Alejandro Korn, and a group of lesser figures answered that the poem was both the pinnacle of Argentine literature and the incarnation of the national spirit.[88] Only a few writers, none of whom enjoyed a wide reputation, objected that the gaucho could not possibly represent a nationality composed increasingly of immigrants.[89]

Among the intellectual opponents of the nostalgic nationalism that was permeating the Argentine climate of opinion after 1910 were occasional elite figures who maintained the traditional faith in immigration. Examples are Norberto Piñero and Rodolfo Rivarola, two respected university professors who affirmed their faith that cosmopolitanism and ethnic heterogeneity were fundamental factors of Argentine progress. Both men urged Argentina to experiment with new forms of social organization brought by the immigrants rather than preserve institutions inherited from the past.[90] Socialist writers attacked cultural nationalism as class nationalism and claimed that the upper class promoted reverence for values that would justify its continued political control. "New social phenomena such as the working-class

[88] "¿Cuál es el valor de *Martín Fierro?*" *Nosotros*, X (June, 1913), 427–429; XI (July, 1913), 81–83; XII (October, 1913), 59.
[89] Ibid., X (June, 1913), 428–429, 431–433; XI (August, 1913), 186–189.
[90] Norberto Piñero, "Nacionalismo y raza," *Revista Argentina de Ciencias Políticas*, IV (June, 1912), 262; Rodolfo Rivarola, *Fernando en el colegio (educación moral y cívica)*, pp. 12–13. Another intellectual who opposed nostalgic nationalism was Rómulo Carbía, who later became a well-known historian. See his "El alma nuestra," *Nosotros*, III (November–December, 1908), 269, 271.

movement are made to appear exotic, to have an odor of the gringos,"
complained an editorial in *La Vanguardia.*[91]

Young writers descended from Italian immigrants formulated the
most searching critique of Argentine cultural nationalism. Disturbed
by Rojas' *La restauración nacionalista*, Eduardo Maglione published
an article late in 1909 contending that Argentine national traditions,
which included violence and civic anarchy, were not worth preserving.
Attempts to assimilate the immigrants to the "indolent and ignorant
creole mentality" would only retard progress; the development of nationalism to integrate the immigrant would lead only to chauvinism
and militarism. Maglione concluded that the immigrants threatened
not the Argentine nationality, but the privileges of the "rural bour-
geoisie."[92] Joining Maglione to protest Rojas' book was Roberto F.
Giusti, who had arrived from Italy at the age of seven and had begun
to edit *Nosotros* in 1907. He too pointed out that the Argentine past,
allegedly glorious, was "full of vices." Argentina, believed Giusti,
should forget its past and concentrate on founding a future based on
contributions that the diverse native and immigrant races might make.[93]
The cogent objections writers like Maglione or Giusti raised against the
glorification of the gaucho heritage had little effect, for cultural nationalism dominated Argentine social thought by 1914. In Chile, intellectuals also began to reject cosmopolitanism and to turn toward
nationalism during the decade preceding World War I. This nascent
Chilean nationalism, however, tended to be more economic than cultural. Like their Argentine neighbors, Chileans rehabilitated the image
of the native-born mestizo and degraded that of the immigrant, but
they did not develop a national archetype.

Nicolás Palacios did more than any other author to foster the Chilean

[91] *La Vanguardia*, July 10–11, 1911, p. 1; April 25, 1912, p. 1. Similar comments made by socialist intellectuals are Alfredo L. Palacios, *La evolución
argentina y la patria*, p. 16, and Antonio de Tomaso, in "¿Cuál es el valor de
Martín Fierro?" *Nosotros*, XI (August, 1913), 190.

[92] Eduardo F. Maglione, "Cosmopolitismo y espíritu nacional," *Renacimiento*, II (November, 1909), 320–326.

[93] Roberto F. Giusti, "*La restauración nacionalista* por Ricardo Rojas," *Nosotros*, V (February, 1910), especially 148, 154.

people's esteem for their own "race." This physician-turned-social-essayist had learned to admire the strength and endurance his mestizo countrymen displayed when he served in the War of the Pacific and later when he practiced medicine in the Tarapacá nitrate towns. Unable to tolerate the disdain nineteenth-century Chilean intellectuals heaped upon the mestizo, Palacios in 1904 published *Raza chilena*, a strident defense of the Chilean people.[94] Palacios, who used biological determinism to his own ends, maintained that Chileans were racially superior to other South American peoples and to Latin Europeans as well (see Chapter 4). By celebrating the heritage of the Spanish conquerors and of the Araucanians, Palacios rescued the Chilean mestizo from the disdain he had long suffered and awakened many Chileans to a new pride in their past.[95] The book was immediately successful, and its author died in 1911 one of the nation's most revered intellectuals.[96] Palacios' ideas lived on to influence later generations of Chilean writers. Particularly influential were his racial theories, which Francisco A. Encina incorporated into his highly nationalistic twenty-volume *Historia de Chile*. Published between 1940 and 1952, this monumental work has enjoyed popularity and prestige, particularly among the Chilean upper and middle classes.[97]

While Palacios was rehabilitating the image of the mestizo, another writer, Benjamín Vicuña Subercaseaux, attempted to portray the *roto*, the common laborer of Chile, as a symbolic national hero. The *roto*,

---

[94] For an account of Palacios' career with specific reference to the formulation of his nationalistic social philosophy see the article by his brother Senén Palacios, "El autor de 'Raza Chilena,' Dr. Nicolás Palacios," *Revista Chilena*, III (1918), 54–65. Also see Virgilio Figueroa, *Diccionario histórico, biográfico y bibliográfico de Chile*, IV, 457–458.

[95] Nicolás Palacios, *Raza chilena*, especially pp. 4, 32, 48–52.

[96] Tributes paid to Palacios' work included Guillermo González M., "Don Nicolás Palacios," *Revista de Educación Nacional*, VII (October, 1911), 424–425; Francisco A. Encina, "Don Nicolás Palacios," *Revista Chilena de Historia y Geografía*, I (second quarter, 1911), 305–307.

[97] Charles C. Griffin, "Francisco Encina and Revisionism in Chilean History," *Hispanic American Historical Review*, XXXVII (February, 1957), 7–8; José Vicente Mogollón, "Francisco Antonio Encina: Su personalidad y sus ideas sobre la raza, la economía, y la educación. Escenario: Chile, 1910," *Atenea*, CLV (July–September, 1964), 11.

wrote Vicuña, was "one of the strongest of humans," and the "best sol-
dier in the world."[98] But Chilean intellectuals did not follow Vicuña's
lead in idealizing the *roto*, a figure far from romantic who in real life
was crushed by sickness, alcoholism, and ignorance.

Neither did Chileans emphasize nationalistic education. After many
years of protest that foreigners dominated education in Punta Arenas,
Chilean nationalists forced the government to establish a state secondary school in that city. A brief flutter of controversy appeared in 1913,
when *El Mercurio* charged that German schools in southern Chile
were ignoring national subjects. After a few of these institutions modi-
fied their curricula to conform to those in the state schools, the agitation
subsided.[99]

While Chilean writers did not press for government-sponsored programs of cultural nationalism, they did begin to advocate economic
nationalism to protect Chileans from the impact of foreign businessmen and entrepreneurs. Chilean economic nationalism, mainly an intellectual movement before 1914, urged the government to promote
the welfare of the native-born working classes, to emphasize national
rather than foreign colonization of state lands, and to prevent foreigners from assuming complete control over several key economic activities. Underlying the concern for economic nationalism was a growing
conviction that liberal theory was responsible for the stagnation of the
Chilean economy. Such disillusionment with the prevailing economic
system had not yet appeared among Argentine writers, with the exception of a few isolated figures. In fact, unbounded optimism over the
future of the free-trade, export economy still gripped most Argentine
intellectuals in 1914. Their colleagues in Chile, in sharp contrast, were
urging that the privileges immigrants and foreign capital enjoyed under
the liberal economic system contributed strongly to Chile's poverty.

Economic nationalists in Chile urged the government to end its
support of immigration. Pointing to the large sums of money that the

[98] Benjamín Vicuña Subercaseaux, *Un país nuevo (cartas sobre Chile)*, pp.
104–105.
[99] Alberto Fagalde, *Magallanes: El país del porvenir*, p. 379; *El Mercurio*,
August 27, 1913, p. 3, August 28, 1913, p. 3, September 20, 1913, p. 16.

state spent to bring in a few thousand immigrants each year, some writers argued that these resources should be devoted to improving the productive capacity of the native born.[100] A bellwether of this change of opinion was *El Mercurio*, which in 1910 dropped its enthusiasm for immigration and began to editorialize, "Instead of immigration we ought to prefer the protection and betterment of our own people."[101] Concern for the welfare of the masses became a more common intellectual theme in Chile than in Argentina, where many writers glorified the national race but where few besides Bialet Massé advocated practical reforms to better the living conditions of the native-born working classes. Argentine intellectuals developed cultural nationalism to protect the traditional social hierarchy and to fortify the landowning elite's power, but Chilean nationalists were concerned with a very different problem, that of national economic independence, and they realized that a more productive working class was essential to achieve this goal.

Abandoning the positivist conception that immigration was the most feasible method to improve the "race," Chilean economic nationalists proposed government action to help the national worker develop his productive capacity. The government might begin, Luis Navarrete suggested, by suppressing alcoholism, an action that Navarrete was convinced would benefit the Chilean people far more than immigration.[102] A campaign against excessive drinking was essential, argued the nationalists, for this vice was causing thirty thousand deaths annually and was responsible for reducing national productivity by one-fourth.[103]

In like vein, several Chilean intellectuals became concerned with

---

[100] *La Lei*, September 29, 1907, p. 1, December 5, 1909, p. 1; Jermán Muñoz, "Necesidad de fundar una sociedad que se ocupe de proteger a la raza chilena," *Revista de Educación Nacional*, VI (September–October, 1910), 204–205; "Brazos, inmigración, mortalidad," *Boletín de la Sociedad Nacional de Agricultura*, XLII (December 15, 1911), 739.

[101] *El Mercurio*, June 29, 1910, p. 3; see also editorials of November 30, 1911, p. 3, November 4, 1912, p. 3.

[102] Navarrete, "El alcoholismo, la inmigración i la falta de brazos," *Revista de Educación Nacional*, III (November, 1907), 265–266.

[103] Ibid., pp. 266, 267, 270–271; also speech of Darío Sánchez M., *B.S.S.*, sesiones extraordinarias, November 15, 1906, p. 349.

wiping out illiteracy, calculated at 60 per cent of the national population in 1907. The novelist Fernando Santiván, for example, complained, "We are thinking of harnessing our rivers to irrigate the land and to produce electrical power, but we are not thinking about developing the intellects of our lower classes." He went on to argue that "the most elementary civic spirit" dictated that the government should form industrial schools to train Chilean workers rather than import skilled workers.[104]

An equally great problem was the shocking inadequacy of Chilean public health, for whose betterment some writers urged the government to devote the sums spent on immigration. Pointing out that Chile's birth rate of forty-eight per thousand was among the highest in the world, but that its death rate of thirty-one per thousand contrasted sharply with Argentina's nineteen, economists argued that government investment in sanitation to reduce the death rate would supply all the population Chile required.[105] "It is simply absurd to spend gold to import individuals to populate the nation when in the same country half the population is dying because of the government's negligence," complained El Mercurio.[106]

Besides advocating government concern with alcoholism, education, and public health, Chilean economic nationalists urged the state to colonize its empty southern lands with the native born, not with foreigners. Since the late 1840's Chileans inhabiting the southern provinces had been virtually outcasts in their own land. The government had granted rich lands to thousands of European colonists, but it did not establish colonization programs for Chileans, many of whom were squatting without titles on state lands. To prevent migration of agricultural workers out of the central valley to the south, one law of 1874 excluded all Chilean citizens from colonization projects in the frontier

[104] Fernando Santibáñez (pseud.), El crisol, pp. 49, 50, 93; for similar remarks, see La Lei, December 5, 1909, p. 1, and Pinochet Le-Brun, La conquista de Chile en el siglo XX, pp. 61–62, 66. Literacy statistics may be found in Chile, Oficina Central de Estadística, Censo . . . de 1907, pp. 1304–1305.

[105] "Población," Boletín de la Sociedad Nacional de Agricultura, XLV (August 15, 1914), 455; El Mercurio, October 22, 1910, p. 3.

[106] El Mercurio, November 9, 1912, p. 5.

provinces.[107] Not until 1898 did the state authorize distribution of parcels of southern land to Chileans. But the minister of colonization revealed the administration's real intent when he stated in 1902 that "the national interest in the division of land among the native born is secondary compared with the encouragement of foreign immigration."[108] Of the 6,000 Chileans who applied for land under the 1898 law, only 289 received final title by 1910.[109] Meanwhile, several ministers of colonization concocted grandiose schemes of foreign colonization involving agreements with shady speculators who had little intention of settling the land.

Such favoritism toward the foreigner provoked opposition in both Congress and the press. The Conservative party and the Democratic party, both of which claimed to represent the laboring classes, led the congressional opposition and condemned the government's policy incessantly. During the 1890–1920 period, as Frederick B. Pike points out, "The Conservative party compiled the best record of any political group in introducing social-reform legislation." The party's interest in national colonization reflects the concern for the masses some of its leaders expressed.[110] By 1911 major newspapers, including *La Unión* and *El Mercurio* had turned against further foreign colonization in the south. A more proper policy, said the Edwards newspaper, would offer land to lure back Chileans who had migrated to Argentina.

Responding to Conservative criticism, Congress sent a bicameral investigating committee to the southern provinces in 1913. After several months of study and travel, this group reported that the national interest required the government to favor the native born. While foreigners still should be eligible to receive land, stated the congressmen, they should receive no official encouragement nor any subsidized

[107] Chile, Ministerio de Relaciones Exteriores, Culto y Colonización, *Memoria . . . presentada al Congreso Nacional el 1° de junio de 1910*, p. 446.

[108] Chile, Ministerio de Relaciones Exteriores, Culto y Colonización, *Memoria . . . de 1902*, I, 245.

[109] Chile, Ministerio de Relaciones Exteriores, Culto y Colonización, *Memoria de la Inspección Jeneral de Colonización e Inmigración*, (Santiago, 1910), 5.

[110] Frederick R. Pike, *Chile and the United States, 1880–1960*, p. 115. See also *La Unión*, April 18, 1911, p. 3; *El Mercurio*, July 10, 1911, p. 3.

passage.[111] The committee seemed to agree with Nicolás Palacios, one of whose posthumously published articles asserted that foreign colonization was "the most ruinous and discredited business that the country ever has made."[112] When the congressional report appeared, the government had already abandoned further interest in foreign colonization and instead was encouraging national ownership. The Ministry of Colonization canceled most of the discredited colonization contracts in 1910.[113] During the following three years, the government granted final title to nearly 1,100 native-born farmers who for years had squatted on government land, as well as to 376 individuals who qualified as national colonists. This was a greater number than had received land during the first fourteen years after passage of the 1898 law. In the 1912–1913 period only 12 foreign colonists received clear title.[114] Thus, for the first time since the 1840's, the government's colonization policy officially identified with the interests of the native born.

During the decade preceding World War I, several young Chilean intellectuals were also pleading for government action to prevent an immigrant takeover of industry and commerce. These writers linked immigration to the penetration of foreign capital and rejected them both as exploitative. The immigrant, they contended, had not come to settle permanently, but was usually only the agent of greedy imperialistic interests that sapped the country of most of the profits it produced.[115] Chilean economists were finally openly admitting what English writers had recognized decades before—that immigrant businessmen in Chile often sent huge profits back to Europe. As one

[111] Chile, Congreso, Comisión parlamentaria de colonización, *Informe, proyectos de ley, actas de las sesiones y otras antecedentes*, p. xxvi.

[112] Nicolás Palacios, "Algunos efectos de la colonización estranjera," ibid., p. 391.

[113] Chile, Ministerio de Relaciones Exteriores, Culto y Colonización, *Memoria . . . de 1910*, insert facing p. 444.

[114] Chile, Ministerio de Relaciones Exteriores, Culto y Colonización, *Memoria . . . octubre de 1911–julio de 1914*, p. 370; Chile, Ministerio de Relaciones Exteriores, Culto y Colonización, *Memoria de la Inspección Jeneral de Colonización e Inmigración*, (Santiago, 1913), 22, 41.

[115] Hernán Ramírez Necochea, *Historia del imperialismo en Chile*, pp. 250–252.

Englishman noted in 1891, "If we no longer carry off bars of silver in our warships, . . . we do manage to make, and take, a great deal of money out of the country.[116]

By 1914 a number of Chilean intellectuals had decided that economic nationalism was the only effective defense against foreign encroachment. Julio Saavedra, for example, feared that, lacking policies to protect domestic economic interests, "we will be fatally absorbed and eliminated by the foreigner."[117] Tancredo Pinochet pointed out, "All nations are tending more and more to protect themselves, to fortify their individualities, to become self-sufficient, to create nationally owned industry, and to develop commerce so as to benefit the native born." But Chile, he bitterly observed, "not only abdicates in this struggle, but gives up its arms, its encampment, and its flag."[118] Guillermo Subercaseaux, a young economist and politician, expanded the argument for economic nationalism. Prosperity, he warned, was possible only if the nation would abandon "cosmopolitan economics" by taking ownership of economic activity away from foreigners and restoring it to Chilean citizens.[119] From his congressional seat, he called in 1912 for a comprehensive government program of economic nationalism to restrict the operations of foreign banks, create a national merchant marine, promote national ownership of the nitrate industry, and prohibit sale of Magallanes lands to foreigners.[120]

A strong intellectual reaction against foreign economic control of the Magallanes region was already under way when Subercaseaux spoke. Nationalists were convinced that the almost complete monopoly both of land ownership in Magallanes and of Punta Arenas' commerce damaged Chile's economic progress and possibly threatened Chilean sovereignty over the region. Throughout an extensive editorial campaign in 1912, *El Mercurio* complained that foreigners exploited Ma-

---

[116] "Cosas de Chile—The Gringo," *The Saturday Review of Politics, Literature, and Art*, LXXII (October 3, 1891), 388.

[117] Julio Saavedra, "La educación utilitaria en Chile," *Revista de Educación Nacional*, III (March, 1907), 13.

[118] Pinochet Le-Brun, *La conquista de Chile en el siglo XX*, pp. 61–62, 66.

[119] Guillermo Subercaseaux, "Política nacionalista," *Revista de Educación Nacional*, IX (July, 1913), 269–271.

[120] B.S.C.D., sesiones ordinarias, July 17, 1912, pp. 830-831.

THE ANTIDOTE 165

gallanes "as the white Europeans exploit their Central African colonies." The newspaper meant that foreign businessmen cared little about the region's long-range economic development and sent the wealth they garnered in Magallanes back to Europe.[121]

No aspect of cosmopolitanism in Magallanes troubled Chileans more than the huge landholdings foreigners had acquired in the region. To encourage development of the grazing industry, the government during the 1890's had leased land to foreign individuals or companies, in return for an annual rental. Since the state retained title, Congress approved the lease proposals with little discussion.[122] The newspapers remained silent in 1903 when the government granted ownership of one million hectares of state land to foreign interests. Praising the "energetic, hardworking, and valiant" foreigners, *El Mercurio* argued that they had every right to own the land they had been developing as renters.[123] Ten years later Chilean opinion on the question of Magallanes land ownership had shifted dramatically in favor of nationalism. When the government announced plans to subdivide and sell most of the rest of its lands in the territory, congressmen and journalists loudly protested that most of the purchasers would be foreigners. The net result of the plan, it was held, would be to strengthen foreign dominance over the territory and to accelerate the flow of Magallanes wealth to Europe. The Radical political writer Francisco Rivas Vicuña also pointed out that the plan would dispossess at least fifteen hundred Chilean families who had squatted on the lands. Congress refused to approve the administration's proposal and instead in 1913 enacted a law permitting rental of the lands only to concerns whose stockholders were at least 80 per cent Chilean citizens or foreigners domiciled in the republic.[124] The practical impact of this law was to shift control

[121] *El Mercurio*, October 15, 1912, p. 3; Alberto Fagalde, *Magallanes: El país del porvenir*, p. 377.

[122] Lucas Bonačić-Dorić B., *Historia de los yugoeslavos en Magallanes*, I, 143, 185; Briones Luco, *Glosario de colonización*, pp. 25–26.

[123] *El Mercurio*, January 10, 1903, p. 4; see also ibid., December 19, 1903, p. 4, and Briones Luco, *Glosario de colonización*, p. 62.

[124] *El Mercurio*, October 15, 1912, p. 3, October 16, 1912, p. 3, October 20, 1912, p. 3; Francisco Rivas Vicuña, *Política nacional*, p. 25; B.S.S., sesiones extraordinarias, October 31, 1912, p. 247, January 2, 1913, p. 1103.

over much of Magallanes to the one large Chilean-owned interest in the territory, the Sociedad Explotadora de Tierra del Fuego. A group of Valparaíso capitalists together with the leading Chilean citizens of Punta Arenas had formed this joint-stock corporation during the Balmaceda administration.[125] *El Mercurio* reflected Chile's growing nationalist mood when it loudly applauded the 1913 law as a major step away from foreign dominance over the south.[126]

Three thousand miles north of Magallanes lay the rich nitrate mines of Tarapacá and Antofagasta, over 60 per cent of whose output English mining interests controlled by 1890.[127] The power and wealth that the English possessed in Chile's far north became a focal point of irritation for Chilean nationalists. Since 1889, when President Balmaceda complained that English dominance of the industry damaged the Chilean national interest,[128] economic nationalists had been demanding nationalization of the mines, by which was meant not government expropriation, but increased ownership by Chilean citizens. Balmaceda was soon overthrown in the bloody Civil War of 1891, and the hostility of English mine operators contributed to his fall. But during the 1890's, some Chileans who had opposed Balmaceda because of his attempt to establish presidential supremacy over Congress resumed his policy of working toward national ownership of the nitrate mines. Noting that nearly all the wealth produced in Tarapacá went into foreign pockets, the Conservative newspaper *El Porvenir* urged the government to end the sale of nitrate lots to foreigners. The Radical party's *La Lei* suggested that the state favor Chilean rather than foreign ownership by setting up easy payment schemes for national purchasers of the government's nitrate lands.[129]

But general apathy together with the predominance of individualist

---

[125] Ramón Serrano Montoner, "La chilenización de Magallanes," *Revista Chilena de Historia y Geografía*, LXXVII (May–August, 1935), 21–23.

[126] *El Mercurio*, January 20, 1913, p. 3.

[127] J. R. Brown, "Nitrate Crises, Combinations, and the Chilean Government in the Nitrate Age," *Hispanic American Historical Review*, XLIII (May, 1963), 234.

[128] Julio César Jobet, *Ensayo crítico del desarrollo económico-social de Chile*, p. 86.

[129] *El Porvenir*, April 30, 1893, p. 1; *La Lei*, June 17, 1894, p. 1.

economic theories quashed these suggestions to favor national ownership, and not for another fifteen years did intellectuals become concerned over the issue. Then, in 1908, Nicolás Palacios revived the question when he published an impassioned plea for national ownership entitled *Nacionalización de la industria salitrera.* The following year, Tancredo Pinochet echoed Palacios' arguments, and, in 1913, the Radical party's spokesman, Rivas Vicuña, began to contend that foreign mining capital "is investment that harms us, not helps us." These nationalist writers agreed that the foreigners who owned and operated the nitrate industry had no interest in settling or remaining in Chile and instead wished only to ship the nation's wealth back to Europe.[130] Furthermore, as Benjamín Vicuña Subercaseaux claimed, the English mine operators exploited the unfortunate Chileans who toiled in the mines. "The English have resolved to maintain their profits by treating the peon like a slave."[131] What Vicuña Subercaseaux and other writers who objected to the English presence did not emphasize was the Chilean government's open cooperation with foreign investors in order to discourage workers who protested. "In Tarapacá," one Englishman mentioned, "the local judges drop in periodically at the leading oficinas to receive a little testimonial destined to facilitate any legal action that may have to be taken against recalcitrant workers, squatters, and the like."[132]

Agitation for increased national ownership culminated in 1912 when the government announced an auction of exploitation rights for Tarapacá's Peña Grande nitrate fields. *El Mercurio* called on the government to exclude foreigners from the bidding, holding that the takeover of Chilean commerce and industry must halt. In the Chamber of Deputies, Guillermo Subercaseaux argued passionately in favor of limiting foreign participation.[133] The government compromised and de-

[130] Nicolás Palacios, *Nacionalización de la industria salitrera,* p. 3; Pinochet LeBrun, *La conquista de Chile en el siglo XX,* pp. 121, 123; Francisco Rivas Vicuña, *Política nacional,* pp. 23, 27, 93.

[131] Vicuña Subercaseaux, *Un país nuevo,* p. 246.

[132] "Cosas de Chile—The Gringo," p. 388.

[133] *El Mercurio,* September 4, 1912, p. 3, November 9, 1912, p. 5; *B.S.C.D.,* sesiones ordinarias, August 28, 1912, p. 1659, sesiones extraordinarias, October 17, 1912, p. 29.

creed that foreigners could participate in the auction for approximately one-half the Peña Grande fields.[134] This pre-World War I opposition to foreign ownership of Chilean extractive industry began a nationalist tradition that since has become steadily more vociferous.

Disillusionment with cosmopolitanism and with the achievements of immigration was generally deeper in Chile than in Argentina. While some Argentine writers continued to support cosmopolitanism right up to the eve of World War I, almost the only well-known Chilean intellectual who did not react against the foreigner was Enrique Molina, an educator who was to found the University of Concepción in 1917. Disagreeing with writers like Pinochet and Subercaseaux, Molina argued that cosmopolitan policies always produced economic prosperity. Pointing to the Old World, he noted that the wealthiest areas were the most cosmopolitan, and he claimed the same was true in Chile, where Punta Arenas, Valdivia, and Valparaíso headed the nation both in cosmopolitanism and affluence.[135]

The intellectual reaction against immigration took basically different forms in the two countries. Argentine nationalism during the period ending in 1914 was romantic and nostalgic; it created a symbol derived from the past to represent the values that the Argentine upper class wished to impose upon the immigrant masses. In Chile the immigrants were too few to disrupt the "national character," and no campaign took place to impose national values upon the foreigners. The Chilean reaction against cosmopolitanism, however, differed from Argentina's by challenging the validity of liberal international economics. Chilean intellectuals were becoming increasingly convinced that official acceptance of economic liberalism impoverished the nation by allowing foreigners to dominate ownership of commerce, industry, and mining. By 1914 Chilean nationalists had rejected immigration and were advocating positive state action both to raise the productivity of the native born and to develop a nationally owned economic system to free Chile from the foreigners' grasp.

[134] *El Mercurio*, November 24, 1912, p. 3.
[135] Enrique Molina, *La cultura i la educación jeneral*, pp. 42–43, 47.

Conclusion: The Tragedy of Argentine and Chilean Immigration Policies

>>

THE NATIONALISTIC REACTION against immigration that swept Argentina and Chile early in the twentieth century contrasted sharply with the liberal, cosmopolitan principles long accepted in both countries. Since the mid-nineteenth century, Argentine and Chilean intellectuals had developed elaborate theories to justify immigration, and, by 1890, writers in both countries were praising it with almost mystical fervor. European immigration, according to the cosmopolitan ideology, would not only stimulate rapid economic development, but would foster civilization and political stability, thereby shattering the national cultural heritage, which most writers belittled and which some equated with barbarism.

Although intellectuals in both countries were proclaiming that immigration presented unique opportunities for national development, Argentina and Chile did not tailor their immigration policies with the long-run national interest in mind. In Argentina the ruling elites valued immigration primarily as a source of cheap agricultural labor and failed to enact land distribution policies that would have encouraged immigrant farmers to settle the nation's vast and empty interior.

Many immigrants became discouraged by the lack of opportunity to own land in rural Argentina and eventually migrated to the Buenos Aires metropolitan region, where they joined thousands of other foreigners who had remained in Buenos Aires since their arrival. Partly as a result of the elite's tragically shortsighted land policies, after a quarter century of massive immigration, the Argentine interior remained sparsely populated and the nation's enormous agricultural potential had not developed to its capacity.

Meanwhile, the immigrants who crowded into the Argentine cities set in motion social, economic, and political changes that weakened the monopoly of power the landed elites had held. By about 1910 the Argentine upper class found itself in a dilemma. Immigrants and their descendants were challenging the traditional elite's political and social predominance, but immigration also was essential to the prosperity this elite was enjoying. Ending immigration did not appear feasible; indeed, Argentina placed no important limitation on entry, other than a few restrictions against anarchists, until the Great Depression shattered the international economic system.

Painfully aware of the dilemma it faced, the Argentine elite attempted to use cultural nationalism to justify its continued dominance. The aim of the Argentine nationalism of this era was to teach the immigrant masses to revere essentially aristocratic cultural values, symbolized by the gaucho, which upper-class intellectuals claimed constituted the true Argentine character. The assumption was that the immigrants would eventually accept the hierarchical structure of Argentine society and would abandon such "foreign" ideas as popular democracy, socialism, and anarchosyndicalism. The public school became the vehicle that transmitted traditional creole cultural values to the immigrants and their children.

The campaign to promote cultural nationalism successfully taught patriotism but failed to prevent the shift of social and political power away from the traditional ruling elements toward the middle class and the masses. By the 1930's first-generation immigrant children were fervently identifying with creole culture. The sons of Italians, Spaniards, and Russians enthusiastically studied gauchesque literature, shouted patriotic slogans, and even adopted some old Argentine customs, the drinking of mate, for example. Politicians of all parties were quick to employ gauchesque symbols and myths to appeal to this patriotism, but the political leader most skillful in their use was Juan Perón, whose nationalist-oriented dictatorship (1946–1955) integrated the masses into Argentine political life. Ironically, less than four decades after the Argentine elites attempted to protect their privileged position with nationalistic education and the gauchesque symbol, Perón utilized similar techniques of cultural nationalism as part of his campaign to destroy the landed oligarchy's monopoly of power.

In Chile, immigration policy was as irrational and shortsighted as in Argentina. In sharp contrast with the neighboring republic, Chile possessed relatively little arable land. This land, moreover, already supported a dense population that the government could have trained and educated to supply the manpower needed for economic development. But rather than utilize its own people, the Chilean government subsidized immigration and thereby reduced the opportunities for the native born to rise economically and socially.

Unlike Argentine nationalism, which the ruling elite contrived to serve its own interests, Chilean nationalism expressed the resentment the national middle class held against the government's favoritism of the foreigner. Since immigration in Chile never reached the volume that might threaten the established political and social structure, the Chilean elites generally did not join the middle groups in opposing immigration. But a number of the nation's leading intellectuals, many of middle-class background, sharply attacked Chile's policy of leaving its gates open to foreign immigrants and capitalists. To prevent a foreign economic takeover, these nationalist writers urged the government to protect citizens who entered industry and commerce and to restrict to nationals the development of the republic's principal resources, especially the nitrate mines, the agricultural lands of the frontier region, and the grazing lands in Magallanes Territory. Intellectuals who pleaded for government action to restrict foreign businessmen and to protect national economic interests found little official support before 1914, and the government placed few restrictions on immigration or on the economic activities of foreigners until the 1930's. But the ideas expressed by writers like Palacios and Encina during the first decade of the twentieth century endured to provide the intellectual roots for the vigorous economic nationalism that characterizes the contemporary Chilean outlook.

BIBLIOGRAPHY

A. Unpublished Material

Bagú, Sergio. "Evolución histórica de la estratificación social en la Argentina." Mimeographed. Department of Sociology, University of Buenos Aires, 1961. [Concentrates on the 1890–1914 period. This valuable study contains a great deal of data on Argentine social change and particularly on the development of a mass society.]

Bejarano, Manuel. "La política colonizadora en la provincia de Buenos Aires (1854–1930)." Mimeographed. University of Buenos Aires, 1962.

Beyhaut, G.; Cortes Conde, R.; Gorostegui, H.; and Torrado, S. "Inmigración y desarrollo económico." Mimeographed. Department of Sociology, University of Buenos Aires, 1961.

Castro, Donald. "The Development of Argentine Immigration Policy, 1862–1914." Doctoral dissertation manuscript, University of California, Los Angeles, 1968.

Tigner, James L. "The Okinawans in Latin America." Doctoral dissertation, Stanford University, 1956.

B. Government Documents

Argentina

Argentine Republic. *Segundo censo de la República Argentina: Mayo 10 de 1895.* 3 vols. Buenos Aires, 1898.

―――. *Tercer censo nacional, leventado el 1° de junio de 1914.* 10 vols. Buenos Aires, 1916–1917.

―――. Congreso Nacional. *Debates parlamentarios sobre instrucción pública.* Buenos Aires, 1904.

―――. Congreso Nacional. *Diario de sesiones de la Cámara de Diputados.* Buenos Aires, 1890–1914.

―――. Congreso Nacional. *Diario de sesiones de la Cámara de Senadores.* Buenos Aires, 1890–1914.

―――. Departamento General de Inmigración. *Memoria del Departamento General de Inmigración correspondiente al año 1891.* Buenos Aires, 1892.

―――. Departamento General de Inmigración. *Memoria del Departamento General de Inmigración correspondiente al año 1895.* Buenos Aires, 1896.

————. Ministerio de Agricultura. *Memoria presentada al Honorable Congreso, enero de 1899–octubre de 1900.* Buenos Aires, 1900. [Pages 55 through 218 include the report of the Dirección de Inmigración for 1899.]

————. Ministerio de Agricultura. Dirección de Comercio e Industria. *Censo industrial y comercial de la República Argentina, 1908–1914.* Buenos Aires, 1915.

Buenos Aires (City). *Censo general de población, edificación, comercio e industrias de la Ciudad de Buenos Aires.* 2 vols. Buenos Aires, 1889. [This census was taken in August and September, 1887.]

————. *Censo general de población, edificación, comercio é industrias de la Ciudad de Buenos Aires . . . levantado en . . . octubre de 1909.* 2 vols. Buenos Aires, 1910.

Rosario de Santa Fe. *Tercer censo municipal: Levantado el 26 de abril de 1910.* Rosario, 1910.

Tucumán (City). *Censo de la Capital de Tucumán: 1913.* Buenos Aires, 1914.

Tucumán (Province). *Anuario de estadística de la Provincia de Tucumán correspondiente al año de 1910.* Buenos Aires, 1913.

Chile

Chile. *Boletín de las leyes i decretos del gobierno.* Santiago, 1890–1918.

————. Cámara de Diputados. *Boletín de sesiones.* Santiago, 1890–1914.

————. Comisión Central del Censo. *Censo de la República de Chile levantado el 28 de noviembre de 1907.* Santiago, 1908.

————. Congreso. Comisión Parlamentaria de Colonización. *Informe, proyectos de ley, actas de las sesiones y otras antecedentes.* Santiago, 1912.

————. Ministerio de Relaciones Exteriores, Culto i Colonización. *Memoria . . . presentada al Congreso Nacional en 1894.* Santiago, 1894.

————. Ministerio de Relaciones Exteriores, Culto i Colonización. *Memoria . . . presentada al Congreso Nacional de 1902.* 2 vols. Santiago, 1902.

————. Ministerio de Relaciones Exteriores, Culto y Colonización. *Memoria . . . presentada al Congreso Nacional el 1° de junio de 1910.* Santiago, 1910.

————. Ministerio de Relaciones Exteriores, Culto y Colonización. *Memoria . . . octubre de 1911–julio de 1914.* Santiago, 1917.

————. Ministerio de Relaciones Exteriores, Culto y Colonización. *Memoria de la Inspección Jeneral de Colonización e Inmigración.* Santiago, 1910.

————. Ministerio de Relaciones Exteriores, Culto y Colonización. *Memoria de la Inspección Jeneral de Colonización e Inmigración.* Santiago, 1913.

————. Oficina Central de Estadística. *Anuario estadístico de la República de Chile.* (1914). 10 vols. Santiago, 1915.

————. Oficina Central de Estadística. *Sétimo censo jeneral de la población de Chile; levantado el 28 de noviembre de 1895.* 4 vols. Santiago, 1900–1904.

————. Presidente. *Lei de presupuestos de los gastos jenerales de la administración pública de Chile.* Santiago, 1890–1914.

————. Senado. *Boletín de sesiones.* Santiago, 1890–1914.

C. BOOKS AND ARTICLES

Abad de Santillán, Diego. *La F.O.R.A. Ideología y trayectoria del movimiento obrero revolucionario en la Argentina.* Buenos Aires: Ediciones Nervio, 1933.

————, ed. *Gran enciclopedia argentina.* 8 vols. Buenos Aires: Ediar Soc. Anon. Editores 1956–1963. [Provided biographical information for many Argentines mentioned in this study.]

Abarca, Florentino. *La decadencia de Chile.* Valparaíso: Imprenta L. de la Cruz y Ca., 1904.

Abeille, Luciano. *Idioma nacional de los argentinos.* Paris: E. Bouillon, 1900.

Aguirre Cerda, Pedro. *Estudio sobre instrucción secundaria.* Santiago: Faculty of Legal and Social Sciences, University of Chile, 1904.

Aguirre de Olivera, Hermosina. "La enseñanza de la historia," *El Monitor de la Educación Común,* XXXI (December 31, 1909), 698–709.

Alarcón Pino, Raúl. *"La clase media en Chile": Orígenes, características e influencias.* Santiago: Faculty of Legal and Social Sciences, University of Chile, 1947.

Alberdi, Juan B. *Bases y puntos de partida para la organización política de la República Argentina.* Buenos Aires: "La Cultura Argentina," 1915. [First published 1852.]

Aldunate B., Santiago. "Inmigración i propaganda," *Boletín de la Sociedad de Fomento Fabril,* XXVI (May 1, 1909), 238–239.

"Un alemán en Chile," *Zig Zag,* II (June 24, 1906), 26; (July 8, 1906), 10; (September 2, 1906), n.p.; (September 16, 1906), n.p.

Alsina, Juan A. *La inmigración en el primer siglo de la independencia.* Buenos Aires: F. S. Alsina, 1910.

————. *La inmigración europea en la República Argentina*. Buenos Aires: Impr. Calle México, 1898.

————. *Población, tierras y producción*. Buenos Aires: Impr. Calle México, 1903.

Álvarez, José S. *Cuentos con policias*. Buenos Aires: Sur, 1962. [A compilation of several short stories, originally published 1897–1906.]

————. *En el Mar Austral*. Buenos Aires: Administración General: Vaccaro, 1920. [First published 1898.]

————. *Obras completas*. Edited by F. J. Solero. Buenos Aires: Editorial Schapire, 1954.

Álvarez, Juan. *Ensayo sobre la historia de Santa Fe*. Buenos Aires: Estab. tip. E. Molina, 1910.

————. *Estudio sobre las guerras civiles argentinas*. Buenos Aires: J. Roldán, 1914.

————. *Historia de Rosario, (1689–1939)*. Buenos Aires, 1943.

————. "Observaciones sobre el procedimiento para naturalización de extranjeros," *Revista Argentina de Ciencias Políticas*, V (October, 1912), 51–56.

Álvarez Andrews, Oscar. *Historia del desarrollo industrial de Chile*. Santiago: Imp. y Lit. La Ilustración, 1936.

Álvarez Suárez, Agustín. *Breve historia de la provincia de Mendoza*. Buenos Aires: Talleres de Publicaciones de la Oficina Meterológica Argentina, 1910.

————. *¿Adónde vamos?* Buenos Aires: "La Cultura Argentina," 1915. [First published 1904.]

Antequeda, Manuel P. *Breve exposición sobre las escuelas ruso-alemanas é israelitas; escuelas nacionales (ley Lainez) de la provincia de Entre Ríos*. Buenos Aires, 1909.

Ara, Guillermo. *Leopoldo Lugones*. Buenos Aires: Editorial La Mandrágora, 1958.

Avalos, Baltazar. "La naturalización de los extranjeros," *Revista de Derecho, Historia y Letras*, V (November, 1899), 23–28.

————. "Proyecto italiano de colonización: La nacionalidad de los extranjeros," *Revista de Derecho, Historia y Letras*, IV (October, 1899), 572–578.

Ayarragaray, Lucas. *La anarquía argentina y el caudillismo*. Buenos Aires: J. Lajouane & Cía., 1925. [First published 1904.]

————. *La constitución étnica argentina y sus problemas*. Buenos Aires: J.

Lajouane & Cía., 1910. [Perhaps the most extensive intellectual argument that immigration was needed in order to improve the Argentine race.]

――――. *Socialismo argentino y legislación obrera.* Buenos Aires: J. Lajouane & Cía., 1912.

Bagú, Sergio. "Estratificación social y estructura nacional del conocimiento en la Argentina (1880–1930)," *Revista de la Universidad Nacional de Córdoba,* Second Series, Year III (March–June, 1962), 7–29.

――――. *Estructura social de la colonia.* Buenos Aires: Librería "El Ateneo" Editorial, 1952.

――――. *Julián Martel y el realismo argentino.* Buenos Aires: Revista Comentario, 1956.

――――. *La sociedad de masas en su historia.* Córdoba: República Argentina, Dirección General de Publicidad, 1961.

Baily, Samuel L. *Labor, Nationalism, and Politics in Argentina.* New Brunswick, N.J.: Rutgers University Press, 1967.

de la Barra, Eduardo. *La vida nacional: El embrujamiento alemán.* Santiago, 1899. [De la Barra published this collection of his newspaper articles in order to further his campaign against German teachers in Chile.]

Baur, John E. "The Welsh in Patagonia: An Example of Nationalistic Migration," *Hispanic American Historical Review,* XXXIV (November, 1954), 468–492.

Bavio, Ernesto A. "Las escuelas extranjeras en Entre Ríos," *El Monitor de la Educación Común,* XXVII (November 30, 1908), 597–604; XXVIII (January 31, 1909), 3–44. [These articles precipitated a widespread campaign against Jewish immigrant schools. Such institutions must be closed, argues Bavio, because they impede immigrant assimilation.]

――――. "Instrucciones sobre la semana de Mayo," *El Monitor de la Educación Común,* XXIX (May 31, 1909), 326–335.

Becher, Emilio. *Diálogo de las sombras y otras páginas.* Buenos Aires: Facultad de Filosofía y Letras, Instituto de Literatura Argentina, 1938.

Belín Sarmiento, Augusto. *Una república muerta.* Buenos Aires: Imp. Lit. y Enc. "Mariano Moreno," 1892.

Bellesort, André. *Le jeune Amerique: Chili et Bolivie.* Paris: Perrin et cie., 1897.

Belloni, Alberto. *Del anarquismo al peronismo: Historia del movimiento obrero argentino.* Buenos Aires: A. Peña Lillo, 1960.

Beltrán, Juan G. "La educación primaria en la República Argentina," *El Monitor de la Educación Común,* XXXVII (May 31, 1911), 317–371.

Bezé, Francisco de. *Tarapacá en sus aspectos físico, social y económico.*
Santiago, 1920.
Bialet Massé, Juan. *Informe sobre el estado de las clases obreras en el interior de la república.* 3 vols. Buenos Aires, 1904. [A massive study of
labor conditions in the Argentine interior, done under commission of
the Ministry of the Interior. One of the first important Argentine works
to vindicate the reputation of the creole worker at the immigrants' expense.]
Bonacič-Dorič B., Lucas. *Historia de los yugoeslavos en Magallanes.* 3 vols.
Punta Arenas: Imprenta "La Nacional," 1941–1946.
Branca, Baltazar C. *Al márgen de un problema: Nuestro partido socialista:
Su cosmopolitismo ante la nacionalidad argentina.* Buenos Aires, 1913.
Bray, Donald W. "The Political Emergence of Arab-Chileans, 1952–
1958," *Journal of Inter-American Studies,* IV (October, 1962), 557–
562.
"Brazos, inmigración, mortalidad," *Boletín de la Sociedad Nacional de Agricultura,* XLII (December 15, 1911), 739.
Briones Luco, Ramón. *Glosario de colonización.* Santiago, 1902. [An encyclopedic collection of information on immigration and colonization.]
Brown, J. R. "Nitrate Crises, Combinations, and the Chilean Government
in the Nitrate Age," *Hispanic American Historical Review,* XLIII (May,
1963), 230–246.
Bunge, Alejandro E. "Los desocupados y la distribución de trabajo," *Estudios,* VII (October, 1914), 298–311.
Bunge, Carlos O. "Cuestiones jurídicas: El anarquismo y su terapeútica
social," *Renacimiento,* VII (April, 1911), 304–326.
———. "El derecho en la literatura gauchesca," *Anales de la Academia
de Filosofía y Letras,* II (1914), 3–32.
———. *La educación.* Madrid: D. Jorro, 1902[?]
———. "La enseñanza nacional," *Archivos de Pedagogía y Ciencias Afines,*
IV (September, 1908), 354–373.
———. "La educación patriótica ante la sociología," *El Monitor de la
Educación Común,* XXVII (August 31, 1908), 67–70.
———. "La enseñanza de la tradición y la leyenda," *El Monitor de la Educación Común,* XXXVI (February 28, 1911), 263–281.
———. *Nuestra América.* Barcelona: Henrich y Cía., 1903. [Reflects the
profound pessimism with which Argentine intellectuals viewed the mestizo race while the cosmopolitan ideology dominated.]
"Buscando carta de ciudadanía," *Caras y Caretas.* XI (June 20, 1908), n.p.

Caballero, Ricardo. *Discursos y documentos políticos del Dr. Ricardo Caballero*. Edited by Roberto A. Ortelli. Buenos Aires: Sociedad de Publicaciones El Inca, 1929.

———. *Yrigoyen: La conspiración civil y militar del 4 de febrero de 1905.* Buenos Aires: Editorial Raigal, 1951.

Calzada, Alejandro. "Enseñanza de la crisis," *Revista Argentina de Ciencias Políticas*, VIII (August 12, 1914), 493–500.

Camón Gálvez, Francisco. "Idioma nacional," *Revista de Educación (La Plata)*, LXIV (October–November, 1913), 1047–1052.

del Campo N., Felix. *La inmigración europea en Chile como servicio del estado*. Valparaíso, 1910. [One of the most complete statements of the Chilean cosmopolitan ideology.]

———. "Pro inmigración," *Boletín de la Sociedad de Fomento Fabril*, XVI (May 1, 1904), 187.

Campolieti, Roberto. *La chacra argentina*. Buenos Aires, 1914.

Cané, Miguel. *Discursos y conferencias*. Buenos Aires: Vaccaro, 1919.

———. *Expulsión de extranjeros (apuntes)*. Buenos Aires, 1899.

———. *Notas é impresiones*. Buenos Aires: "La Cultura Argentina," 1918. [First published 1901.]

———. *Prosa ligera*. Buenos Aires: "La Cultura Argentina," 1919. [First published 1903.]

Cantón, Dario. "El parlamento argentino en épocas de cambio: 1889, 1916 y 1946," *Desarrollo Económico*, IV (April–June, 1964), 21–48.

Carbía, Rómulo D. "El alma nuestro," *Nosotros*, III (November–December, 1908), 269–273.

Carbonell, Cayetano. *Orden y trabajo*. 2 vols. Buenos Aires: J. Lajouane & Cía., 1910.

Cárcano, Miguel Ángel. *Sáenz Peña: La revolución por los comicios*. Buenos Aires: Talleres Gráficos CEPEDA, 1963.

Carrasco, Gabriel. *De Buenos Aires al Neuquén*. Buenos Aires, 1902.

Casadevall, Domingo F. *El tema de la mala vida en el teatro nacional*. Buenos Aires: Editorial Guillermo Kraft Limitada, 1957.

Chuaqui, Benedicto. *Memorias de un emigrante*. Second Edition. Santiago: Editorial Nascimento, 1957. [This autobiography of a Syrian immigrant's early days in Chile reveals a great deal about the problems of adjustment immigrants faced and about Chilean prejudice.]

Chueco, Manuel C. *La República Argentina en su primer centenario*. 2 vols. Buenos Aires: Compañía Sud-Americana de Billetes de Banco, 1910.

de Cires, E. "La criminalidad en Buenos Aires," *Revista Argentina de Ciencias Políticas*, IV (July, 1912), 493–503.

———. "La inmigración en Buenos Aires," *Revista Argentina de Ciencias Políticas*, IV (September, 1912), 735–746.

"Colonización e inmigración," *Anales de la Sociedad Rural Argentina*, XLV (November–December, 1910), 139–143.

Comisión de Homenaje. *Lucio Vicente López: En el cincuentenario de su muerte*. Buenos Aires, 1944.

Cordero, Clodomiro. *El problema nacional*. Buenos Aires, 1911.

Cornblit, Oscar E. "European Immigrants in Argentine Industry and Politics," in Claudio Veliz, (ed.), *The Politics of Conformity in Latin America*, pp. 221–248.

Cornblit, Oscar E.; Gallo, Ezequiel (hijo); and O'Connell, Alfredo A. "La generación del 80 y su proyecto: Antecedentes y consecuencias," in Di Tella, *Argentina, sociedad de masas*, pp. 18–58.

Correa Bravo, Agustín. *Los extranjeros ante la ley chilena*. Santiago: Imprenta Cervantes, 1894.

"Cosas de Chile—The Gringo," *The Saturday Review of Politics, Literature, Science, and Art*, LXXII (October 3, 1891), 388.

Crawford, William Rex. *A Century of Latin American Thought*. New York: Frederick A. Praeger, 1966.

"¿Cuál es el valor de *Martín Fierro?*" *Nosotros*, X (June, 1913), 425–433; XI (July, 1913), 74–89; XI (August, 1913), 186–190; XII (October, 1913), 59–74. [Opinions of Argentina's best-known intellectuals about the value of the gauchesque poem *Martín Fierro*. The strong praise most writers give illustrates the predominance of cultural nationalism in the Argentine intellectual climate by 1913.]

Daireaux, Godofredo. *Las cien hectáreas de Pedro Villegas*. Buenos Aires: Ediciones Argo, 1945. [First published 1914.]

———. *Las dos patrias*. Buenos Aires: Imp. de "La Nación," 1908 [First published 1906.]

Díaz, Raúl B. *La educación en los territorios y colonias federales. Propaganda. Educación y viajes*. Buenos Aires, 1907.

Díaz Garcés, Joaquín. *Páginas chilenas*. Third Edition. Santiago: Zig Zag, 1947. [First published 1908.]

Díaz Lira, Javier. *Observaciones sobre la cuestión social en Chile*. Santiago: Faculty of Legal and Social Sciences, University of Chile, 1904.

Dickmann, Enrique. "Inmigración y latifundio," *Revista Argentina de Ciencias Políticas*, X (May, 1915), 160–178. [Oligarchic control of

Argentina's best land has prevented the rise of an immigrant farmer class and has encouraged the growth of a huge foreign-born urban proletariat.]

―――. *Recuerdos de un militante socialista.* Buenos Aires: Editorial La Vanguardia, 1949.

Di Tella, Torcuato S.; Germani, Gino; Graciarena, Jorge; et al., eds. *Argentina, sociedad de masas.* Buenos Aires: Editorial Universitaria de Buenos Aires, 1965. [A key work for study of social change and economic development in Argentina since 1880. Several essays important to this monograph are entered separately in the Bibliography.]

Donoso, Ricardo. *Alessandri: Agitador y demoledor.* 2 vols. Mexico: Fondo de Cultura Económica, 1952.

Edwards Bello, Joaquín. *El inútil.* Santiago: Soc. Imprenta y Litografía "Universo," 1910.

Edwards Vivas, Alberto. *La fronda aristocrática.* Fifth Edition. Santiago: Editorial del Pacífico, 1959.

E. M. "Vendedores ambulantes," *Pacífico Magazine,* II (November, 1913), 668.

Encina, Francisco A. *Nuestra inferioridad económica.* Santiago: Editorial Universitaria, 1956. [First published 1911. One of the most influential Chilean books of its time, this work warned that continued cosmopolitanism and immigration might cost Chile its economic and political independence. Practical and utilitarian education is Encina's answer.]

―――. "Don Nicolás Palacios," *Revista Chilena de Historia y Geografía,* I (Second Quarter, 1911), 305–312.

―――. *La educación económica y el liceo.* Santiago: Imprenta Universitaria, 1912.

"En Pillanlelbum," *Zig Zag,* I (September 3, 1905), 39.

"La enseñanza del idioma nacional," *El Monitor de la Educación Común,* XIV (September 30, 1896), 817–818.

"La escasez de brazos," *Boletín de la Sociedad Nacional de Agricultura,* XLIII (June 15, 1912), 333–334.

Escobar, Saúl M. *Inmigración.* Buenos Aires: Faculty of Law, University of Buenos Aires, 1907.

―――. "Orientación patriótica de la educación primaria," *El Monitor de la Educación Común,* XXXIV (September 30, 1910), 488–542.

"La escuela en el centenario," *El Monitor de la Educación Común,* XXXIII (June 30, 1910), 1040–1494.

"Las escuelas israelitas en Entre Ríos," *Caras y Caretas*, XI (December 5, 1908), n.p.

Espejo, Anjel C. *El partido radical, sus obras y sus hombres.* Santiago, 1911.

"Exportación e inmigración," *Anales de la Sociedad Rural Argentina*, XXX (January 31, 1896), 148–150.

Eyzaguirre, Jaime. *Chile durante el gobierno de Errázuriz Echaurren, 1896–1901.* Second Edition. Santiago: Empresa Editora Zig-Zag, 1957.

————. *Fisonomía histórica de Chile.* Third Edition. Santiago: Editorial del Pacífico, 1965.

Ezcurra, Pedro, "Inmigración," *Revista de Derecho, Historia y Letras*, XLIV (April, 1913), 575–606.

Fagalde, Alberto. *Magallanes: El país del porvenir.* Valparaíso: Talleres Tipográficos de la Armada, 1901.

Fantozzi, M. "La 'colonia' italiana en la Argentina, conversación con el Comendador Cittadini," *Revista de Derecho, Historia y Letras*, XXIV (June, 1906), 561–567.

Feliú Cruz, Guillermo. *Chile visto a través de Agustín Ross.* Santiago: Imp. Encuadernación "Pino," 1950.

Ferrarotti, Juan Luis. "Algunas reflexiones sobre la defensa social: La ley 7029," *Renacimiento*, VII (April, 1911), 230–260.

Figueroa, Virgilio. *Diccionario histórico, biográfico y bibliográfico de Chile.* 5 vols. Santiago: Establecimientos Gráficos "Balcells & Cía," 1925–1931. [A source of biographical information for most Chileans in the present study.]

Fliess, Alois E. *La producción agrícola y ganadera de la República Argentina en el año 1891.* Buenos Aires: Impr. de "La Nación," 1892.

Foerster, Robert F. *The Italian Emigration of Our Times.* Cambridge, Mass.: Harvard University Press, 1924.

Fontanella, Agustín. *El secreto de la virgen.* First performed 1903. In *Bambalinas*, No. 48 (March 8, 1919).

Funes, Silvano. *Inmigración y colonización.* Córdoba: Faculty of Law, University of Córdoba, 1902.

Galdames, Luis. *Educación económica e intelectual.* Santiago: Imprenta Universitaria, 1912. [Another appeal for practical education to prevent foreigners from driving Chileans out of middle-class clerical and office positions.]

————. "El espíritu de la enseñanza commercial," *Revista de Educación Nacional*, VIII (June, 1912), 185–198.

————. *A History of Chile.* Translated by Isaac Joslin Cox. Chapel Hill, N.C.: University of North Carolina Press, 1941.

————. *Temas pedagójicos.* Santiago, 1913.

————. *Valentín Letelier y su obra, 1852–1919.* Santiago: Imprenta Universitaria, 1937. [An encyclopedic compilation of Letelier's thought, this work also is a useful contribution to Chilean intellectual history.]

Galletti, Alfredo. *La política y los partidos.* Buenos Aires: Fondo de Cultura Económica, 1961.

Gallo, Ezequiel (hijo). "Santa Fe en la segunda mitad del siglo XIX. Transformaciones en su estructura regional," in Rosario, Universidad Nacional del Litoral, Facultad de Filosofía y Letras, *Anuario del Instituto de Investigaciones Históricas,* VII (1964), 127–161.

———— and Sigal, Silvia. "La formación de los partidos políticos contemporáneos: La U.C.R. (1890–1916)," in Di Tella, *Argentina, sociedad de masas,* pp. 124–176. [Presents important data on relationships between immigration and the rise of mass political parties in Argentina.]

Gálvez, Manuel. *El diario de Gabriel Quiroga: Opiniones sobre la vida argentina.* Buenos Aires: Arnoldo Moen & Hno., 1910. [A blistering attack on cosmopolitanism. Cultural nationalism is necessary to save Argentina from the alien values immigrants are introducing.]

————. *El solar de la raza.* Buenos Aires: "Nosotros," 1913.

————. "Los himnos de la nueva energía," *El Monitor de la Educación Común,* XXXIX (October 31, 1911), 69–73.

García, Belisario. "Chile como país colonizador," *La Revista de Chile,* III (November 15, 1899), 306–309; (December 1, 1899), 340–344; (December 15, 1899), 369–376. [An extensive statement of the pro-immigration ideology, revealing the great faith liberals placed on immigration as a force for change and progress.]

García Ledesma, H. *Lisandro de la Torre y la pampa gringa.* Buenos Aires: Editorial Indoamerica, 1954.

Gautier, Ferdinand. *Chile et Bolivie.* Paris: E. Guilmoto, 1906.

Gerchunoff, Alberto. *Los gauchos judíos.* Fourth Edition. Buenos Aires: Editorial Sudamericana, 1950. [First published 1910. With deep emotion, Gerchunoff argues that the Jewish agricultural colonists were good Argentines, who were assimilating into national life while retaining their religious heritage.]

Germani, Gino. "Las repercusiones de la inmigración en la estructura social de los paises. El ejemplo de un país sudamericano." *Inmigración,* No. 7 (1963), pp. 22–30.

————. "La movilidad social en la Argentina," in Lipset and Bendix, *Movilidad social*, pp. 317–365. [Included as an appendix to the Spanish translation of a North American work, Germani's study is fundamental to understanding the relationships among immigration, social mobility, and class structure in Argentina.]

————. *Política y sociedad en una época de transición*. Buenos Aires: Editorial Paidos, 1962. [Contains much information on the social and economic impacts of immigration.]

Gil, Federico G. *The Political System of Chile*. Boston: Houghton Mifflin Co., 1966.

Giusti, Roberto F. "*La restauración nacionalista* por Ricardo Rojas," *Nosotros*, V (February, 1910), 139–154. [An attack on cultural nationalism. Domestic values ought to replace the reactionary traditions inherited from the Argentine past.]

Glauert, Earl T. "Ricardo Rojas and the Emergence of Argentine Cultural Nationalism," *Hispanic American Historical Review*, XLIII (February, 1963), 1–13.

Glazer, Nathan and Moynihan, Daniel Patrick. *Beyond the Melting Pot*. Cambridge, Mass.: M.I.T. Press, 1963.

Gómez, Eusebio. *Criminología argentina*. Buenos Aires: M. A. Rosas y Cía., 1912.

————. "La mala vida en Buenos Aires," *Archivos de Psiquiatría y Criminología Aplicados a las Ciencias Afines*, VI (1907), 431–442.

————. *La mala vida en Buenos Aires*. Buenos Aires, 1908. [One of Argentina's most respected criminologists argues that immigration is a principal cause of Buenos Aires' crime.]

Gómez García, Agustín. *Viaje de un chileno a Magallanes en 1914*. Santiago: Imprenta Universitaria, 1914.

González, Joaquín V. *La Argentina y sus amigos: Discursos sobre política internacional, 1906–1910*. In González, *Obras completas*, IX, 171–455.

————. *El juicio del siglo ó cien años de historia argentina*. Buenos Aires: Libreria "La Facultad" de Juan Roldán, 1913.

————. *Obras completas*. 25 vols. Buenos Aires: Imprenta Mercateli, 1935–1937.

González, Pedro Luis. "La inmigración," *Boletín de la Sociedad de Fomento Fabril*, XX (September 1, 1903), 315.

González Castillo, José. *El grillete*. First performed 1914. In *La Escena*, II (March 20, 1919).

González M., Guillermo. "Don Nicolás Palacios," *Revista de Educación Nacional*, VII (October, 1911), 424–426.

Gori, Gaston. *El pan nuestro.* Buenos Aires: Ediciones Galatea, 1958.

Gotschlich, Bernardo. "Reseña de la colonización de las provincias australes," *Boletín de la Sociedad de Fomento Fabril*, XVIII (November 1, 1901), 404–405.

Grandmontagne, Francisco. *Teodoro Foronda.* 2 vols. Buenos Aires: Tipografía La Vasconia, 1896.

Greve, Ernesto. *Historia de la ingeniería en Chile.* 4 vols. Santiago: Imprenta Universitaria, 1938–1944.

Griffin, Charles C. "Francisco Encina and Revisionism in Chilean History," *Hispanic American Historical Review*, XXXVII (February, 1957), 1–27.

Guana, D. "Enseñanza del castellano," *El Monitor de la Educación Común*, XXXI (October 31, 1909), 164–175.

Gudiño Kramer, Luis. "Colonización judía en el litoral," *Davar.* No. 14 (November, 1947), 5–28.

Guelfi, Cesarina Lupati. *Vida argentina.* Translated by Augusto Riera. Barcelona: Casa Editorial Maucci, 1910.

Guglieri, Pablo. *Las memorias de un hombre del campo.* Buenos Aires, 1913.

Güiraldes, Carlos (hijo). "La cuestión de la ciudadanía," *Anales de la Facultad de Derecho y Ciencias Sociales*, III (Second part, Second series), 211–263.

Halperin Donghi, Tulio. *Historia de la Universidad de Buenos Aires.* Buenos Aires: Editorial Universitaria de Buenos Aires, 1962.

Hayes, Carleton J. H. *A Generation of Materialism.* New York: Harper & Brothers, 1941.

Hoerll, Alberto. "La colonización alemana en Chile," in Hoerll, *Los alemanes*, pp. 1–62.

———. ed. *Los alemanes en Chile.* Santiago, 1910.

Hoyo, Enrique. "Espíritu partriótico en la escuela," *Revista de Educación (La Plata)*, LXIV (October–November, 1913), 1027–1030.

Huret, Jules. *La Argentina de Buenos Aires al Gran Chaco.* Translated by E. Gómez Carrillo. 2 vols. Paris: Eugène Fasquelle, 1910[?] [An extremely perceptive French traveler narrates his Argentine tour, commenting with insight on creole-immigrant relationships.]

Imaz, José Luis de. *La clase alta de Buenos Aires.* Buenos Aires: Universidad de Buenos Aires, 1962.

————. *Los que mandan.* Second Edition. Buenos Aires: Editorial Universitaria de Buenos Aires, 1965. [A study of the groups which direct Argentine society, with much valuable data on their immigrant backgrounds.]

Ingenieros, José. *Socialismo y legislación del trabajo.* Paris: Eduard Cornely, 1906[?]

————. *Sociología argentina.* Madrid: D. Jorro, 1913. [Points out that immigration has formed a new urban middle class which is contesting the old landed elites for power.]

"La inmigración," *Boletín de la Sociedad Nacional de Agricultura,* XXXVII (November 15, 1906), 768–769.

"Inmigración," *Boletín de la Unión Industrial Argentina,* XXVI (April 15, 1912), 4–6.

"Inmigración: Importante proyecto con este fin," *Revista Económica,* Third epoch, I (August 10, 1899), 211–214.

"Inmigración libre," *Boletín de la Sociedad de Fomento Fabril,* XVII (December 1, 1900), 362.

"Inmigración peligrosa," *Caras y Caretas,* XII (June 12, 1909), n.p.

"Inmigración y emigración," *Boletín de la Unión Industrial Argentina,* VII (June 1, 1895), 19–20.

"La inmigración y la industria," *Boletín de la Unión Industrial Argentina.* III (March 27, 1890), 1.

Irigoin, Helena. "Enseñanza patriótica," *El Monitor de la Educación Común,*" XXXII (March 31, 1910), 847–856.

"Los italianos en Buenos Aires," *Caras y Caretas,* II (September 23, 1899), n.p.

Jefferson, Mark. *Peopling the Argentine Pampa.* New York: American Geographical Society, 1926.

————. *Recent Colonization in Chile.* New York: Oxford University Press, 1921.

Jobet, Julio César. *Ensayo crítico del desarrollo económico-social de Chile.* Santiago: Editorial Universitaria, 1955. [This scholarly work by a distinguished socialist intellectual pays particular attention to foreign economic penetration.]

————. *Luis Emilio Recabarren: Los orígenes del movimiento obrero y del socialismo chilenos.* Santiago: Prensa Latinoamericana, 1955.

————. "Notas sobre tres sociólogos nacionales," *Atenea,* LXXXIX (March, 1948), 235–250. [Points out some of the basic ideas of Letelier, Palacios, and Encina.]

————. *Precursores del pensamiento social de Chile.* 2 vols. Santiago: Editorial Universitaria, 1955–1956.

Johnson, John J. *Political Change in Latin America: The Emergence of the Middle Sectors.* Stanford: Stanford University Press, 1958.

"La jura de la bandera por las escuelas de los consejos escolares de la capital," *El Monitor de la Educación Común,* XXX (July 31, 1909), 102–173.

Kaempffer Villagrán, Guillermo. *Así sucedió: Sangrientos episodios de la lucha obrera en Chile.* Santiago, 1962.

Labarca H., Amanda. *Historia de la enseñanza en Chile.* Santiago: Imprenta Universitaria, 1939.

Lagos, Bismark. "Escuelas particulares: La orientación de su enseñanza," *El Monitor de la Educación Común,* XXXI (November 30, 1909), 313–332.

Lahitte, Emilio. "Correspondencia sobre nuestra inmigración," *Anales de la Sociedad Rural Argentina,* XXVIII (January 31, 1894), 46–48.

————. "La verdad sobre 'El mal de latifundio,' el gran problema de la población rural," *Anales de la Sociedad Rural Argentina,* XXIX (1905), 88–104.

Lancelotti, Miguel A. *La criminalidad en Buenos Aires.* Buenos Aires, 1914.

————. "La herencia en la criminalidad," *Revista Nacional,* XXV (May, 1898), 326–333; (June, 1898), 395–402, XXVI (August, 1898), 156–159; (September, 1898), 233–236; (October, 1898), 300–304; (November, 1898), 369–375.

Larra, Raúl. *Lisandro de la Torre.* Fourth Edition. Buenos Aires: Editorial Futuro, 1950.

————. *Payró: El novelista de la democracia.* Buenos Aires: Editorial Quetzal, 1952.

Larreta, Enrique. *Discursos.* Buenos Aires: Talleres Gráficos Argentinos, 1939.

Latzina, Francisco. *Diccionario geográfico argentino.* Second Edition. Buenos Aires: Compañía Sud-Americana de Billetes de Banco, 1892.

Leguina, Ezequiel. "A propósito de la naturalización de extranjeros," *Renacimiento,* I (June, 1909), 55–69.

Leiserson, Alcira. *Notes on the Process of Industrialization in Argentina, Chile, and Peru.* Berkeley: University of California Institute of International Studies, 1966.

Letelier, Valentín. *La lucha por la cultura.* Santiago: Impr. i Encuadernación

Barcelona, 1895. [Chilean cultural progress depends on close contact with Europe, and particularly with German teachers.]

Levillier, Roberto. "La delincuencia en Buenos Aires," in Buenos Aires (City), *Censo general . . . de 1909*, III, 393–420.

Lillo, Baldomero. *Sub terra*. Twelfth Edition. Santiago: Editorial Nascimento, 1963. [First published 1904. Starkly realistic short stories about life around the coal mines of Lota and Coronel. "El grisu," (pp. 23–45) strongly condemns foreign mine bosses.]

Lipset, Seymour Martin and Bendix, Reinhard. *Movilidad social en la sociedad industrial*. Buenos Aires: Editorial Universitaria de Buenos Aires, 1963.

———— and Solari, Aldo, eds. *Elites in Latin America*. New York: Oxford University Press, 1967.

López, Heriberto. "El germanismo en Chile," *Revista Nacional* (Buenos Aires), XXIX (April, 1899), 346–354; (May, 1899), 440–447; XXX (August, 1899), 121–127.

López, Lucio V. "Discurso pronunciado por el Dr. Lucio V. López en la colación de grados de la Facultad de Derecho el 24 de mayo de 1890." In Comisión de homenaje, ed., *Lucio Vicente López*, pp. 25–32.

————. *La gran aldea*. Buenos Aires: Editorial Universitaria de Buenos Aires, 1960. [First published 1884.]

"Los que vienen a ilustrarnos: ó los sabios golondrinos," *Caras y Caretas*, XV (June 22, 1912), n.p.

Lugones, Leopoldo. "A campo y cielo," *Nosotros*, VII (May, 1913), 225–235.

————. "Ciencia y moral práctica," *El Monitor de la Educación Común*, XLII (September 30, 1912), 185–189.

————. *Obras poéticas completas*. Madrid: M. Aguilar, 1948.

————. *Odas seculares*. In Lugones, *Obras poéticas completas*, pp. 427–484. [First published 1910. Particularly important for this study was the poem "A los ganados y las mieses," in which Lugones celebrates Argentine agricultural prosperity and the immigrants' labor that helped make it possible.]

————. *El payador*. Buenos Aires: Ediciones Centurion, 1961. [First published 1916. Amplified version of a lecture series delivered in 1913. Thoroughly rehabilitates the gaucho and the *Martín Fierro* legend, and claims that Argentina's national character derives from the gaucho.]

————. *La reforma educacional*. Buenos Aires, 1903.

McBride, George M. *Chile: Land and Society*. New York: American Geographical Society, 1936. [A brilliant study of the Chilean land system and of the rural oligarchy.]

McGann, Thomas F. *Argentina, Estados Unidos y el sistema interamericano, 1880–1914.* Translated by Germán O. Tjarks. Buenos Aires: Editorial Universitaria de Buenos Aires, 1960. [The first five chapters brilliantly characterize the generation that ruled Argentina between 1880 and 1914.]

Maglione, Eduardo F. "Cosmopolitismo y espíritu nacional," *Renacimiento,* II (October, 1909), 191–196; (November, 1909), 320–329. [An important article attacking cultural nationalism. Claims that nationalists oppose cosmopolitanism because immigrants are threatening the power monopoly of the landed oligarchy.]

Malbrán, M. E. "Los italianos en la República Argentina," *Revista de Derecho, Historia y Letras,* V (January, 1900), 406–412.

Mamalakis, Markos and Reynolds, Clark Winston. *Essays on the Chilean Economy.* Homewood, Ill.: R. D. Irwin, 1965.

"Manifestaciones de duelo en Buenos Aires," *Caras y Caretas,* III (September 20, 1900), n.p.

Mansfield, Robert E. *Progressive Chile.* New York: Neale Publishing Co., 1913.

Mansilla, Lucio V. *Mis memorias: Infancia-adolescencia.* Buenos Aires: Librería Hachette, 1955. [First published 1904.]

———. *Un país sin ciudadanos.* Paris, 1907. [Mansilla is divided on the issue of immigration; he truly wants population, but he fears that the ever-growing masses of unnaturalized foreigners may ruin the nation.]

Marie-Anne (pseud.). "Buenos Aires social," *Revista de Derecho, Historia y Letras,* XXXIV (September, 1909), 5–7.

Marín Vicuña, Santiago. *Al través de la Patagonia.* Santiago, 1901.

———. *Nuestros ingenieros.* Santiago: Editorial Nascimento, 1935.

Marotta, Sebastián. *El movimiento sindical argentino: Su génesis y desarrollo.* 4 vols. Buenos Aires, 1960–1963. [The first two volumes, which cover the 1857–1920 period, are an excellent source of factual information on the growth of the Argentine working-class movement.]

Martínez, Albert B. and Lewandowski, Maurice. *The Argentine in the Twentieth Century.* Translated by Bernard Miall. London: T. F. Unwin, 1911. [This survey of Argentine life provides a good example of the cosmopolitan ideology. Very optimistic about the impact of immigration.]

Martínez Cuitiño, Vicente. *Los Colombinos.* First performed 1912. In Martínez Cuitiño, *Teatro*, III, 111–197. [An entertaining comparison of the different achievement motives that Argentine creoles and Italian immigrants held.]

———. *Teatro*. 3 vols. Buenos Aires: M. Gleizer, 1923.

Mattar, Ahmad H., ed. *Guía social de la colonia árabe en Chile (Siria-Palestina-Libanesa)*. Santiago: Impr. "Ahues Hnos" 1941.

Melgar, Ramón. *La nacionalización de la instrucción primaria*. Buenos Aires, 1911.

Miró, José (pseud. Julián Martel). *La Bolsa*. Buenos Aires: Editorial Guillermo Kraft Limitada, 1959. [First published 1890. This novel reveals bitter hostility against immigrant businessmen, particularly Jews.]

Mogollón, José Vicente. "Francisco Antonio Encina: Su personalidad y sus ideas sobre la raza, la economía y la educación. Escenario: Chile, 1910," *Atenea*, CLV (July–September, 1964), 3–21.

Molina, Enrique. *La cultura i la educación jeneral*. Santiago, 1912.

"El monumento sirio-otomano," *Zig Zag*, VIII (September 28, 1912), 45.

Morante, Pedro G. *Grandezas*. Buenos Aires, 1897.

Mörner, Magnus. *Race Mixture in the History of Latin America*. Boston: Little, Brown and Co., 1967.

Moya Figueroa, Luis. *Estudio comparativo de la lei de municipalidades de 22 de diciembre de 1891*. Santiago: Faculty of Legal and Social Sciences, University of Chile, 1901.

Moyano Gacitúa, Cornelio. *La delincuencia argentina ante algunas cifras y teorías*. Córdoba: F. Domenici, 1905.

———. "La delincuencia argentina ante algunas cifras y teorías," *Archivos de Psiquiatría y Criminolgía Aplicados a las Ciencias Afines*, IV (1905), 162–181.

Muñoz, Jermán. "Necesidad de fundar una sociedad que se ocupe de protejer a la raza chilena," *Revista de Educación Nacional*, VI (September–October, 1910), 201–206.

Napolitano, Emma. "Francisco A. Sicardi," *Instituto de Literatura Argentina: Sección de Crítica*, II, No. 6 (1942), 375–528.

Navarrete, Luis. "El alcoholismo, la inmigración i la falta de brazos," *Revista de Educación Nacional*, III (November, 1907), 263–271. [This strong appeal for the protection of the Chilean race rather than the encouragement of immigration typifies the thinking of Chilean nationalists around 1910.]

Nichols, Madeline W. *The Gaucho: Cattle Hunter, Cavalryman, Ideal of Romance*. Durham, N.C.: Duke University Press, 1942.

Novión, Alberto. *La cantina.* First performed 1908. In *Revista Teatral*, No. 29 (1920).

Ocantos, Carlos María. *El peligro.* Buenos Aires: Imp. de "La Nación," 1916. [First published 1911.]

———. *Promisión.* Buenos Aires: Imp. de "La Nación," 1914. [First published 1897.]

Oddone, Jacinto. *Historia del socialismo argentino.* 2 vols. Buenos Aires: Talleres Gráficos "La Vanguardia," 1934.

Ojeda, Honorio. *Detalles completos de los sucesos de Osorno, 10 de noviembre de 1894.* Valparaíso, 1895.

"Operarios estranjeros para los ferrocarriles del estado," *Boletín de la Sociedad de Fomento Fabril*, XIX (May 1, 1902), 182.

Orrego Luco, Luis. *Casa grande.* Santiago: Zig Zag, 1953. [First published 1908. A valuable portrait of contemporary upper-class society by one of Chile's greatest novelists.]

Pacheco, Carlos M. *Los equilibristas.* First performed 1912. In *Argentores*, III (June 11, 1936). [Humorously portrays creole hostility against rapid immigrant economic rise.]

———. *Los fuertes.* First performed 1906[?] In *Bambalinas*, No. 200 (1922).

Palacios, Alfredo L. *La evolución argentina y la patria.* Buenos Aires, 1910.

Palacios, Nicolás. "Algunos efectos de la colonización extranjera," in *Informe*, Chile: Comisión parlamentaria, pp. 383–395.

———. *Nacionalización de la industria salitrera.* Santiago, 1908. [The national middle class suffers because foreigners dominate industry, commerce, and mining.]

———. *Raza chilena.* Valparaíso: Impr. de G. Schäfer, 1904. [One of the most influential books ever published in Chile. Besides strongly attacking immigrants and the cosmopolitan spirit, this work marked the first intellectual attempt to rehabilitate the image of the Chilean mestizo.]

Palacios, Senén. "El autor de 'Raza chilena,' Dr. Nicolás Palacios," *Revista chilena*, II (1917), 535–540; III (1918), 47–69.

———. *Hogar chileno.* Santiago: Imp. de Lathrop Hnos., 1910.

Paleró Escamilla, Adolfo. "'Modificaciones al idioma," *Caras y Caretas*, III (May 12, 1900), n.p.

Panettieri, José. *Los trabajadores en tiempos de la inmigración masiva en la Argentina (1870–1910).* La Plata: Universidad Nacional de La Plata, 1966.

Patroni, Adrián. *Los trabajadores en la Argentina.* Buenos Aires, 1898.

Payró, Roberto J. *La Australia argentina.* Buenos Aires: Imp. de "La Nación," 1898.

———. *El casamiento de Laucha.* Fourth Edition. Buenos Aires: Librerías Anaconda, 1933. [First published 1906.]

———. *Crónicas.* Buenos Aires: M. Rodríguez Giles, 1909.

———. *En las tierras de Inti.* Buenos Aires: Editorial Universitaria de Buenos Aires, 1960. [First published 1909.]

———. *Los italianos en la Argentina.* Buenos Aires, 1895.

———. *Marco Severi.* First performed 1905. In Payró, *Teatro completo,* pp. 131–187. [A strong protest against the anti-immigrant Residence Law of 1902.]

———. *Teatro completo.* Edited by Roberto F. Giusti. Buenos Aires: Librería Hachette, 1956.

"Un pedagogo alemán," *Zig Zag,* I (June 11, 1905), 22.

Peralta, Alejandro N. "El pueblo quiere principios," *Revista Argentina de Ciencias Políticas,* VI (May 12, 1913), 133–149.

Pérez Rosales, Vicente. *Recuerdos del pasado.* Santiago: Impr. Gutenberg, 1886.

Pico, Pedro. *Así empieza una historia.* First performed 1914. In *El teatro Nacional,* No. 35 (1914).

———. *Ganarse la vida.* First performed 1907. In *Bambalinas,* No. 183 (October 8, 1921).

Pike, Frederick B. *Chile and the United States, 1880–1960.* Notre Dame: University of Notre Dame Press, 1963.

Piñero, Norberto. "Nacionalismo y raza," *Revista Argentina de Ciencias Políticas,* IV (June, 1912), 261–264.

Pinochet Le-Brun, Tancredo. *La conquista de Chile en el siglo XX.* Santiago: Imp., Litografía y Encuadernación "La Ilustración," 1909. [A bitter attack on the immigrant and on other foreign influences in Chile as well as a call for nationalism.]

———. *La obra.* Santiago: Imprenta "La Ilustración," 1911.

Platt, D. C. M. "British Agricultural Colonization in Latin America," *Inter-American Economic Affairs,* XIX (Summer, 1961), 23–42.

"Población," *Boletín de la Sociedad Nacional de Agricultura,* XLV (August 15, 1914) 455.

Prieto, Adolfo. *La literatura autobiográfica argentina.* Santa Fe: Universidad Nacional del Litoral, Facultad de Filosofía y Letras, n.d.

"El problema de la inmigración," *Boletín de la Sociedad Nacional de Minería,* Third Series (October–November, 1906), 364–368.

Quesada, Ernesto. *El 'criollismo' en la literatura argentina.* Buenos Aires: Coni Hermanos, 1902.

———. *El problema del idioma nacional.* Buenos Aires: Revista Nacional, 1900.

Rahola, Federico. *Sangre nueva: Impresiones de un viaje a la América del Sud.* Barcelona: Tipografía "La Académica," 1905.

Ramírez Necochea, Hernán. *Balmaceda y la contrarrevolución de 1891.* Santiago: Editorial Universitaria, 1958. [Marxist oriented, this study is especially valuable for identification of interest groups prominent in the 1891 Civil War.]

———. *Historia del imperialismo en Chile.* Santiago: Colección Realidad Americana, 1960.

———. *Historia del movimiento obrero en Chile: Siglo XIX.* Santiago: Austral, 1956.

Ramos, Juan Abelardo. *Revolución y contrarrevolución en la Argentina.* 2 vols. Buenos Aires: Ediciones Plus Ultra, 1965.

Ramos, Juan P. *Historia de la instrucción primaria en la República Argentina, 1810–1910.* 2 vols. Buenos Aires: J. Peuser, 1910.

Ramos Mejía, José M. *Las multitudes argentinas.* Buenos Aires: Talleres Gráficos Argentinas, 1934. [First published 1899. Bitter denunciation of middle-class immigrants.]

———. *Los simuladores del talento en las luchas por la personalidad y la vida.* Buenos Aires, 1904. [Chapter 5 of this volume of psychological theory is a strong condemnation of immigrants, particularly Jews, who had high achievement motives.]

Ratti, Anna Maria. "Italian Migration Movements, 1876 to 1922," in Willcox, *International Migrations,* II, 440–490.

Rennie, Ysabel F. *The Argentine Republic.* New York: Macmillan Company, 1945. [Perhaps the most insightful and readable history of modern Argentina in English.]

Repetto, Nicolás. *Mi paso por la política.* Buenos Aires: S. Rueda, 1956.

Reynal O'Connor, Arturo. *Paseos por las colonias.* Buenos Aires, 1908.

———. "Por las colonias," *Revista nacional,* XXXI (June, 1901), 511–518; XXXIII (January, 1902), 41–49.

Reynolds, Clark Winston. "Development Problems of an Export Economy: The Case of Chile and Copper," in Mamalakis and Reynolds, *Essays on the Chilean Economy.*

Río, Francisco Aníbal. "Alma gaucha," *Caras y Caretas*, X (October 19, 1907), n.p.

Rivarola, Horacio C. *Las transformaciones de la sociedad argentina y sus consecuencias institucionales (1853 á 1910)*. Buenos Aires: Impr. de Coni Hermanos, 1911.

Rivarola, Rodolfo. *Fernando en el colegio (educación moral y cívica)*. Buenos Aires, 1913.

Rivas Vicuña, Francisco. *Política nacional*. Santiago, 1913. [An example of intellectual nationalism which by 1914 was calling for domestic ownership of extractive industries.]

Rodríguez del Busto, Francisco. *Problemas económicos y financieros*. Córdoba, 1905.

Rojas, Ricardo. *Blasón del Plata*. Buenos Aires: Editorial Losada, 1954. [First published 1910. A strong appeal for cultivation of an Argentine nationalism based on Hispanic and Indian cultural values. The immigrants must be assimilated into this cultural tradition.]

————. *La restauración nacionalista*. Buenos Aires: Ministerio de Justicia e Instrucción Pública, 1909. [Immigration and the cosmopolitan spirit threaten the very roots of Argentina's national character. Rojas' solution is cultural nationalism and particularly nationalistic education. Perhaps the most influential Argentine book published during the decade preceding World War I.]

Roldán, Belisario. *Discursos completos*. Buenos Aires: "Sarmiento" Casa Editora, 1922.

Romero, José Luis. *Argentina: Imágenes y perspectivas*. Buenos Aires: Editorial Raigal, 1956. [In this collection of essays the author comments meaningfully on the influence of immigration upon Argentine society and culture.]

————. *A History of Argentine Political Thought*. Third Edition. Translated by Thomas F. McGann. Stanford: Stanford University Press, 1963.

————. "La realidad argentina y el análisis sociológico a comienzos del siglo," *Revista de la Universidad (La Plata)*, V (December, 1958), 49–59.

Roquendo, Miguel. *Los saguaypes*. First performed 1912. In *Bambalinas*, No. 163 (1921). [Immigrant businessmen are portrayed as greedy, lustful, and dishonest.]

Rossi, José Gregorio. "La criminalidad profesional en Buenos Aires," *Archivos de Psiquiatría y Criminología Aplicados a las Ciencias Afines*, II (1903), 169–176.

Ruas, Enrique M. "Cuento para immigrantes," *Caras y Caretas*, X (November 2, 1907).

Saavedra, Julio. "La educación utilitaria en Chile," *Revista de Educación Nacional*, III (March, 1907), 7–14.

Saavedra Lamas, Carlos. *Economía colonial*. Buenos Aires, 1910.

Sáenz Peña, Roque. *Escritos y discursos*. 2 vols. Buenos Aires: J. Peuser, 1914–1915.

Salaverría, José M. "El miedo," *Caras y Caretas*, XVI (April 19, 1913), n.p.

————. *Tierra argentina*. Madrid: F. Fé, 1910.

Sánchez, Florencio. *La gringa*. First performed 1904. In Sánchez, *Teatro completo*, 106–144. [A key work that portrays the clash of immigrant and creole cultures in rural Argentina.]

————. *La pobre gente*. First performed 1904. In Sánchez, *Teatro completo*, 201–223.

————. *Teatro completo de Florencio Sánchez*. Edited by Dardo Cúneo. Third Edition. Buenos Aires: Editorial Claridad, 1964.

Sánchez Aguilera, Víctor. *El pasado de Osorno, la gran ciudad del porvenir*. Osorno, 1948.

Sánchez Viamonte, Carlos. *Biografía de una ley antiargentina: Ley 4144*. Buenos Aires: Nuevas Ediciones Argentinas, 1956.

Santibáñez, Fernando (pseud. Fernando Santiván). *El crisol*. Second Edition. Santiago: Editorial Nascimento, 1926. [First published 1913. The author defends Chilean middle- and working-class creoles while attacking the upper class and the foreigners.]

————. "El desalojamiento del nacional," *Pacífico Magazine*, III (June, 1914), 705.

Sarmiento, Domingo F. *Facundo: Civilización y barbarie*. Garden City, N.Y.: Doubleday & Co., 1961. [First published 1845.]

Saráh, Roberto. *"Los turcos."* Second Edition. Santiago: Editorial del Pacífico, 1961.

Scardín, Francisco. *La Argentina y el trabajo*. Buenos Aires: J. Peuser, 1906. [Primarily a compilation of Italian commercial and industrial activity in Argentina.]

Schneider, Samuel. *Proyección histórica del gaucho*. Buenos Aires: Ediciones Procyón, 1962.

Schobinger, Juan. *Inmigración y colonización suizas en la República Argentina en el siglo XIX*. Buenos Aires: Instituto de Cultura Suizo-Argentino, 1957.

Schwarz, Ernst and Te Velde, Johan C. "Jewish Agricultural Settlement in Argentina: The ICA Experiment," *Hispanic American Historical Review*, XIX (May, 1939), 185–203.

Scobie, James R. *Revolution on the Pampas: A Social History of Argentine Wheat, 1860–1910*. Austin, Texas: University of Texas Press, 1964.

Sebreli, Juan José. *Buenos Aires: Vida cotidiana y alienación*. Fifth Edition. Buenos Aires: Ediciones Siglo Veinte, 1965.

Serrano Montoner, Ramón. "La chilenización de Magallanes," *Revista Chilena de Historia y Geografía*, LXXVII (May–August, 1935), 14–32.

"Servicio de inmigración," *Boletín de la Sociedad Nacional de Agricultura*, XXXVIII (December 15, 1907), 724–725.

Silva, Victor Domingo. *La pampa trágica*. Santiago: Imp. de Masgrán y Cía., 1921. [First published 1912.]

Silva Castro, Raúl. *Carlos Pezoa Véliz (1879–1908)*. Santiago: Ministerio de Educación Pública, 1964. [Includes the complete works of one of Chile's great poets.]

————. *Don Eduardo de la Barra y la pedagogía alemana*. Santiago, 1943.

————. *Prensa y periodismo en Chile (1812–1956)*. Santiago: Ediciones de la Universidad de Chile, 1958.

Silvert, Kalman H. *La sociedad problema: Reacción y revolución en América Latina*. Translated by Noemí Rosenblat. Buenos Aires: Editorial Paidos, 1962. [Originally published in English as *The Conflict Society: Reaction and Revolution in Latin America*.]

————. "Los mitos sociales chilenos," *Revista de la Universidad (La Plata)*, III (January–March, 1958), 105–117.

Simon, S. Fanny. "Anarchism and Anarcho-syndicalism in South America," *Hispanic American Historical Review*, XXVI (February, 1946), 38–59.

Smith, W. Anderson. *Temperate Chile*. London: Adam and Charles Black, 1899. [Many insightful comments on the impact of immigration and on the problems foreign colonists faced in southern Chile.]

Snow, Peter. *Argentine Radicalism*. Iowa City: University of Iowa Press, 1965.

Sociedad de Fomento Fabril. *Inmigración libre*. Santiago, 1893.

Sommi, Luis V. *La revolución del 90*. Second Edition. Buenos Aires: Ediciones Pueblos de América, 1957.

Stach, Francisco. "La República Argentina y la defensa social," *Estudios*, V (November, 1913), 359–368.

Stewart, Watt. "El trabajador chileno y los ferrocarriles del Perú," *Revista*

Chilena de Historia y Geografía, LXXXV (July–December, 1938), 128–171.

Subercaseaux, Guillermo. *Historia de las doctrinas económicas en América y en especial en Chile*. Santiago: Soc. Imp. y Lit. Universo, 1924.

————. "Política nacionalista," *Revista de Educación Nacional*, IX (July, 1913), 267–277.

Taborda, Hector A. "El clandestinismo en las prisiones," *Archivos de Psiquiatría y Criminología Aplicados a las Ciencias Afines*, VII (1908).

Thayer Ojeda, Luis. *Elementos étnicos que han intervenido en la población de Chile*. Santiago: "La Ilustración," 1919.

Thedy, Enrique. "Índole y propósitos de la Liga del Sur," *Revista Argentina de Ciencias Políticas*, I (1909), 76–95.

El Tiempo, ed. *La naturalización de los extranjeros: Opiniones y proyectos*. Buenos Aires: "El Tiempo," 1900.

Tigner, James L. "The Ryukyuans in Argentina," *Hispanic American Historical Review*, XLVII (May, 1967), 203–205.

"Todos al Colón," *Caras y Caretas*, XVI (April 5, 1913), n.p.

Tornquist, Ernesto & Cía, Ltda. *El desarrollo económico de la República Argentina en los últimos cincuenta años*. Buenos Aires, 1920.

"Los turcos en Buenos Aires," *Caras y Caretas*, V (March 1, 1902), n.p.

Ugarte, Manuel. *Cuentos de la pampa*. Madrid: Biblioteca Mignon, 1903.

————. *El porvenir de América Latina*. Buenos Aires: Editorial Indoamerica, 1953. [First published 1911.]

Unsain, Alejandro M. "La ley de defensa social," *Renacimiento*, VIII (May, 1911), 20–37.

Urien, Carlos M. and Colombo, Ezio. *La República Argentina en 1910*. 2 vols. Buenos Aires: Maucci Hermanos, 1910.

Vaca-Guzmán, Santiago. *La naturalización de los extranjeros (conversación familiar)*. Buenos Aires, 1891.

Vattier, Carlos. "Apuntes sobre la industria nacional en Chile," *Boletín de la Sociedad Nacional de Minería*. Third Series (January 21, 1901), 26.

de Vedia, Enrique. "Educación patriótica," *El Monitor de la Educación Común*, XXVII (September 30, 1908), 169–175.

————. *Educación secundaria*. Buenos Aires, 1906.

————. *La enquête Naón*. Buenos Aires, 1909.

————. "La escuela," *El Monitor de la Educación Común*, XXXV (October 31, 1910), 21–30.

————. "La nueva tendencia," *El Monitor de la Educación Común*, XXXV (December 31, 1910), 584–589.

Vega, E. M., ed. *Album de la colonie française au Chile*. Santiago: Impr. et Lithogr. Franco-Chilienne, 1904.

Veliz, Claudio, ed. *The Politics of Conformity in Latin America*. New York: Oxford University Press, 1967.

Venegas, Alejandro. (pseud. J. E. Valdes Cange.) *Cartas al excelentísimo Señor Don Pedro Montt*. Second Edition. Valparaíso, 1909.

——. *Sinceridad: Chile íntimo en 1910*. Santiago: Imprenta Universitaria, 1910. [This critique of contemporary Chilean life strongly opposed middle-class immigrants and the German professors but argued that agricultural colonists are a progressive force.]

Venturino, Agustín. *Grandes familias chilenas descendientes de ingleses, franceses e italianos*. Santiago: Impr. Franco-Chilena, 1918.

——. *Sociología chilena: Con comparaciones argentinas y mejicanas*. Barcelona: Editorial Cervantes, 1929.

de Veras, Jil (pseud.). *Los incendiarios, ó sea narración completa de los sucesos de Osorno*. Santiago, 1895.

Vicens Vives, Jaime. *Historia social y económica de España y América*. 5 vols. Barcelona: Editorial Teide, 1957–1959.

Vicuña Mackenna, Benjamín. *Bases del informe presentado al supremo gobierno sobre la inmigración estranjera por la comisión especial nombrada con ese objeto y redactada por el secretario de ella*. Santiago: Imprenta Nacional, 1865.

Vicuña Subercaseaux, Benjamín. *Un país nuevo (cartas sobre Chile)*. Paris: A. Eyméoud, 1903.

——. *El socialismo revolucionario y la cuestión social en Europa y en Chile*. Santiago: Soc. Impr. Universo, 1908.

Viñas, David. *Literatura argentina y realidad política*. Buenos Aires: Jorge Álvarez, 1964. [Analyzes in detail the relationships of intellectuals in pre-World War I Argentina with the upper classes. A Marxist viewpoint.]

Weber S., Alfredo. *Chiloé: Su estado actual, su colonización, su porvenir*. Santiago: Impr. Mejía, 1903.

Whitaker, Arthur P. and Jordan, David C. *Nationalism in Contemporary Latin America*. New York: Free Press, 1966.

Willcox, Walter F. "Increase in Population of the Earth and of the Continents since 1650," in Willcox, *International Migrations*, II, 33–82.

——, ed. *International Migrations*, 2 vols. New York: National Bureau of Economic Research, 1929–1931. [The first volume contains statistics, and the second consists of interpretive essays, some of which this bibliography lists separately.]

Winsberg, Morton D. *Colonia Baron Hirsch: A Jewish Agricultural Colony in Argentina.* Gainesville, Fla.: University of Florida Press, 1963.

Zea, Leopoldo. *Dos etapas del pensamiento en Hispanoamérica.* México: El Colegio de México, 1949. [This work later appeared in English under the title *The Latin American Mind,* trans. James H. Abbott and Lowell Dunham.]

Zeballos, Estanislao S. "Problemas conexos con la inmigración," *Revista de Derecho, Historia y Letras,* XV (June, 1903), 544–552.

Zuccarini, Emilio. "Los exponentes psicológicos del carácter argentino: evolución del gaucho al atorrante," *Archivos de Psiquiatría y Criminología Aplicados a las Ciencias Afines,* III (1904), 179–196.

D. NEWSPAPERS

El Diario Ilustrado. 1913. Santiago. [This conservative-oriented daily had a large circulation but still lacked prestige before 1914.]

El Estandarte Católico. 1890–1891. Santiago. [Reflected the interests of the Catholic church and the Conservative party. Replaced by *El Porvenir* in 1891.]

La Lei. (Title varies, sometimes spelled *La Ley.*) 1894–1910. Santiago. [The voice of the Radical party. Like the party, this paper became increasingly hostile to immigration after 1905.]

El Mercurio. 1890–1900, Valparaíso; 1900–1913, Santiago. [Chile's oldest and most distinguished newspaper, probably also the most influential. Owned by the wealthy Edwards family, it generally reflected the views of banking and commercial interests.]

La Nación. 1890–1914. Buenos Aires. [Founded by General Bartolomé Mitre and owned by the Mitre family, this was one of the two Argentine newspapers of the period which enjoyed national prestige. Its editorial opinions represented the views of the Buenos Aires elite.]

El Porvenir. 1891–1906. Santiago. [This conservative and strongly proclerical newspaper opposed immigration in general and foreign teachers in particular. Replaced by *La Unión in* 1906.]

La Prensa. 1890–1914. Buenos Aires. [The property of the Gainza Paz family, this newspaper enjoyed national and worldwide prestige. It generally viewed Argentine issues from the perspective of the Buenos Aires elite.]

El Pueblo Obrero. 1906–1910. Iquique. [Reflected the views of Chilean business interests in the far north.]

La Unión. 1906–1914. Santiago. [In the tradition of *El Estandarte Católico* and *El Porvenir,* this paper faithfully represented the interests of the rural oligarchy and the church. A good source for conservative views on immigration during the decade preceding World War I.]

La Vanguardia. 1898–1914. Buenos Aires. [Founded in 1894, this influential newspaper faithfully reflected the views of the Argentine Socialist party. Its editorials, written by such party leaders as Juan B. Justo and Alfredo L. Palacios, frequently challenged the views of *La Prensa* and *La Nación.*]

INDEX

Abeille, Luciano: 139, 140

acculturation. SEE assimilation of immigrants

Aconcagua (Chilean province): 46, 59

Agote, Luis: 147

agriculture (Argentina): disdain of cattlemen for, 11; economic importance of, 11, 17; and immigrant labor, 12, 13, 14, 17, 26, 37, 44, 111, 115, 169, 170; dominance of elite landowners in, 52; immigrant ownership of specialized, 55; native-born workers in, praised, 152; immigrant contribution to, 154; failure to develop potential, 170. SEE ALSO colonists (Argentina); farmers (Argentina); landownership (Argentina)

agriculture (Chile): native-born labor in, 15; stagnation of production in, 14, 27. SEE ALSO colonists (Chile); farmers (Chile); landownership (Chile)

Aguirre Cerda, Pedro: 79–80

Alberdi, Juan Bautista: 7, 17

alcoholism: 93, 101, 102, 160

Aldunate B., Santiago: 21

Allessandri, Arturo: 64

Allessandri, Jorge: 64

alfalfa: 12

Alsina, Juan: 26, 135–136, 153

Álvarez, José S.: 99

Álvarez, Juan: 154

Álvarez Suárez, Agustín: 30

anarchist movement (Argentina): popularity of, 93; emergence of, 102; appeal to unskilled workers of, 108, 120; newspapers of, 108; organization of, 108; strikes called by, 108; denounced by intellectuals, 108–115 *passim*; legislation against, 110, 114, 170; suf-

fers repression, 112, 113; fear of, 132; use of nationalism to combat, 170; mentioned, 141. SEE ALSO labor movement (Argentina)

anarchist movement (Chile): 104, 107, 132. SEE ALSO labor movement (Chile)

anarchosyndicalism. SEE anarchist movement (Argentina); anarchist movement (Chile)

anti-Semitism (Argentina): 88, 113, 114, 148–149. SEE ALSO Jewish immigrants (Argentina); nationalistic education (Argentina)

anti-Semitism (Chile): 70–71. SEE ALSO Jewish immigrants (Chile)

Antofagasta (Chilean city): 39

Antofagasta (Chilean province): nationality of population of, 46; nationality of real estate ownership in, 58, 59; Chinese businessmen in, 70; mining capital in, 166; mentioned 6

Araucanian Indians: loss of lands of, 15; venerated by cultural nationalists, 99, 158; decline of, 101, 102. SEE ALSO nationalism (Chile)

Arauco (Chilean province): 46, 59

architects: 61, 73

Archivos de Psiquiatría y Criminología (Argentine scholarly journal): 98

Arica (Chilean city): 10

Armenian immigrants: 21

army (Argentina): 62

arrendatarios: 55

artisan skills: scarcity of, 52

Asiatic immigrants. SEE Chinese immigrants (Chile); Japanese immigrants (Argentina); Japanese immigrants (Chile)

Atacama (Chilean province): 46, 59